KAI LEHIKOINEN

STEPPING QUEERLY?

Discourses in Dance Education for Boys in Late 20th-Century Finland

PETER LANG

Oxford · Bern · Berlin · Bruxelles · Frankfurt am Main · New York · Wien

Bibliographic information published by Die Deutsche Bibliothek
Die Deutsche Bibliothek lists this publication in the Deutsche National-
bibliografie; detailed bibliographic data is available on the Internet at
‹http://dnb.ddb.de›.

British Library and Library of Congress Cataloguing-in-Publication Data:
A catalogue record for this book is available from The British Library,
Great Britain, and from The Library of Congress, USA

Cover design: Milla Järvipetäjä

Photo: Markus Lahtinen

ISBN 3-03910-572-8
US-ISBN 0-8204-7599-8

© Peter Lang AG, International Academic Publishers, Bern 2006
Hochfeldstrasse 32, Postfach 746, CH-3000 Bern 9, Switzerland
info@peterlang.com, www.peterlang.com, www.peterlang.net

Printed in Germany

Contents

Preface

My interest in dance was sparked by John Travolta's dancing in the 1970s film *Saturday Night Fever*. At the age of fourteen, my first experience of an organised dance class was a disco dance course at a private school of social dancing in Turku, my hometown in Finland. Soon after that, a friend introduced me to tap dancing and classes in tap followed. In autumn 1980, a newly established dance theatre in Turku, Tanssiteatteri Miimos, advertised in a local newspaper for free classes for males who would like to assist in their productions. I decided to sign up. No more than a couple of months later, a group of us boys was on stage in Turku City Theatre, performing hunters in Jane Koskinen's *The Wolf's Bride*, a dance theatre piece based on Aino Kallas' (1928) book about a hunter's wife who turns into a wolf at night to dance with other wolves in the woods.

I was happy to notice that two other boys from my school had taken up dance as well. When our dance interest came out at school, at first we faced some mockery. However, our dancing gradually became more accepted – partly, perhaps, due to the dirty punk tango that we performed with three female classmates at a school party, and partly because our dance teachers managed to organise an introductory course on different dance forms for our male classmates.

At home, my grandparents fully supported my dance interest. My mother remained neutral but she was always happy to help with making costumes for the performances. My father reacted positively towards my tap interest but remained reserved about other theatrical dance forms. Once my dancing became more known to others through public performances and reviews of the choreographies performed, he attacked me with a verbal torrent of abuse: I had made myself a public laughing stock, he shouted at me. It was my love of the 'magic' of stage, the joy of moving in a non-competitive way (unlike in PE at school), the musicality of dancing and the fact that I had become close friends with other boys and girls who shared my dance interest that

7

made me continue. The dedication that my teachers showed towards dance gave me an uncompromising model, and the encouragement I received from them led me to embark on a dance career eventually.

Besides my tap training with Helvi Anias in Tanssitiimi – a private school of theatrical dance in my hometown – and classes in jazz, tap and ballet at Verla Flower's Dance Arts in Seattle during my exchange year in the United States, I gained most of my early dance training in the all-male group of Turku Dance Association. Mirja-Liisa Herhi, Riitta Saastamoinen and other female teachers in the school of the association taught ballet and jazz to the all-male class once or twice a week. However, many of us boys also took classes together with girls and women because we wanted more training. Thus, we entered the female realm of dancing and our presence turned a number of all-female classes co-educational.

Later, during my years of professional training, I studied with several outstanding female teachers including Janice Brenner, Ruth Currier, Jane Darling, Betty Jones, Karen Levy, Gun Roman, Cilla Roos, Lynn Simonson, Ernestine Stodelle and Jeanne Yasko. But I also had the opportunity to study with charismatic male teachers such as Vanoye Aikens and Thomas Berggren in the University College of Dance in Stockholm and with Alan Danielson, Jim May and Clay Taliaferro in Ruth Currier Dance Studio in New York. A variety of masculinities were performed in their dance classes, but the focus of my learning, as I recall it, was not on the embodiment of masculinities but on the embodiment of particular styles of jazz and modern dance these men taught.

After receiving a Bachelor of Fine Arts degree in Dance Education in 1989, I first taught for a year in Kuopio Conservatory and then worked for a period of five years as a regional dance artist in the Regional Arts Council of Turku and Pori Province. On several occasions, dance teachers approached me to ask how to get more boys to take up dance. There seemed to be uncertainty about what the content of boys' dance classes should be and what kind of teaching methods should be used. I found it difficult to answer these questions because my dance background was grounded almost entirely in co-educational training. For me, gendered dance pedagogy seemed like the mysterious Holy Grail: a hidden secret that I had no access to. In

8

my search for this 'Grail', I collaborated with the Board of Dance in the Province of Turku and Pori to organise a seminar on boys' dance education in Turku in autumn 1992. I was also hoping to learn about the teaching of boys from more experienced colleagues who worked in the Dance Camp for Boys in Siilinjärvi. Thus, I enrolled to teach modern dance, improvisation and dance composition in the camp on three subsequent summers. I learned enormously from conversations with Leena Jääskeläinen, Ilkka Lampi and Harri Setälä, three of the key people from the camp. Even more so, I learned directly from the boys (see Lehikoinen 1993).

My perception on dance and gender changed radically when I encountered feminist ideas at the University of Surrey in the UK where I completed a Master of Arts degree in Dance Studies in 1997. One of the first things I was told by a female lecturer was that I should not expect 'special treatment' just because I was male. I had come to England with a serious intention to study – 'special treatment' was not what I was expecting. Yet, because of my gender, I was already treated differently from my female fellow students. As I grew more familiar with feminist thinking and Foucault's (1972, 1980a, 1982) ideas on discursive knowledge, I could see the attack as discursively constructed through certain feminist ideas on men. As the year progressed, I learned more about dance and gender. I applied a gender-critical perspective to my choreographic praxis and to my coursework in dance analysis. I also gained a complex understanding on men and masculinity through my MA dissertation, a dance analysis on masculine representations in Kenneth Kvarnström's *Fem Danser*. Drawing from critical and psychoanalytical texts that emerged as part of the second wave in sociology of masculinity, I saw masculinities as multiple, socially constructed and fragile (Lehikoinen 1996, 1999).

Eventually, I started paying attention to gender in dance education. Inspired by Joseph Pleck's (1981) critique on sex role theory, I presented a paper on fragile masculinities and the influence of sex role theory in boys' dancing at the 7th dance and the Child international conference in Kuopio, Finland (Lehikoinen 1997). I had become aware of the tensions between masculinity and boys' dance education, albeit, I was still quite unable to articulate these tensions. Nevertheless, my curiosity about the power of masculine discourses in

9

boys' dancing had been aroused.[1] I wanted to study further and write a PhD thesis, and subsequently this book, on this phenomenon.[2]

Thus, the early foundations of this book have been built from my personal experiences as a male dance student, my earlier search for the 'Holy Grail' of boys' dancing and the understanding I have gained on gender through dance studies. These studies have made me see choreographies, dance educational practices and the male dancer as historically situated within wider contextual and discursive frameworks provided by society and culture.[3]

1   'Discourse' is not a transparent concept as its uses in everyday language and in academia vary. For different definitions, see, for example: Foucault (1972) and (1984a); Jarowski & Coupland (1999); Mills (1997); Wetherell et al (2001a) and (2001b). This book follows a Foucauldian line of thinking, which sees that power operates in society through historically specific discourses (Foucault 1980a, 1984b, 1995). Discourse is a more or less coherent body of statements that produce and regulate social practices, such as dance teaching or performing gender. It is also the relationship between linguistic and embodied knowledge that makes a specific social act and the material objects involved meaningful (Philips & Jørgensen 2002b). Discourses are kept in circulation through a nexus of practices while other practices try to resist or asphyxiate certain discourses (Mills 2003).

2   See Lehikoinen (2003).

3   See, for example, Adshead (1981), Burt (1995), Foster (1995), Hodgens (1988), Hanna (1988).

Acknowledgements

My PhD thesis, and subsequently this book, would not have been possible without those funding bodies whose generous support was essential for me to accomplish this goal. I would like to extend my warmest thanks to the Arts and Humanities Research Board, the Emil Aaltonen Foundation, the 100th Anniversary Foundation of Helsingin Sanomat, Oscar Öflund Foundation and the Turku Polytechnic.

I am indebted to the many people who have helped in various ways in my research and in this book project. First and foremost, I would like to thank all the dance students and their teachers who took part in focus groups or shared their experiences informally in other conversations. Only a fraction of their accounts could be included as examples in this book. However, every account was invaluable during the research process. I would also like to thank the Finnish National Opera Ballet School, the Kuopio Dance Festival, the Outokumpu Learning Centre, the Theatre Academy, the Turku Arts Academy, the Turku Conservatory and the Vantaa Dance Institute for allowing me to carry out research with their students and teachers. I would like to thank N'Fanly Camara, Donna Jewell, Outi Kallinen, Minna Karesluoto, Juuso Kauppinen, Ilkka Lampi, Juha Lampi, Kaisa Nevalainen and Isto Turpeinen for letting me observe their classes.

As this book is based upon my PhD thesis, I am particularly grateful to Professor Janet Adshead-Lansdale and Professor Jennifer Brown at the University of Surrey, Guildford, UK, whose knowledge, guidance and encouragement were truly invaluable throughout the research project. Professor Adshead-Lansdale taught my first classes in Dance Analysis, and introduced me to poststructuralist thinking and intertextuality. She has guided my work throughout different stages, read and commented on various versions of the manuscript. Also, she helped me to find funding for the research from the UK. Professor Brown's help in the area of social psychology was indispensable. She advised me on questions of identity, focus groups and discourse analysis. She also read through the manuscript and contributed with useful comments.

An important contribution to this research has come from colleagues and friends who have helped me access literature, articles, photographs and videos, and who have helped me with technical problems. Special thanks to Heikki Jauhiainen in the Finnish National Opera archive, Pasi Leppänen and Merja Snellman in the Finnish National Opera Ballet School, Tiina Jalkanen and Aarne Mäntylä in the Vantaa Dance Institute, Chris Jones and Helen Roberts in the National Resource Centre for Dance at the University of Surrey as well as Ritva Bergsström, Sari Hannula, Markus Lahtinen, Kirsti Nurmela, Ritva Saastamoinen, Minna Palokangas-Sirviö, Monica Richardsson, Marja Salminen, Satu Sihvoin, Tiina Suhonen, Johanna Turunen and Marketta Viitala. Also, I want to thank Adrian Coyle, Tiina Holopainen, Jonathan Kane, Tuija Liikkanen, Jaana Lämsä, Anne Makkonen and Christina Sami, whose questions, comments and linguistic remarks have been invaluable at different stages of the research process. Additionally, many thanks to Milla Järvipetäjä in the Arts Council of Southwest Finland for her invaluable contribution to the visual design of this book.

I am eternally grateful to my dear friends Vesa Orava and Christina Sami in Wimbledon for their generous hospitality during my visits to the UK over the period of my research process. Finally, I would like to thank my partner Kari Salminen for his forbearance and support throughout this project.

List of Tables and Figures

Tables

Figures

14

Chapter One
Introduction

Analysing Dance Education of Males as a Site of Oppression

Since the 19th century, male dancers have been subjected to (social prejudices) in the West (Hanna 1988; Burt 1995; Au 2002). In masculinist culture, the stereotype of the male dancer as an (effeminate homosexual) has limited young males' participation in dance. Thus, gender-specific dance educational approaches have been developed in Finland and elsewhere in an attempt to get more boys involved (Mumaw & Sherman 1982, Hanna 1988, Räsänen 1995, Mitchell 1999, Turpeinen 1997; Foster 2001, Lampi et al 2002). However, dance education can also provide a prime site for the oppression of boys.

Any education that makes students embody and perform gender and sexuality in a limited heteronormative manner violates non-heterosexual students' constitutional right to be treated equally.[1] Enforcing heterosexual masculinity, as the only socially acceptable way of performing maleness, is not equal treatment – it is heteronormative indoctrination. This kind of oppressive practice can influence how males in dance construct their identities and how they limit themselves to perform in certain ways. To make dance a democratic site, where every student can participate on equal terms, requires that we, as dance educators, recognise oppressive gender-

---

1 The new Constitution of Finland that came into force in 2000 is very clear about discrimination: 'No one shall, without an acceptable reason, be treated differently from other persons on the ground of sex, age, origin, language, religion, conviction, opinion, health, disability or other reason that concerns his or her person' (FINLEX, 2003).

political discourses and politics of sexuality in dance education and do something to change them. Thus, this book aims to 'unsettle' heteronormative masculinism as a 'doxa' in boys' dance education and choreography.

While 'dance for boys' has been a widely discussed topic in Finland, such discussion has taken place almost entirely outside academia. This discussion has lacked a critical perspective on gender, sexuality and other, more complex, topics such as the discursive underpinnings of dance education and identities of dance students. Thus, this book investigates the relationship between boys and dance education in theatrical dance with the objective of illuminating the underpinning discourses that produced 'gender order' and performed masculinities in boys' dancing in Finland during the latter half of the 20th century.

Five interrelated questions are asked:

1. How are 'boys' constructed as a concept in dance educational discussions?
2. How are boys' dance educational practices constructed?
3. How is gender embodied in these practices and what kind of masculinities are performed through the dancing male body?'
4. How do individual male subjects in dance negotiate their social position in relation to gender and sexuality?
5. How do masculine embodiments and performances operate as a political rhetoric on personal and institutional levels?

By investigating these questions, this book aims to provide new understanding on young males' oppression in dance. The book can help dance teachers and administrators to recognise oppressive practices, which will hopefully lead to the search for more humane and democratic approaches that appreciate students as subjects who identify themselves in multiple ways.

Following recent suggestions in the sociology of masculinity (Brod & Kaufman 1994; Frosh 1994; Horrocks 1994; Connell 1995; Mac an Ghaill 1996; Segal 2001) and in dance research (Thomas 1995, Adshead-Lansdale 1999b, Green & Stinson 1999), an interdisciplinary approach was chosen to expose discourses that

16

produce embodiments and performances of gender in boys' dancing. An interdisciplinary approach that draws from dance studies, masculinity studies, queer theory, discourse analysis, social constructionism as well as Finnish cultural and political history seemed valid because dance and gender are part of social practices and because 'the grounding of who and what we become as women and men can be seen as operating at so many different levels' (Segal 2001, 236-237). However, there are limitations to an interdisciplinary approach as far as ontological and epistemological underpinnings of different methodologies are concerned (Thomas 1995, Green & Stinson 1999). Still, as epistemologically and ontologically consistent methodologies, which were relevant to the research questions, could be found and they yielded 'conclusions which are compatible with the theory' (Breakwell & Rose 2000, p. 20), an interdisciplinary approach seemed justified in this research project.

Because discourses in dance education leave marks on various forms of data – written, spoken, choreographed and embodied – a nexus of methodologies that would work for all these different forms of data was applied. The outlining of the context was done first through a literature review on boys' dance education and also on males in theatrical dance. Primary data was collected through a nexus of methodologies, including fifteen focus groups, informal and formal discussions, observation of dance classes and dance analytic descriptions of seven choreographies.

Discourse analysis (as described in Carabine 2001, Taylor 2001a and Parker 1992) was used first to pick out recognisable themes on boys' dancing in primary and secondary data. Then, texts in each topic area were subjected to a detailed scrutiny to see how these topics were addressed from various discursive positions. This analysis provided an illustrative chart of discourses recognised in the texts (see Figure 1 in Chapter 2).

The investigation of dance educational accounts, the observation of dance classes and the dance analytic examination of choreographies helped to identify discursive strategies and technologies in boys' dance education. Further, the attempt to look for absences, silences, resistances and counter-discourses in the data helped to recognise the dominant position of heteronormative masculinism in boys' dancing:

non-heterosexual positions were either missing from the statements examined, or such positions were marginalised and marked negatively. The examination of dance educational practices, seven choreographies and boys' self-narratives helped to identify consequences of the discourses. The key discourses recognised were elaborated upon through intertextual analysis to make sense about the worldviews that they put forward and, also, to make the consequences of these discourses visible. The illustrative chart helped trace relevant intertexts from different discursive realms when the intertextual analysis was produced. Intertextuality (as described in Adshead-Lansdale 1999 and Frow 1990), which treats all data as 'text', was used as the overarching methodology that made possible the juxtaposition of a vast range of texts from different theoretical contexts.

Gender, Masculinities and Masculinism

Gender has become an increasingly discussed topic in the field of dance studies during the past fifteen years or so (Cooper Albright 1997, 1998; Bond 1994; Burt 1995, 2001a, 2001b; Desmond 2001, Foster 1996, 2000; Hanna 1988; Thomas 1993). This discussion stems, to a large degree, from more than thirty years of feminist research and is focused on female representations, experiences and positions in dance (Adair 1992; Cooper Albright 1990; Banes 1998; Briginshaw 1998, 1999; Brown 1994a, 1994b; Carter 1993, 1996; Daly 1984, 1987, 1991, 1992, 1998, 2000; Dempster 1988, English 1980; Shapiro 1998; Stinson 1984, 1993, 1998; Stinson et al 1990). Recently, some writers have approached gender and sexuality in dance from a 'queer theory' point of view (Briginshaw 2001, Burt 2001a; Case, Brett & Foster 1995, Desmond 2001).[2] Within dance studies, as

2   Queer theory has emerged during the past ten years or so as a nexus of feminist, poststructuralist and psychoanalytic theories to interrogate the notion of fixed

well as in feminist and gender studies more generally, 'gender' is a multiply defined concept.[3] In this book, it is understood as a social practice that 'refers to bodies and what bodies do' (Connell 2001, p. 34) within the existing 'gender order'.[4] In addition, gender is seen as a 'parody' and a 'performative' (Butler 1990, 1993, 1997).

Butler (1990, 1997) refers to Althusser's (1971) theory of ideology to explain how the subject becomes 'subjugated'.[5] Our sex is announced at birth, and from then on our social environment keeps reminding us about what it is to be a 'boy' or a 'girl', a 'man' or a 'woman'. We are 'interpellated' into gender from birth through speech acts and other forms of discursive practices that operate 'in a network of authorization and punishment' (Butler 1997, p. 11). The very idea of an original in reference to gender is a myth: people imitate

identity. Its 'target is … the assumption of unity or harmony or transparency within persons or groups' (Phelan 1997, p. 2). It affirms 'the indeterminacy and instability of all sexed and gendered identities' (Salih 2000, p. 9). One of the key tasks of this critical perspective is 'to investigate formulations of straightness in order to reveal the "queerness" underlying particularly those identities which aggressively present themselves as straight, straightforward, singular and stable' (Ibid).

3   For concise and critical accounts on how gender is defined through different theoretical positions including liberal feminism, Marxist feminism, radical feminism, socialist feminism, French feminism, feminism of colour, lesbian feminism, postfeminism and queer theory, see, for example, Brooks 1997 or Burr 1998.

4   Following Bob Connell, 'gender order' can be defined as 'a historically constructed pattern of power relations between men and women and definitions of femininity and masculinity … the structural inventory of an entire society' (Connell 1987, p. 99).

5   Althusser (1971) uses the concept of 'interpellation' to talk about the process of subjugation. Briefly: 'ideology "interpellates" – or "hails" – individuals as subjects of the system: it gives them the identity necessary to the functioning of the existing state of affairs. This identity is constituted materially, concretely in various practices … "Obviousness" – taken-for-grantedness – is quite characteristic of ideological practices; and it is so because these practices are inseparable from the way that people live out the spontaneous and immediate aspect of their "existence". No one is unaffected by ideology in this sense' (Lechte 1994, 40).

meanings that this myth produces. The imitation becomes a 'parody' because it displaces 'the meaning of the original' (Butler 1990, p. 138) and imitates 'the myth of originality itself' (ibid.). Thus, gender identity emerges as

> a personal/cultural history of received meanings subject to a set of imitative practices which refer laterally to other imitations and which, jointly construct the illusion of a primary and interior gendered self or parody the mechanism of that construction. (Butler 1990, p. 138)

Human 'expressions' have been traditionally taken as products of identity. However, Butler sees them as a 'performatively constituted' (1990, p. 25) identity.[6] Gender as 'performative' is

> the repeated stylisation of the body, a set of repeated acts within a highly rigid regulatory frame that congeal over time to produce the appearance of substance, of a natural sort of being. (Butler 1990, p. 33)

Gender is a performative 'insofar as it is the effect of a regulatory regime of gender differences in which genders are divided and hierarchized under constraint' (Butler 1997, p. 16).

Drawing from Foucault, Butler acknowledges that political life is regulated in 'negative terms' by juridicial systems of power. Negative in this context suggests statements that prohibit, limit, control and so on. These systems, Butler argues, '*produce* the subjects they

---

6   For a person, the idea that s/he is either a woman or a man, heterosexual or homosexual emerges from the 'metaphysics of gender substances ... [that locates] the notion of gender under that of identity ... [which leads] to the conclusion that a person *is* a gender and *is* one in virtue of his or her sex, psychic sense of self, and various expressions of that psychic self, the most salient being that of sexual desire' (Butler 1990, pp. 21-22, emphasis in original). Austin (1962) in his speech act theory suggests that language is a means to do things and to make things happen. An utterance that commits an act is a 'performative'. Following Austin, 'performative acts' can be seen as 'forms of authorative speech' (Butler 1997, p. 11). Butler suggests that 'most performatives ... are statements that, in uttering, also perform a certain action and exercise binding power' (ibid.).

subsequently come to represent' (1990, p. 2, original emphasis). Further,

> the subjects regulated by such structures are, by virtue of being subjected to them, formed, defined, and reproduced in accordance with the requirements of those structures. (ibid.)

The link between power and the subject is all-important for the politics of gender

> because juridical subjects are invariably produced through certain exclusionary practices that do not 'show' once the juridical structure of politics has been established. (ibid.)

Thus, the standards of structures through which subjects are produced are not neutral or natural. Instead, being discursively constructed within a 'heterosexual matrix' of power, such standards

> operate by requiring the embodiment of certain ideals of femininity and masculinity, ones which are almost always related to the idealization of the heterosexual bond. (Butler 1997, pp. 17-18)

The notion of constraint in Butler's theory can be understood as any form of belief, value statement, restriction, taboo or warning that works through the reiteration of heteronormative standards that regulate the construction of gender in any given situation. As a 'compulsory' assignment, gender performativity is not entirely 'determining' in the sense that it 'is never quite carried out according to expectation, whose addressee never quite inhabits the idea s/he is compelled to approximate' (Butler 1997, p. 17). This does not mean, however, that gender is a voluntary practice or a matter of choice: a performance of an actor.[7] On the contrary, Butler underlines that gender performativity is

---

7   Butler emphasises that '[t]here is no subject who is "free" to stand outside …
     [social] norms … on the contrary, the subject is retroactively produced by these
     norms in their repetition, precisely as their effect … Freedom, possibility,

a compulsory repetition of prior and subjectivating norms, ones that cannot be thrown off at will, but which work, animate, constrain the gendered subject, and which are also the resources from which resistance, subversion, displacement are to be forged. (1997, p. 17)

For this book, and for dance studies more generally, the usefulness of Butler's definition of gender lies in its ability to theorise how performances of the body are in-/formed by culturally constructed accounts of masculinity and femininity. Her theory reveals, 'how the apparently "natural" body turns out to be a "naturalized effect" of discourse' (Salih 2002, p. 80). When bodies mediate culturally constructed meanings of gender in this way, they operate in a Foucauldian sense as 'vehicles' of discursive power (Foucault 1995). Therefore, the body (dancing or otherwise) can be examined

as signified and as signification, a body that can only be known through language and discourse – in other words, a body that is linguistically and discursively constructed. (Salih 2002, p. 80, original emphasis)

Butler's theory of gender is not entirely unproblematic. It has been criticised for paying little attention to material consequences of gender and of being reductionist in its view on heterosexuality (Connell 2000, Jackson 1999). In addition, the use of Althusser's (1971) concept of 'interpellation' in Butler's theory is problematic, from a poststructuralist point of view, because it suggests a critical structuralist framework for 'gender'. However, when the ideological framework and connotations are replaced with a discursive understanding of the subject, the subject as a fabrication of discursive power, her theory can be used along with other poststructuralist tools.

Much of the masculinity research from the last two decades has emerged from (pro)feminist underpinnings (Gardiner 2002; Whitehead 2001). This area of research has proliferated radically, now covering a range of topics including, for example, public institutions

agency do not have an abstract or presocial status, but are always negotiated with a matrix of power' (Butler 1997, p. 17).

such as workplace (Collinson & Hearn 2001) and school (Mac an Ghaill 1994; Haywood & Mac an Ghail 1996; Lehtonen 1999, 2003, Segal 2001). Work on public masculinities can be linked with Pateman's (2002) work on the 'fraternal social contract' as well as research on masculinity in reference to popular culture (Dyer 1989, 1993, 1994, 2002; Lehtonen 1995; Donald 2001, Lehman 2001), sports (Tiihonen 1999; Majors 2001) and dance (Burt 1995 Burt 2001a, Burt 2001b; Lehikoinen 1996, 1997, 1999; Spurgeon 1997; Keyworth 2001; Risner 2002a, 2002b, 2002c; Turpeinen 1990; 1997). On the other hand, work on private masculinities has focused on families (Morgan 2001) and fatherhood (Huttunen 1996, 1999), men's sexuality (Grönfors 1999; Hänninen 1999; Soikkeli 1999) and identities (Dyer 1989; Nardi 2001, Lancaster 2002). In reference to multiple masculinities, Segal (2001) and Halberstam (2002) have introduced the idea of 'female masculinity'. Also, there has been some work published on boys and young men (Sinkkonen 1990; Hoikkala (ed) 1996; Holland et al 1998; Pollack 1998; Lehtonen 1999, 2003; Connell 2000; Frosh et al 2002).

While a complete review of masculinity studies would be outside the scope of this book, the listing above is broad enough to suggest that such vast a range of topics attracts multiple theoretical perspectives. Indeed, masculinity has been addressed from a broad range of theories covering, for example, such disciplines as psychoanalysis, sociology, social psychology, anthropology, cultural studies, history, dance studies as well as different strands of feminisms and gender studies. In this book, I draw from recent masculinity studies in the sense that I perceive masculinities as multiple and discursively constructed (Haywood & Mac an Ghaill 1996, Lehtonen 1999, Segal 2001). In addition, I refer to 'masculinism', a culturally prevalent discourse that

> naturalizes male domination ... Masculinism takes it for granted that there is a fundamental difference between men and women, it assumes that heterosexuality is normal, it accepts without question the sexual division of labour, and it sanctions the political and dominant role of men in the public and private spheres. Moreover ... it tends to be relatively resistant to change. In general, masculinism gives primacy to the belief that gender is not negotiable ... nor, for that matter, does it allow for the possibility that lesbianism and

homosexuality are not forms of deviance or abnormality, but are alternative forms of gender commitment. (Brittan 2001, p. 53-54)

In this book, 'masculinism' is preferred to the commonly used concept of 'hegemonic masculinity', which refers to dominant forms of masculinity, due to the inconsistency that makes the latter term unfit for a poststructuralist 'tool-box' (see Whitehead 2002).[8] Brittan (2001) perceives masculinism as an 'ideology', but the concept can be used along with other poststructuralist tools on the condition that

> [t]he ideological framework and assumptions must give way to a *discursive* understanding of power. Thus masculinism becomes a dominant discourse rather than a dominant ideology. (Whitehead 2002, p. 98, original emphasis)

Males in Theatrical Dance

The appreciation of male dancing has varied radically in different cultural and historical contexts (Hanna 1988; Burt 1995, 2001a, 2001b; Hayashi 1998; Au 2002). While in Finland theatrical dance only dates back to the late 19th century, elsewhere in Europe dancing for an audience goes much further back in history.[9] In Europe, an uneasy relationship between males and theatrical dance emerged in the

---

8   On 'hegemonic masculinity' see for example Carrigan, Connell & Lee 1985; Connell 1995; Bird 1996.

9   Russian ballet ensembles performed several times in Helsinki during the early part of the 20th century and the free-dance movement that linked to German Ausdruckstanz was active. A number of private dance schools operated in Helsinki already in 1911 when the Finnish Opera (from 1956 the Finnish National Opera) was established. The Ballet of Finnish Opera was not established until in 1922. Meanwhile, students from Baroness Maggie Gripenberg's and Toivo Niskanen's dance schools assisted at the Opera (Vienola-Lindfors & af Hällström 1981; Repo 1989; Salmenhaara 1996; Suhonen 1997; Ikäheimo 1998; Pakkanen 2001a).

economic climate of the 19th century. Buzzwords of modernity - rationality, productivity and progress - made the bourgeoisie culture reduce the body to a means of production, highlight self-control, and link theatrical dance with sexuality and emotions (Hanna 1988; Burt 1995, 2001b; Sutinen 1997). |Romantic ballet was constituted as a male directed patriarchal institution and the ballerina was displayed as the eroticised object of desire for the heterosexual male gaze|(Daly 1987; Novack 1993; Burt 1995 and 2001a; Tudeer 1999). In such a context, performing dance was considered inappropriate for men. The male dancer was met with disgust because he interfered with the visual consumption of the eroticised body of the ballerina and blurred the boundary between the homosocial and homosexual gaze of the male audience (Burt 1995 and 2001a). Eventually, in the 1840's, in London and Paris, the male dancer was replaced by a 'danseuse travestie' a female dancer dressed up as a man who partnered the ballerina (Walker 2000).[10] Men's resistance to dance has been evident also in Japan during the 20th century. According to Michie Hayashi (1998), this resistance stems from modernity and those European influences that were imported to Japan in the late 19th century.[11]

Male dancing has been intricately linked to wider social issues in Finland as well. For example, in the 1920s and 1930s, the socially dominant 'white' discourse - a nationalist discourse embedded in agrarian, bourgeois and Christian values and influenced by the discourse of Natural Sciences – produced a culturally dominant masculine ideal that was in conflict with the romantic, aristocratic masculinity and the notion of male individuality that were performed in classical ballets (Ahonen 2000). The healthy male athlete and the effeminate dandy were other male stereotypes that emerged in Finland through a modernist discourse in the 1920s (Ahonen 2000; Hapuli 1995). Finnish male ballet dancers' bodies did not resonate with the

---

10   See also Tiina Rosenberg's (2000) book on travesty roles in theatre and opera.
11   Michie Hayashi (1998) maintains that a discourse on fixed embodiments of gender that underpinned European system of Physical Education eroded a long tradition of Japanese male dancing when this system was implemented in Japan in the 1870's.

highly celebrated male athlete's winning body that signifies physical power and competition. Moreover, male dancing embodied soft, round and lyrical movement material that could be interpreted as feminine (Ahonen 2000). The effeminate form of masculinity was despised and perceived as a cultural threat because markers that appeared as feminine on men were taken to signify a renunciation of power. Also, effeminacy in men was regarded as a threat because feminine markers were taken to signify homosexuality, which was a crime in Finland in the 1920s (ibid.).

It has been suggested that boys who dance have faced significant social prejudice at different points during the 20th century (Rodgers 1966, Alkins 1994, Van Ulzen 1995/96, Keinänen 2003, Nykänen 2003). Comments about dance not being a male pursuit come from peers at school but sometimes also within the family. Rodgers, for example, notes how '[m]any parents discourage their sons from dancing because they are afraid it might "sissify" them' (1966, p. 36). When it comes to peers, as Van Ulzen (1995/96) suggests, harsh bullying can be involved because boys who dance stand out from what is commonly considered as the socially acceptable culturally dominant male stereotype.[12] In Finland, dance teacher Aarne Mäntylä's inquiry among secondary school children revealed that only one boy out of ten shows interest towards dance while most boys reject the idea entirely (Nykänen 2003). Dance teacher Ilkka Lampi points out that many boys have to hide their dance interest particularly in small municipalities where male dancing is not common (ibid.).

Various texts show that male dancers' sexuality is an uneasy topic and that homosexuality is often discussed in negative terms in relation to male dancing (Rodgers 1966, Grant 1985, Van Ulzen 1996, Koegler 1995, Hamilton 1999). For example, Rodgers sees homosexuality as an 'emotional disturbance', more 'likely to be a handicap than a help to anyone who is having to lead a disciplined life, such as that of a dancer' (1966, p. 36). Grant suggests '[t]here's

---

12 Bullying can be defined as 'a subset of aggressive behaviour that involves an intention to hurt another person by a variety of means, including physical and verbal assaults and social exclusion' (Boulton 1997, p. 223).

26

an|assumption that men in dance are either gay or else only there to ogle or pick up women'|(1985, p. 20). Van Ulzen notes how in Australia some male dancers have 'learned, sometimes through bitter experience, simply to keep quiet about their occupation in certain company' (1996, p. 17). Koegler maintains that Western theatrical dance has been 'in the closet' for an 'unusually long time' (1995, p. 231). Even in a relatively recent American article the topic of 'coming out' in dance is introduced apologetically:

> We realize that some readers may be uncomfortable with the topic of homosexuality. However we believe that *Dance Magazine* has a responsibility to provide useful information for those dancers who may be dealing with this issue... (Hamilton 1999, p. 72)

As Spurgeon suggests,

> [w]hat is germane for the issue of men and dance is the *assumption* that any male interested in dance must be either a homosexual or 'effeminate – sissy' and more importantly *the consequent derision, even hatred, heaped upon such men.* (1997, p. 12, emphasis in original)

It has been suggested that the link between the male dancer and homosexuality is, partially at least, due to Diaghilev's influence in the early part of the 20th century but also due to the fact that discourse on homosexual identity was constructed first in the late 19th century (Burt 2001a, Foucault 1998b). What Burt calls 'the performance of the queer male dancing body' (2001a, p. 214) transgresses the dominant heterosexual norms of masculinity. In that sense, performing non-heterosexual masculinity is subject to '[t]he threat of punishment for transgression of heterosexual norm' (ibid.). Indeed, constructing the male dancer as a top athlete can be seen, by boys and men in dance as a means to fight the stereotypical image of the male dancer as gay.[13] This speaks clearly about culturally prevalent heteronormative

---

13   Anthropologist Daniel O'Connor's work from the 1980's points out a number of rhetoric strategies, which male dancers in New York City use, despite their sexual orientation, to avoid being labelled as gay (Hanna 1988).

discourses that oppress and marginalise gays, not just in dance, but also more generally in society.

Indeed, Wulff's (1998) multi-locale ethnography shows that homosexuality was commonly concealed in some large-scale ballet companies in the 1990s in the West. It is telling that gay couples in dance are not invited to various promotional functions such as dinners and receptions at embassies (ibid.). This kind of social injustice is something that Hanna seems to miss entirely with her focus on the question 'why male homosexuals are disproportionately attracted to dance' (1988, p. 136). From a position that seems to lack an understanding of gay lives, she suggests that the ballet world of the 20th century has functioned as some kind of a safe haven for psychologically torn escapist gay males who choose a dance career because they do not have 'as much to lose as other males' (Hanna 1988, p. 136). Her speculative list about reasons why homosexuals are attracted to dance is a perfect example of heteronormativity that constructs homosexuality in negative terms as a problem, not just for heterosexuals but also for gays.[14, 15]

Due to social prejudices, it has not been easy for young males to take up dance in Finland during the 20th century. An extract from dancer Kari Karnakoski's (1908-1985) autobiography provides a good example of this as it shows that theatrical dance was not regarded as a decent occupation for men in the 1930s:

My determined mother had already solved my future career in her mind. "Kari is going to become a dentist!"

---

14 For more critique on Hanna's heteronormative view: Daly (1989); Burt (1995); Risner (2002a).

15 According to Butler, our social world is constructed within a 'heterosexual matrix' of power that produces heteronormativity, a culturally prevalent discourse that demands 'the embodiment of certain ideals of femininity and masculinity, ones which are almost always related to the idealization of the heterosexual bond' (Butler 1997, pp. 17-18). Heteronormativity typically 'renders any alternative sexualities "other" and marginal' (Jackson 1999, p. 163).

I exerted myself bravely for a couple of months. However, I was not a genius, far from it. Eventually I grew angry. One day when I came home from the University, I slammed the books on the table and announced that it is now over.
"What is over?" my mother asked.
"My medical studies", I answered, and I do not know where the courage came from, but I also immediately threw out my big news.
"I am going to be a ballet dancer!"
The astonishment could not have been greater had I announced I was going to become a circus director. My relatives insisted on a change of name to avoid a scandal. But I had been planning this idea about the career of a dancer in my head for so long that for once I wanted to have it my way. I was steadfast with my stand. (Karnakoski 1993, pp. 27-28)

In 1931, when Karnakoski started his ballet training in the Finnish National Opera Ballet School, the boys and the girls were still taught in mixed groups (Räsänen 1997).[16] The first all-male dance class was established much later, in autumn 1959 (Ahjolinna 1994). The beginning of the autumn term was advertised in *Helsingin Sanomat* on 30 August 1959. The advertisement shows that new female students were not accepted in that year. New boys, however, were asked to report to the director of the school by 15th of September. As dance critic Helena Mäkinen (1959b) writes, the decision to focus on male students that year was because the Ballet of the Finnish National Opera frequently lacked good male dancers. There was a particular shortage of men who could perform the 'prince type', Mäkinen (ibid.) writes and adds that the ballet school had successfully recruited an unusually large number of boys that year.

There were approximately ten new boys who started that year, which made the total number of boys, at the ballet school, around twenty – approximately one sixth of the total number of students at the school (ibid.). Seija Simonen, a female teacher who was in charge of the two classes in the elementary level, is mentioned as the teacher of the boys in Mäkinen's article (ibid.). However, in an obituary that was

16 A ballet school was established at the Finnish Opera in 1922. At first, the school was open for everyone who paid the tuition. However, from 1956 onwards a state subsidy made it possible for the Finnish National Opera Ballet School to focus on training professional ballet dancers (Räsänen 1997).

29

written to commemorate former principal dancer and ballet teacher Uno Onkinen, Aku Ahjolinna (1994) recalls that Onkinen was hired to teach the first all-male ballet class in the Finnish National Opera Ballet School in 1959. It is possible that the boys were handed to Onkinen soon after the crushing comments that Mäkinen (1959b) wrote about their effeminate behaviour in Simonen's class.

Mäkinen's (ibid.) article instigated a response in Ludvig Nyholm, a dancer in the Finnish National Opera and the chairman of the Union of Finnish Dance Artists in his article that was published in a journal of the union later the same year (see Nyholm 1959). As Nyholm's article is investigated more carefully in Chapter Eight, it is sufficient to say here that he, too, attacks effeminacy in males and welcomes the then discussed idea about sports training as a means to teach dance for boys. The sports discourse in Mäkinen's (1959a, 1959b) and Nyholm's (1959) articles links these texts with the 'desissifying' gender politics that can be seen in Western theatrical dance history more generally.

Research in sports sociology suggests that sports are formed as a male field of activity (McKay 1992). As Solway suggests, the idea of dance as sport has been used strategically to 'demystify the world of dance' (quoted in Hanna 1988, p. 145). That is, male dancers have been constructed as athletes to make boys and young men interested in dance. Ted Swawn's all-male dance project in the 1930's, Jacques d'Amboise's project in American schools during the early 1980's and Jorden Morris' work with male students in Canada in the 1990's provide some examples (Mumaw & Sherman 1982, Hanna 1988, Foster 2001, Mitchell 1999).

Jean Carroll and Peter Lofthouse's (1969) handbook *Creative Dance for Boys* is also a good example although the authors make a clear distinction between sports and dance:

> Athletics arise from the child's delight in running, jumping and throwing in measurable situations … in dance, movement is used for the inner purpose of expression. (1969, p. 10-11)

The authors seek ways to teach dance so that boys do not have to 'feel foolish or unmanly' (ibid.). This is done, Carroll and Lofthouse suggest, by introducing 'material ... [that] will re-assure them of their masculine rôle when dancing' (ibid.). Male dance students' concern about their social position is also mentioned in Rodgers (1966) and Grant (1985). Such concern shows, it can be argued, that performances of masculinity have been strongly regulated during the 20th century in the West. Moreover, the above mentioned 'demystification' projects can be perceived as a form of a gender politic that aims to 'desissify' and 'heterosexualise' the male dancer (Risner 2002a, 2002b). Indeed, as Burt (1995) suggests, heterosexual sturdiness is a key characteristic of performed masculinities in American modern dance tradition during the 20th century.

Central-European modern dance tradition, or free-dance, had great significance in Finland during the first three decades of the 20th century. However, free-dance was very much a female realm and those few men who wanted to take classes from a Dalcroze-influenced Maggie Gripenberg did so in private (Pakkanen 2001a). 'Plastic movement' was not considered as a male pursuit, which made some people see it as a non-serious art form.[17] Thus, men's participation was used in the 1920's to measure the legitimacy of different art forms (Pakkanen 2001c). Unlike ballet, free-dance did not have an established training method nor an institutional safe-haven in Finland, which made it to the fight for its position as a legitimate art form very difficult, particularly in the strong anti-German political climate after the World War II. Ausdruckstanz was linked with Nazism (Ikäheimo 1998).

Modernism never faded entirely in Finnish dance. The American modern dance tradition picked up from where the Central-European free-dance movement had ended (Makkonen 1990, 1991). However, free-dance and modern dance movements remained a female realm up until 1960's. Even if male students constituted a small minority in the schools of modern dance, their overall number increased gradually during the 1960's (Pakkanen 2001c). More men got involved with

17   See Rajala quoted in Pakkanen 2001a.

31

theatrical dance in the 1970's when the first dance theatres were established.[18]

Ballet education for boys gained new impetus in Finland in the early 1980's when Ilkka Lampi took over the teaching of male students in the Finnish National Opera Ballet School. Lampi was trained in the teaching programme at the Vaganova Institute in Leningrad but instead of being dogmatic to the Russian approach, he has introduced games and athletic elements including sports training and its terminology as well as various martial arts forms to his male students (Räsänen 1995, 2000).[19] In addition, he worked to integrate sports and dance medical knowledge into the teaching of ballet to prevent dance injuries and to build stronger dancers (Raisko 1990, Räsänen 1995). Lampi is also one of the founding members and he has been the artistic director of the dance camp for boys that Kuopio Dance and Music Festival has organised since 1987.[20]

The initiative to set up a special dance course just for boys came from Leena Jääskeläinen who, in the 1980s, was the Chief Inspector of Physical Education for the National Board of Education. Her son was one of the group of disappointed young males who marched to the office of the Kuopio Dance and Music Festival to claim back their course fees in the summer of 1986. They felt they were being overrun by girls and women in the course that they had attended (Janhonen 1996a; Jääskeläinen 1993). Eventually, a curriculum for male dance students was constructed in collaboration with Lampi. The first boys' dance camp took place 1-13 June 1987 under the title of 'The Course for Developing the Dance Art of Boys' (Kuopio Dance Festival, dance camp for boys brochure 1987). Ever since, this camp was established, it has been running annually with approximately twenty to thirty boys attending every year. In the summer of 2003, 87 boys from Finland and Holland participated in the two courses: one for beginners to

---

18   More on the Dance Theatre Raatikko: Suhonen 1997; Ikäheimo 1998.
19   More on combat forms, see Chapters 5 and 6 of this book.
20   The Kuopio Dance and Music Festival (since 2002 the Kuopio Dance Festival) is one of the largest dance events in Scandinavia. It was first organised in 1970. See: Hietaniemi (1992); Miettinen (1994).

intermediate level, the other for boys who had extensive experience in dancing (Lankolainen 2003, Mäkinen 2003, Kuopio Dance Festival programme 2003).

Almost every year since the beginning, ballet training has been the core component of the camp. Other genres of dance, including tap, jazz, break, contemporary dance and African dances, have been introduced in the camp in different years. In addition, Orff-based music education has been part of the summer camp every year. Classes in dance improvisation and composition, acrobatics, mental training, fitness training and some martial arts forms such as shaolin and capoeira have also been included in the programme. Visits to see dance performances in the Kuopio Dance Festival have also been part of the boys' dance camp experience (Kuopio Dance Festival, the Dance Camp for Boys brochures 1987-2003).

A 'boom' in Finnish male dancing took place during the early 1990's when the number of men who entered the professional field of theatrical dance suddenly increased. It has been suggested that this younger generation of male dance artists was able to benefit from the formal educational routes that were established for dance in vocational and higher education systems during the 1980's and early 1990's (Sarje 1999). However, in the area of basic arts education system, the number of male dance students has remained remarkably low.[21] At the end of the 20th century, more than 95 % out of the total of 21,785 students who were studying dance within this system were female (Porna 2000). Thus less than 5 % were males. This figure is in line with the average percentage of male students found studying in the area of basics arts education more generally. The low number of boys in the basic arts education suggests that the relationship between young males and the arts is generally an uneasy one in Finland. Yet,

---

21 Basic arts education system is a goal-oriented and gradually advancing education for different art forms that was created by the law that came into force in 1992. The system is aimed primarily for children and young people and one of its objectives is that it provides the necessary skills for the students to apply into arts education in vocational and higher levels. Curriculum guidelines are provided by the National Board of Education (Opetushallitus 1992; Porna & Korpipää 1992).

there are some art forms that appeal to young men. Porna's (ibid.) report shows that 48.9% of the students who study architecture and video art in the area of basic arts education are male. Also in the basic education of circus art 42%, and in music 30.4%, of the students are male.

Several institutions of dance education have worked zealously in Finland to get more boys and men involved in dance. In addition to the Finnish National Opera Ballet School in Helsinki, and the Dance Camp for Boys in the Kuopio area, the Vantaa Dance Institute (formerly the Dance School of Raatikko) in South Finland also needs to be mentioned. In Vantaa, dance has played an increasingly important role for boys and young men since the early 1990's when the directors of the Vantaa Dance Institute, Aarne Mäntylä and Isto Turpeinen established a project with two local kindergartens and a local elementary school. Subsequently, their project brought hundreds of boys into contact with contemporary dance (Turpeinen 1997, Mäntylä personal information 29.3.2001). Turpeinen, who regarded his work with boys as a 'mission', developed a particular teaching method. This so called 'raw timber method' has been elaborated upon in a number of articles (see for example Turpeinen 1994, 1997, 1998).[22] In addition, Turpeinen is known for his large-scale choreographies that have been performed by his students and that have gained major recognition in Finland and abroad.

In addition to Lampi, Mäntylä and Turpeinen, the question on how to get boys and men engaged in dance has intrigued many other Finnish dance teachers, such as Marketta Viitala (1998), Eeva Anttila (1994) and Minna Palokangas-Sirviö for example, who have worked in their respective areas of children's dance in Pyhäjärvi, Kajaani and Helsinki to find ways to teach dance for boys and young men. Viitala, Anttila and Palokangas-Sirviö are in many respects excellent examples of female dance teachers who have successfully involved boys in dance.

22   On Turpeinen's 'raw timber method' see Chapter 4.

Discussion on Boys in Dance

Gender differences between male and female dance students have been reported by a number of teachers and scholars from different countries (see for example: Carroll & Lofthouse 1969, Alkins 1994, Bond 1994, Plummer 1995, Wigert 1999). Russell Alkins, a ballet teacher and Grade Examiner for the Royal Academy, suggests that boys develop differently from girls: they can have problems with posture and their feet are often 'difficult' (1994, p. 49). In addition, boys perform masculinity 'with a tense and stiff body that will not "move"' (ibid.) and when they spring and leap, 'they often attempt to use their arms and shoulders' (ibid.). Anne Wigert's (1999) observational studies on dance in Swedish elementary school support Carroll and Lofthouse's (1969) view on gender differences in the ways children solve movement tasks. According to her, boys find high energy, speed and transitions enjoyable and they tend to use more space than girls. Karen Bond (1994) has acknowledged in her observational studies in Australia that free transitions, explosive energy, high speed, the use of body weight and loudness are typical of boys' way of moving. Plummer's (1995) thesis on gendered codes in modern dance suggest that female dance students enjoy (gentle and indirect use of kinesphere and their steps and gestures are performed with isolated parts of the body) while male students are more focused on elevation, locomotory movements and holistic ways of using the body. In addition, male dance students' direct and strong actions take often place in general space (Plummer 1995, see also Spurgeon 1997).

Sometimes, the notion of male aggression has been used to explain male dance students' behaviour and movement qualities. Wigert (1999), for example, refers to the winter issue of *Dance Perspectives* (40/1969) where a number of male dancers consider aggression as a positive source of energy. She then proposes that boys and men need to find ways to express their aggressive emotions. Perhaps boys' aggressions and their desire to use a lot of space are some of the qualities that make Alkins propose that dance teachers should not let boys 'dominate at the expense of the girls' (1994, p. 48).

Apart from Turpeinen's (1994, 1997, 1998) articles, there is very little academic or pedagogic literature that has been published directly on boys and dance in Finland. It is more common that authors make short references to males in dance. For example, Aino Sarje (1997) takes up young schoolboys' responses to dance in her survey on schoolchildren's relation to creative dance in four elementary schools that participated in a particular 'artists in schools'–project in Central Finland in 1996. Sarje (ibid.) assumes that all boys connect the dance studio with femininity and uses statistical analysis to show that dance is 'easier' and 'more natural' for girls than for boys. She also writes about children's attitudes towards dance and dancers. Boys, she suggests, are slightly reserved towards those who dance and they have a 'remarkably' more negative view on dance than girls. She calls for ideas on how to get boys to overcome their preconceptions and how to get them excited about dance.

Eeva Anttila (1997) shares with Sarje (1997) the concern that it is important to find out why boys have more negative experiences with dance than girls. She refers to a series of dance classes that were offered to eight groups of 5-9 year-old children as part of her work towards the licentiate thesis. In these classes, boys were often more self-confident than girls and they came up with more 'original' movement ideas than girls. In addition, boys had more problems with concentration and were less able to bring their tasks to a conclusion than girls. Moreover, older boys had difficulties in freeing themselves to move expressively (Anttila 1997).

Finnish boys take up dance significantly later than girls, generally around 15 years of age, reports Pipsa Nieminen (1998a) in her PhD thesis on non-professional dancers' socialisation, participation motives, attitudes and stereotypes.[23] In addition, as far as taking up dance was concerned, both boys and girls in dance found the influence of their mothers more significant than that of their fathers. This distinguishes the socialisation in dancing from the socialisation

---

23   See also Nieminen 1998b.

in sports. Moreover, other siblings who already dance make it 'easier' and 'more evident' for their brothers to take up dance (Nieminen 1997).

Marketta Viitala (1998), a Finnish dance educator in the area of children's dance, calls for the right for boys to try out dance without unnecessary social pressures. Such pressures link to common ignorance, which, as Viitala suggests, is one of the main reasons why dance is undervalued in Finnish society. In addition, boys need role models if they are to dance but Finnish society seldom provides such models (ibid.). In the search for a scapegoat, Viitala points her finger at theatrical dancing and asks whether too much gracefulness in certain male dancers at a critical point in history distanced men from dance.[24] She calls for boys' right to be sensitive and suggests that public action should be taken to replace old biases with new strategies. She highlights the importance of media in implementing new values and believes that children should have equal opportunities to learn dance at school (ibid.).

In the spring of 2002, a task force that was set up by the Finnish National Opera Ballet School and the Vantaa Dance Institute published a memo on dance pedagogy for boys (see Lampi et al 2002). The objective of the memo was to create guidelines for boys' dance education within the framework of the basic arts education in dance. The memo focuses on two key pointers: the balanced structure of dance classes and some special features of young males. In addition to the guidelines and some practical ideas, the memorandum also contains four short reflections on boys and dance, one from each of the task force members.[25] In the memo, Lampi addresses the 'teaching of the man' in a poetic fashion, Turpeinen maps the paths different boys have taken in dance training and Niiranen challenges the notion that a male teacher is the best option for all-male groups. Mäntylä reflects his personal dance history and the problems he faced at the

---

24   Viitala does not specify the period in history she refers to. Neither does she mention any names.
25   More on the memo in Chapter 4.

age of nine due to his ballet interest. His account highlights the existing tensions between males and dance in Finnish culture.

Structure of the Book

This books seeks to investigate some of the key discourses that operate in dance education for boys. Methodologies applied and the corpus of data collected are presented in Chapter Two.

The discourse analysis of accounts of dance teachers and of other dance-related people such as administrators and critics, in Chapter Three, presents how essentialist ideas about boys are constructed from a number of different discursive perspectives in such accounts. Discourses of biology, medicine and evolutionary psychology are picked out from text extracts as key advocates of essentialism. Also, it is shown how essentialist discourses amalgamate with the heroic masculinity, as presented in popular culture and Western history writing, to fix heroic behaviour into male biology while the nexus of nationalist and psychological discourses present young Finnish males as particularly fragile.

The focus then shifts to examine how boys in dance are discursively constructed differently in different contexts. The discourse of otherness introduces the 'freak'. On the other hand, the male dance student is constructed as 'normal' with references to plurality and ordinariness but by constructing him as an athlete. The sports discourse provides the means to construct boys in dance as superior to other males and make them attractive to the military discourse. Male dance students' need for social support is shown to be constructed through a therapeutic discourse that perceives boys in dance as victims and also through the role learning discourse that emphasises boys' need of male role models. The belief that male dance students are competitors to each other is also taken up in Chapter Three.

Boys' dance education is examined in Chapter Four from a Foucauldian point of view as a collection of discursive practices that operate on the student's body. Teacher's accounts in primary and secondary data are investigated to recognise discursive underpinnings of ideas that constitute pedagogical frameworks for the teaching of boys. Formal dance educational documents such as national curricula guidelines are examined for their gender-neutral tone. Essentialist and emancipatory ideas, which underpin claims about all-male groups in dance within the basic arts education, are also studied. This leads to the analysis of texts that perceive boys' dance education – its content and methods – as distinct from other forms of dance education.

Also in Chapter Four, the 'raw timber method' of Isto Turpeinen is introduced as a complex example that draws from discourses of motor skills development, sports training and psychology. A three-stage model, presented by the task force on dance pedagogy for boys, provides another example of the amalgamation of these discourses. Tag is introduced as an example of a play activity in boys' dance education. The discursive underpinnings of its use as a means to handle delirious boys are examined. Discourses of sports training and nutrition are scrutinised as a means through which stronger and healthier bodies that operate as mannequins of modernity are formed in boys' dance education. The rhetoric act of renaming ballet to get more boys to take up dance is examined at the end of Chapter Four.

In Chapter Five, the notion of adventure is presented as an overarching idea that connects themes and practices of boys' dance education. The teaching of male students is analysed in the light of dance teacher Ilkka Lampi's poetic elaboration upon the theme. In addition, the rich intertextuality that opens up on a page from Isto Turpeinen's choreographic notebook of *True Stories* is examined. Glimpses from the Dance Camp for Boys, in the summer of 2001, reveal the camp as a site where various masculinities – the ballet dancer, the entertainer, the warrior, the soldier and the West-African black masculinity – intermingle. Turpeinen's (1998) account of his 'mission' in boys' dance education and some female dance teachers' accounts show that the teaching of boys can appear from the teacher's point of view as an adventure. A female performance of masculinity as an attempt to gain legitimacy in front of an all-male student group is also taken up. An examination of different views on boys dancing in public closes the chapter.

Chapter Six looks at which gendered positions are available for male students to inhabit in the choreographies that they perform. Performances of masculinity are examined by scrutinising dance analytic descriptions of seven choreographies and a critic's review of one dance. In addition, performances of sexuality are analysed. Also, choreographies that subject homosexual masculinity and intimate male bonding to heteronormative social control are examined.

Underpinned by a social constructionist view of the subject, Chapter Seven scrutinises self-narratives of boys in dance to see how young males position themselves inside and outside the dance context. Extracts from focus groups are examined to see how boys discuss their relations with significant others. A self-narrative of a male dance student in the Higher Education is analysed to see how a strong heteronormative masculinist background can make it difficult for a young male to solve a conflict between a traditional masculinist identity and a more open-ended male identity in theatrical dance. Self-narratives of two other students are studied to see how dance practices can both enable and limit the performances of diverse identities. Some linguistic strategies that boys in dance use to address bullying, and to protect themselves from bullying, are examined in the final section of Chapter Seven.

The recognition of the oppressive power of heteronormativity in the examined accounts of male dance students in Chapter Seven leads, in Chapter Eight, into a more detailed analysis of the rejection of effeminacy and the fear of dancing 'queerly' in dance educational accounts on boys' dancing. A discourse analysis undertaken on Ludvig Nyholm's (1959) article is used to point out how a gender political strategy that rejects effeminacy and homosexuality emerges through the interplay of discourses of modernity, eugenics, psychiatry and nationalism. The use of sports discourse in Nyholm's account is examined as a means to 'wash' dance from these marks of 'degeneracy'. More recent text extracts are used to demonstrate that texts on male dancing from the late 1990s and early 2000s resonate with the late 1950s view that rejects homosexuality and male performances of effeminacy as damaging. The chapter shows how

40

particular constructions of the male dance student and certain performances of masculinity and sexuality have appeared to be politically more advantageous than others in distinctive social and historical contexts. Concluding remarks and reflections in Chapter Nine bring the book to a closure.

Chapter Two
Research Methodologies

Dance Education as Discourse

There is much more than just the physicality of dancing involved in dance education.[1] Learning dance involves embodying movement codes and mastering their performance in the dancing body. In the area of theatrical dance, learning dance commonly takes place through social interaction in a dance class through formal teaching-learning situations. In such a context, teaching and learning involve generally both verbal and non-verbal communication (Gray 1989). These two modes of communication are often used in a complementary manner and/or interchangeably. In addition, discussion on dance teaching appears verbally from informal coffee table discussions to formal seminars and in written form from scholarly papers to articles in newspapers and weekly magazines. Reflection on what goes on in dance classes takes place in student groups as well as in the musings of individual students and teachers.

It can be suggested that dancing as a form of embodied understanding and bodily meaning-making amalgamates in a dance class with spoken words and non-verbal signifiers and with what is already 'read' or 'said' to constitute a set of statements that can be regarded as a 'discourse'. Dance discourse is not a single unified set of ideas. Rather, dancing embodies historically specific cultural meanings (Adshead 1981, Hodgens 1988, Foster 1995, Desmond 1997, Shapiro 1998). In that sense, dancing, choreographies and dance educational conventions are formed through and carry traces of other discourses. As Susan Leigh Foster suggests,

---

1   Gray (1989) provides a useful conceptual framework for dance educational research where different variables of dance teaching have been mapped out.

[a]ny standardized regimen of bodily training ... embodies, in the very organization of its exercises, the metaphors used to instruct the body, and in the criteria specified for physical competence, a coherent (or not so coherent) set of principles that govern the action of that regimen. These principles, reticulated with aesthetic, political, and gendered connotations, cast the body who enacts them into larger arenas of meaning where it moves alongside bodies bearing related signage. (1995, p. 8)

I sought a way to make an in-depth analysis of the relationships between dance, gender, identities and institutional politics. This type of research is typically interpretative in the sense that it rejects the positivist stance of revealing the 'truth' about these phenomena through 'objective' methodologies and sees, instead, that our accounts about 'reality' and our practices are socially constructed (Burr 1995; Foucault 1972, 1995; Gergen 1999; Green & Stinson 1999). In my search for a feasible methodology that would work for my research questions and the types of data I had to deal with, I acknowledged that there are limitations to every methodology and that applying a nexus of methodologies can 'compensate for the weaknesses of one methodology in a domain by supplementing or complementing it with another methodology which is stronger in that domain' (Breakwell & Rose 2000, p. 20-21).

Dance educational questions have been typically studied with document analysis, various types of interviews and various forms of observational methods (Gray 1989, Green & Stinson 1999). When considering the different options for working on my research topic, I rejected the idea of designing a survey because surveys and questionnaires tend to provide short replies of a closed nature. Such data is rather useless for research that seeks constructed interpretations (Green & Stinson 1999). I also abandoned the idea of ethnography because of the 'naturalist' underpinnings of ethnographic research.[2] I,

2   Naturalism can be regarded as a philosophical attempt to remain faithful to the nature of the phenomenon that is studied. Within ethnographic literature, '[n]aturalism proposes that, as far as possible, the social world should be studied in its 'natural' state, undisturbed by the researcher" (Hammersley & Atkinson 1995, p. 6).

however, regarded the ethnographer's field methods – observing, listening, asking open-ended questions, taking notes and making recordings - as feasible ways to collect multiple forms of data on boys and dance. I needed to do 'fieldwork' in order to collect data from various dance educational institutions. I hoped to access archives in these institutions to see if there were useful documents for my research. Also, I needed to listen to how dance teachers and male students construct their views on boys' dancing. In addition, I wanted to see how gender operated and how masculinities were embodied and performed in dance educational practice and in choreography.

The Data

To locate secondary data on boys in dance, I ran a data search to trace printed and electronic sources that already existed on boys and dance. I conducted a keyword search with electronic search tools in English and in Finnish. I used libraries with dance collections in Finland and in England to gather relevant articles and other printed data. Additional secondary data were collected from the archives of the institutes visited, particularly in the Finnish National Opera, the Kuopio Dance Festival and the Vantaa Dance Institute. Secondary data collection continued throughout the research process and in some cases colleagues who knew my research interest contacted me to point out additional relevant sources.[3]

Secondary data included dance educational books, articles and Internet pages (Anttila 1994; Lampi 1991; Turpeinen 1994, 1997, 1998, http://www.kolumbus.fi/isto. turpeinen/index2.htm 15.3.2003;

---

3   I am particularly grateful to Tiina Suhonen for bringing Ludvig Nyholm's (1959) article to my attention. I also want to thank Anne Makkonen for providing me with a copy of Piia Ahonen's (2002) MA dissertation and Satu Sihvoin for providing me with a copy of Marika Bergman's (2002) article.

Lampi 1991; Nyholm 1959; Viitala 1998), curricular texts (Lampi et al 2002; Opetushallitus 2001, 2002, Raatikon tanssikoulu n.d.), a choreographer's unpublished notebook (Turpeinen 2000), programme notes (Raatikon tanssikoulu & Tikkurilan teatteri 1996; Sokura 2000) and photographs on choreographies taken by Kari Hakli, Markus Lahtinen, Laura Luostarinen, Kari Liukkunen and Isto Turpeinen and also by some anonymous photographers. Media accounts on boys' dance education and on young males in dance were collected from newspapers and magazines (Af Björkesten 1997; Bask 1992; Bergman 2002; Hankaniemi 1999; Harri 1993; Hietalahti 1996; Hietaniemi 1989, 1992; Härkönen 1999; Innanen 1997; Janhonen 1996; Jokela-Nazimov 1991; Jääskeläinen 1993; Kaikkonen 1996; Kaiku 1996; Kangas 1994; Laakso 1988; Lammassaari 1992; Lehtiranta 1993; Leinonen 1994; Lipiäinen 1996; Miettinen 1994b; Moring 1993; Mäkinen 1959a, 1959b; Nykänen 2003, Pietinen 1997, Reunamäki 2000, Runonen 2001, Räsänen 1986, Räsänen 2000a, 2000b; Räty 2003; Saarela 2001; Sairo 1990; Sarjas 1995; Silenius 1991; Tiihonen 1996; Tenhunen 1994; Talvitie 1990; Tossavainen 1998; Tourunen 1988; Vuori 1996; Yli-Sirniö 1996). Transcriptions of two television documentaries (Rauhamaa 1994; YLE TV1 2003), a television news insert (Keinänen 2003) and two radio programmes (Mattila 2001; YLE RADIO 1 2001) were also used as secondary data. In addition, three male dance students' self-narratives, as constructed in their MA dissertations, were also included as secondary data (Luhtanen 1998, Halonen 2000, Knif 2000).

Primary data collection, which took place between December 2000 and May 2002, included informal and formal discussions, focus groups and observation of dance classes. I limited my research to dance institutions that teach dance for young males who engage with dance either as a serious hobby or as an occupational interest. For practical reasons, and also because my approach was qualitative rather than quantitative, I narrowed the focus down to seven institutions: The Finnish National Opera Ballet School and the Department of Dance at the Theatre Academy in Helsinki, the Dance Camp for Boys in Siilinjärvi, the Department of Dance in the Outokumpu Learning Centre, the Department of Dance in the Turku Conservatory and the Department of Dance in the Turku Arts Academy/Turku Polytechnic and the Vantaa Dance Institute. I chose these institutions because they represented the Finnish arts education system from basic arts education level to upper secondary level vocational dance education up to dance studies in higher education. The fact that these educational locations had male students and that some of these institutions were well known for their emphasis on male dancing were obvious reasons to choose them.

During the fieldwork period, I visited all institutions involved at least once. In most cases, at least two visits were made to each institution. The visits lasted from two hours to several days and included observation of dance classes or dance performances as well as informal discussions and formal focus groups with teachers and students. The longest single period of fieldwork took place in the Dance Camp for Boys in Siilinjärvi in June 2001. I volunteered to work as a supervisor throughout the ten-day camp. I had my meals with the 17 boys (age from 10 to 16) and 5 of their teachers. Together with a female supervisor, I helped with mundane tasks, comforted those who were homesick, tried to make sure that the lights were out by 11pm and so on. This allowed me to establish a good rapport with many of the boys as well as with their teachers, some of whom I knew already before I came to the camp.

Fifteen focus groups were conducted in order to study how discourses that underpin boys' dance education and also to explain how young males in dance construct themselves in their self-narratives. The sample was obtained by contacting administrators in the institutions and asking for their help in recruiting volunteers – male dance students and their teachers - for the focus groups. Separate focus groups were organised for students and teachers.

All together, 33 male dance students aged from 10 to 28 years of age and 24 teachers (12 male, 12 female) aged from 29 to 49 years of age were interviewed. Those participants who are directly quoted in this book are presented in Tables 1 and 2 below. Throughout the book, pseudonyms are used to refer to the participants.

Pseudonym	Age	Institutional Level
Matt	n.a.	Basic
Elliot	41	Basic/vocational
Frank	46	Basic
Jeremy	39	Basic
Janet	46	Higher
Maggie	36	Higher
Tina	32	Higher
Jane	29	Basic

Table 1. Participants of the teacher focus groups who are quoted in the book.

Pseudonym	Age	Institutional Level
Risto	25	Higher
Pekka	28	Higher
Lauri	22	Higher
Kalle	24	Higher
Teemu	13	Basic
Mikko	16	Basic
Eero	13	Basic
Jaakko	14	Basic

Table 2. Participants of the student focus groups who are quoted in the book.

The observation of dance classes included classes in ballet, ballet repertory, contact improvisation, improvisation, jazz dance, modern dance, music, tap and West-African dances in five institutions: the Finnish National Opera Ballet School, the Kuopio Boys' Dance Course, the Turku Arts Academy, the Turku Conservatory and the Vantaa Dance Institute. In addition, two lectures and a panel discussion that were held in a seminar on dance pedagogy in Vantaa 27-29.4.2001 provided additional primary.

Dancing is certainly a central component of dance education and gender can be 'read' from the dancing body (Foster 1995, Carter 1996). Moreover, dance educational institutions tend to organise showings where students perform dances that have been choreographed particularly for them or variations from the existing dance repertoire. Visual data such as video recordings of dances that had been choreographed for male students or mixed-sex groups were found from the archives of the Vantaa Dance Institute, the Finnish National Opera Ballet School and the Turku Conservatory. The researcher's dance analytic descriptions provided primary data about masculinities that were performed in seven choreographies (see Table 3).

Title of the Work	Choreographer	Year	Genre
Seven Brothers	Isto Turpeinen	2002	Narrative dance theatre
General Raiko	Ilkka Lampi	1993	Narrative dance theatre
The Newer Quadrille of the Northern Boys	Marketta Viitala	2000	Narrative dance theatre
White on White	Jorma Uotinen	1991	Contemporary dance
People's Celebration	Ari Numminen	1998	Postmodernist dance theatre
The Last Warning	Katri Soini	1996	Contemporary dance
Reset to zero - coincidental accidents	Sari Hannula	2000	Contemporary dance

Table 3. Choreographies analysed in the book.

Observing Dance Classes

Moore and Yamamoto's (1988) ideas on perception and the 'bodily prejudices' that influence the way the world is perceived by different people made me aware of the perceiver as an active meaning-maker. They emphasise the inter-subjective nature of perception, psychological, somatic and environmental conditions that can influence perception and the activities that observations involve. I discussed these issues with Karen Bond and Sue Stinson during their method course on 'researching meaning in dance education' that was organised in Theatre Academy in Helsinki in the summer of 1997. I furthered my understanding of observational practice by reading

49

through Lofland and Lofland's (1995) book on qualitative observation in social settings. I also became acquainted with Judith A. Gray's (1989) book on dance educational research although her behaviourist oriented framework for observing dance educational settings was designed for the collection of quantitative rather than qualitative data and therefore was less relevant for me.

When I was conducting fieldwork in dance studios and other spaces where actual dancing took place, I tried to find a place in a corner or by the wall, where my presence would not distract the dance class. Generally, I tried to remain neutral but occasionally I was pulled into social interaction with the class. For example, in Minna Karesluoto's all-male ballet class in Turku Arts Academy, I had to participate in the class because two male students insisted on it and I did not want to compromise the rapport I had established with them. Likewise, on the last day in the dance camp, I had to participate in the sharing that involved an African-influenced dance improvisation where everybody participated. In one dance class, I was turned into a judge of a contest that involved two groups and a showing of my videotape was requested to determine the winning group. Personally, I enjoyed participating in the dance activities, however, I also realised that personal participation hindered rather than helped the collection of visual data. Clearly, the situation would have been very different had I had phenomenological aspirations with my research.

A dance class is full of life – it is rich in physical activities and social interaction. During the observational sessions in the field, I followed Bond's advice to 'alternate between perception of part and whole' (1997) to keep track of what was going on. In order to cope with the overwhelming amount of visual data, I also had to focus on particular types of activities that were relevant to my research objectives. Thus, rather than pondering over questions of safety, or some kinesiological concerns of particular dance exercises, for example, I focused on acts that could be regarded as meaningful in terms of embodying and performing gender and sexuality. While observing, I tried to be aware of my 'inner state' as an observer by questioning my shifting discursive positions that directed the choices I made in terms of focus and in terms of interpreting what I saw. Rather than trusting my perception of fading moments, I used a video camera to record actions. These recordings provided visual data that could be used to verify written notes and to produce detailed descriptions of dance activities through multiple viewings.

From a poststructuralist viewpoint, it can be argued that dance educational activities are never limited to their immediate presence. Instead, they are linked through their discursive underpinnings with various contexts that exist outside the immediate boundaries of particular dance events. This makes observational methods that focus merely on what takes place in the immediate teaching-learning situation, in a piece of choreography or in the dancing body inadequate. Therefore, methods that focus on describing spatial and dynamic qualities of movement through a limited conceptual framework, like Laban Movement Analysis does, fall short in analysis if the objective is to trace the discursive underpinnings of embodied signifiers in the dancing body and to link the dance 'text' with social divisions such as gender, class, 'race', sexuality and age within the wider social relations.

Thus, I used my 'own' words - a fragmented corpus of discursive dance languages and other 'language games' (Wittgenstein 1965) – to provide interpretative descriptions of what I observed. Following Loftland and Loftland's (1995) idea on 'jotted' note taking, I scribbled down key words, short phrases and quotes and drew stick-figures. I used these notes as a memory-aid when I later produced full field notes at the end of the day or the next morning. These notes included comments about the institutional environment, observed dance practices, social interaction between the teacher and the students as well as between the students themselves. In addition, my notes included comments on conversations that I had happened to overhear or on informal conversations that I had had with students and teachers. Gradually, during the process of note taking, I started to write down preliminary interpretations about possible discourses that underpinned observed practices and different themes in conversations.

Focus Groups: Interviewing Boys and Their Teachers

In order to enlarge the corpus of primary data and to gain first-hand experience on how discursive ideas on boys and dance emerge through social interaction, I decided to interview male dance students and their teachers. To prepare, I reviewed my notes on interviewing methods from Jennifer Brown's lecture at the University of Surrey (14.9.1999) and also from Karen Bond and Sue Stinson's method course (see above). In addition, I got acquainted with some literature on the subject (Briggs 1986; Flick 1998; Powney & Watts 1987; Smith 1995).

Structured interviewing with a strict interview schedule or a pre-designed questionnaire was clearly unfit for my purposes as my objective was to study discourses that operate in respondents' talk rather than to 'reduce the responses to quantitative categories' (Smith 1995, p. 9). In addition, I wanted to 'capture the richness of the themes emerging from the respondent's talk' (ibid.). Structured interviewing was far too limiting for this. Semi-structured interviewing seemed to allow more opportunities for the respondent 'to tell his or her own story' (Smith 1995, p. 12). Also, as I had to take into consideration that some questions on gender and sexuality could be experienced as sensitive, semi-structured interviewing seemed like a better way to 'establish a rapport with the respondent' (Smith 1995, p. 12).

I chose to use a semistructured approach within a group interview format for the reason that group interviews are less time-consuming but also because 'they stimulate the answers and support … [respondents] in remembering events, and … they can lead beyond the answers of the single interviewee' (ibid.). Within qualitative research, there are various group interviewing techniques that suit different purposes (see Flick 1998). I was not interested merely in *what* people thought but more importantly in *how* and *why* they perceived certain topics the way they did. I was also curious to see how identities are constructed and how social positioning takes place in relation to the discussed topics. Therefore, I decided to use a focus group technique that can be defined as

> a semistructured group session, moderated by a group leader, held in an informal setting, with the purpose of collecting information on a designated topic. (Carey & Smith 1994, p. 124)

Focus groups differ from other group interview methodologies 'by "the explicit use of the group interaction" as research data' (Kizinger 1994, p. 103), which can be seen as one of the great advantages of this approach. The focus group technique is a useful, and also unique, methodology in the sense that it yields rich and detailed descriptions of complex 'experiential information by using group interactions' (Carey & Smith 1994, p. 124). From a discourse analytic point of view, one of the key advantages of this approach is that it gives space for respondents' priorities and their use of language and discourses when they explicate their ideas and make sense about the world in a group (Kizinger 1994).

One of the main weaknesses of focus group methodology is that it compromises privacy and confidentiality (Kitzinger 1995). In addition, psychosocial group dynamics can cause 'censoring and comforting' (Carey & Smith 1994, p. 124). I was acutely aware of these shortcomings. I decided to tackle the issue of confidentiality as I met the respondents face to face before each interviewing session. Also, I thought that tension does not always have to be viewed as something negative in a research setting. Indeed, as Wellings, Branigan and Mitchell (2000, p. 265) suggest,

> conflicts over differences of opinion are rarely accessible to the social researcher in routine observation or in interviews since the presence of the researcher will attenuate or temper expression of discord but may be re-enacted and expressed in the simulated social setting afforded by the focus group.

My original intention was to conduct fourteen focus groups: one group of teachers and one group of students in each of the seven institutions. However, because in two of the vocational institutions some of the boys were out of reach and in one of the institutions there were only two male students enrolled in the dance programme, I decided to conduct additional student focus groups. In one institution it was not possible to schedule a focus group with the teachers despite several attempts. My revised approach ensured that I had enough data to work with.

I prepared two discussion guides: one for the teachers and the other for the students. In both cases, I used open-ended questions that had emerged from the interplay of written sources on boys and dance, literature on gender and masculinity studies, and my personal experiences as a male dance teacher and a student. Following Kitzinger's (1994) suggestion on the use of 'cards', I wrote some key statements on boys' dancing on pieces of paper to stimulate discussion.

I piloted the discussion guides and the use of the card method in one of the institutions. I learned that I needed to limit the number of questions and give more freedom to the respondents for in-depth discussions to emerge. During the pilot for the 'card method', I found some of the respondents held the 'cards' in their hands and repeated the written statements over and over again instead of moving on to discuss these statements. I regarded the written statements as overly dominating in the focus group situation and decided to discard the card method. I revised the discussion guides (see Appendices 1 and 2). In actual focus group situations, the discussion guide functioned merely as a memory-aid: I used it to tick off the discussed topics. It also helped me to use moderator skills to draw the discussion back to the pre-designed topics when a digression did not seem to provide relevant data.

I decided to allow the more sensitive topics to 'emerge gradually over the course of the interview' (Lee 1993, p. 103). Of course, it was quite impossible to know precisely which topics individual respondents regarded as difficult or embarrassing. However, I followed Lee's idea that people can have difficulties in picking up topics, which are 'highly personal, threatening or confidential ... unfamiliar or distasteful' (1993, pp. 102-103). I spotted two topics that might be potentially sensitive to the teachers that I was going to interview: sexuality and speaking about individual students. As for the boys, I thought sexuality and experiences of bullying might be sensitive topics for them. In addition, I thought it might be difficult for them to talk about their teachers. To put the participants more at ease, I followed Wellings, Branigan and Mitchell's advice to work 'from the more neutral and potentially inoffensive [topics] to more personal [ones]' (2000, p. 257). I placed the question about bullying towards the end of the discussion guide before the question that addressed the commonly held stereotype of the male dancer as homosexual. In this way, I was hoping that the respondents themselves might lead the discussion from one topic to another.

In the actual focus groups, I tackled the problem of mentioning names by starting each session with a briefing where I made clear the objectives of the session and of other aspects of my research. I underlined the importance of confidentiality and promised to use pseudonyms. To avoid unnecessary anxieties, I also asked for permission from the respondents to use a video camera. I explained that the video recording would provide me with extra help in case I had difficulties transcribing some parts of the conversation from the audiotape. I made it clear that the videotapes would not be shown to anybody and that both the audio- and videotapes would be stored in a safe place where only I had access. I also made sure that I answered all the questions that the participants might have about the research before I asked for their informed consent. From younger boys, informed consent was asked not only from the boys themselves but also from their parents, in all cases through the respective institutions.

Following Kitzinger's (1995) advice, I decided to make the respondents at ease by making the setting comfortable and relaxed and providing refreshments. Then I started off by introducing a non-threatening question such as 'can you describe to each other how you came to take up dance?' The focus groups lasted from 1.5 hours to 2 hours. Following the idea that in focus groups 'attempts must be made to enable participants to focus on one another, rather than on the researcher' (Wellings, Branigan & Mitchell 2000, p. 257), I tried to function as a moderator or a facilitator of the ongoing conversation. I used my body language and open-ended questioning techniques to ensure that everyone actively participated.

Usually, I tried to avoid intervening by commenting on what the participants said. However, in cases where I knew the teachers quite well, it was more difficult to maintain the traditional independent role of the moderator. While not offering opinions of my own, I had to acknowledge that I was part of their lived history. Moreover, I too had taught boys – sometimes the same young men that were their students. In these cases, I chose to participate in the conversation to maintain the rapport with the group. I do not think that my participation 'damaged' the data in any way. Rather, my accounts became part of the nexus of different voices where multiple views intermingled.

As the interviews came to an end, I asked all participants to fill out a simple questionnaire that contained questions about age, education (teachers) and parents' occupation (students). I also asked them to write down their contact details in case I had to get in touch with them for some reason. The debriefing at the end of the interview also gave me the opportunity to give the participants my contact details in case they wanted to speak to me about anything that they felt uncomfortable in speaking in the group or if they wanted to discuss some of the topics further. Once the tape recorder and the video camera had been turned off and the 'formal' part of the interview was over, many of the participants expressed their contentment at having had the opportunity to participate in the focus group. Many of the boys said they were genuinely happy that they had this opportunity to share their ideas and experiences on dancing and to address also such topics that are in everyday conversations passed by with a silence. In two focus groups, the post-interview conversations started to address such topics that I had to ask for a permission to continue recording.

With almost 30 hours of recorded conversations to transcribe, I developed a more economic method to deal with the audible data by transcribing only those parts of the discussions that I had marked, on the basis of preliminary listening of the tapes, as relevant to my research. While transcribing these sections, I frequently listened through also other sections of the tapes to ensure that I did not lose the meaning of the surrounding context. Also, as the aim of this book was not to provide a detailed conversation analysis but an analysis of discourses that underpin accounts presented in the focus groups, there was no need to use a complex system of transcription symbols. However, a radically simplified version of such symbols was adapted from Wooffitt (2001) to ensure the clarity of the transcript where the conversation was dense or otherwise obscure.[4] Once a transcript was ready, a proof reading was done to confirm that the text matched with the recorded voices.

Dance Analysis: Reading Masculinities from Choreographies

As Hodgens maintains, interpreting dances requires skills of *'recognising, characterising,* and *making sense of* the object of event in question' (1988, p. 61). The interpretative practice involves locating the dance in the broad socio-cultural framework that underpins it. It also involves recognising the context where the dance appears (artistic, educational, social, therapeutic, sacral, etc). Recognising the genre and style of any particular dance is also important as they both convey, even in a post-modern world where barriers between genres erode, important insights about ideologies and values that underpin conventions in different traditions (Hodgens 1988). The viewer studies the embodiment of these discourses in the dance 'text' to construct her/his reading of the choreography. 'The reality of interpretation is', as Adshead-Lansdale suggests,

> that the readers enter at different points, select points of interest and, most usually enter from an interpretive or evaluative stance. The reader then selects (chooses) those 'facts' which support that perspective. In this sense the reader constructs the dance. (1999, p. 19)

Dance analysis, as described in Adshead et al (1988), Adshead-Lansdale (1999) and Carter (1996), was used as a methodology to

4   The transcript marks used include: (.) = a short pause in the speech; [ ] = simultaneously occurring speech; xx = a strong emphasis in the speech; (comment) = focus group facilitator's comments.

describe masculinities performed in seven choreographies (see table 3 above). The process included the following steps:

Each tape was watched through once or twice to get a general idea about the existing visual data and to locate dance examples that were relevant to the research questions.

A choreographic outline of the selected dances was produced. This included a detailed description of the dancers and their movements.[5] Visual elements, such as set design, lighting, costumes and props and also audible elements such as speech and music were described when necessary.

Relationships between dancers were described.

Different sections from a single choreography were juxtaposed when necessary.

I used my 'own' words to describe the dances very much the same way as I did in the field (see above). In the viewing of video recorded dances the same precautions applied regarding perception as in the observations in the field. As I was focused on examining how gender and sexuality were constructed and performed in these dances, it was unnecessary for me to capture everything that went on in them. In that sense my descriptions are partial as descriptions always are (Adshead-Lansdale 1999; Green & Stinson 1999).

I approached the dance examples in this research by following Adshead-Lansdale's (1999) idea of dance descriptions as 'unstable' texts. From the collected dance examples, I examined how masculinities were constructed and performed in relation to male and

---

5   Adshead et al emphasise the acts of '*recognising* and *identifying* the character of the dance, *ascribing* qualities to it and understanding its meaning' (1988, p. 110). However, such interpretative acts are made possible only by '*discerning, describing and naming* the components and the form of the dance' (ibid). In this model, the components of dance are 'movement', 'dancers', 'visual settings', and 'aural elements' and the formal structures emerge from 'relations according to components', 'relations at point in time', 'relations through time', 'relations between the moment and the linear development' and 'major/minor/subsidiary relations' (ibid.).

female characters and 'in relation to the narrative' (Carter 1996, p. 47) or what Barr and Lewin call the 'proto-narrative units' in the dance.[6] I examined how maleness, the notion of being a man, was portrayed through the characters that boys performed. Following Carter (1996), I linked these questions to questions about the characters' social significance in the narrative, their 'destiny' in the story, their mental states and their agency. I also scrutinised other components such as costumes and sound to see how 'masculine actions and qualities' (Carter 1996, p. 52) are endorsed. I focused particularly on the movement material or more precisely on 'how the actual movement contributes to, or constitutes, the "meanings" of dance (Carter 1996, p. 49). Such investigation linked to questions such as

> what kinds of actions are performed by the women and by the men: who lifts, who supports, who leads or guides and who follows, and what is the significance of these actions in terms of notions of dependency and control? (ibid.)

I tried to be aware of the spatial features and dynamics of movement as well as the dancer's orientation in the performance space and even the use of focus to see in what ways these elements contribute to the narrative structure in a meaningful way.

The dance analysis method of Adshead et al (1988) that has been developed further from a feminist perspective by Alexandra Carter (1996) seemed a useful approach for reading how gender operates in the described dance educational practices and choreographies. She argues that

---

6   The proto-narrative unit can be defined as 'a semiotic unit of experience containing elements that lend themselves to being configured with narratives' (Barr & Lewin 1995, p. 20). This concept can be used 'to refer to elements such as themes, schemas, gestures, and postures that, like Mona Lisa's smile, suggest narrative possibilities without specifying what these narratives might be. Such proto-narratives employ recognizable components of everyday life whose meanings remain ambiguous yet suggestive and open to interpretation' (Ibid).

through analysis, dance can be revealed as not just an artistic product but also as a cultural phenomenon which produces, circulates – and has the potential to subvert – dominant constructs of gender in society. (1996, p. 54)

The model of analysis that Carter proposes is formed on the idea that 'the symbols and structures of dance can only be read in relation to the cultural practices of society' (1996, p. 45). This type of analysis does not assume an apolitical or ahistorical position that focuses merely on how the movements are executed by the dancing body. Nor does it 'rest solely in the realm of aesthetics but is a complex interplay between the aesthetic and the social' (ibid). As Carter suggests, the notion of 'shared cultural meanings' (ibid) is central to this type of analysis.

While Carter's model of analysis focuses on 'constructs of femininity' (1996, p. 43), it can be used more generally to interpret 'how gender in all its cultural manifestations and stereotypes is produced and circulated by dance' (ibid). Carter's suggestions provide a number of useful starting points for reading gender. A list of binary oppositions is just one example:

Polarities of delicate/strong; lyrical/forceful; flexible/direct; inner/outer; passive/active; emotional/rational; natural/cultural; private space/public space can be exposed as facets of the male-female binary construction in which one term, one attribute, one way of being is favoured at the expense of another. (Carter 1996, p. 53)

The disadvantage of Carter's model is its feminist commitment to the idea of patriarchy as an omnipresent structure that subordinates women. That is, patriarchy has been subjected to growing critique in academia and one of the problems with the use of this concept is that it

implies a fixed state of male oppression over women, rather than a fluid relationship between men and women which is complex and moves with great speed at times. (Hargreaves as quoted in Whitehead 2002, p. 87)

More importantly, it has been suggested that the concept of patriarchy is reductionist and that it victimises women (Whitehead 2002). Some feminists, including for example Elshtain, Pollert, Kandiyoti and hooks, have maintained that patriarchy 'is unable to explain and analyse male dominance and its differentiations across multiple sites' (Whitehead 2002, p. 87). From a feminist perspective, it would seem particularly problematic that patriarchy 'fails to prise open and illuminate the points of resistance, change and difference' (Whitehead 2002, p. 87). Whitehead elaborates this further with a reference to Pollert's warning, which

> alerts us to the dangers of assuming a concrete structure within which the individual either struggles to little or no avail or, in Althusserian terms, is subsumed under an ideological apparatus that has successfully inculcated any critical faculty and awareness … there is ample evidence to show that women do successfully resist and overcome male dominance across both the public and private spheres and are increasingly doing so across numerous, diverse societies. Likewise, issues of class, race, ethnicity and sexuality need to be introduced into the analysis if one is to capture something of the (localized) experience and dynamic of male dominance, beyond simple overarching description. (2002, p. 88)

In this light, Carter's feminist oriented dance analysis model appears problematic as it aims to pin down quite complex cultural constructions in the dance by forcing them under the overarching title of 'caused by patriarchy'.

A feminist reading practice can sometimes provide fresh interpretations that deconstruct grand narratives. Other times, when this is not possible, Carter suggests, 'we can, at least, look to their origin and their reasons' (1996, p. 48). Depending on the feminist underpinnings, it could be maintained that in the final analysis this type of interpretation tends to end up blaming either men as a group or the capitalist system. What is lacking from Carter's model is the poststructuralist idea that there is no final referent to the dance or the dancing body. This is not to argue, however, that Carter's feminist oriented model is useless. On the contrary, it is a cornucopia of insight about where to start and what to look at when engaging in a gender-oriented dance analysis. In this research, I applied Carter's ideas but, to grasp the complexity of gender relations, I chose to keep the interpretative part of the analysis work more open than is possible when the dance or the dancing body is investigated with the feminist concept of patriarchy in mind.

Discourse Analysis: Tracing Discourses from the Data

I was looking to find a method to pull out discourses from different forms of data. To find a feasible method for this, I consulted a number of books on discourse analysis (Coyle 1995; Jarowski & Coupland 1999; Jokinen et al 1993, 1999; Parker 1992; Philips & Jørgensen 2002a; Potter & Wetherell 1987 and Wetherell et al 2001a, 2001b). Discourse analysis can be described broadly as a research practice that aims to explain how discourses actualise in various social practices and how social reality is being produced through language and other signifying systems (Coyle 1995, Jokinen et al 1993). However, discourse analysis is not a single method or a coherent research practice.[7] All strands of discourse analysis share a common interest in the human meaning making but there is no epistemological and ontological consistency throughout these different approaches. A precise taxonomy of different strands is difficult to produce because not all examples of discourse analytic research fit into clear-cut categories and there is overlap, for example, in the use of theories and methods (Jawroski and Coupland 1999; Mills 1997; Taylor 2001a). Thus, discourse analysis needs to be understood as a complex and relatively heterogeneous area of social and cultural research or 'a

7   Currently, there are at least twelve strands of discourse analysis including speech act theory and pragmatics, conversation analysis and ethnomethodology, discursive psychology, the ethnography of communication, interactional sociolinguistics, narrative analysis, critical discourse analysis, rhetorical analysis, Bakhtinian research, Foucauldian research, deconstructive discourse analysis and Laclau and Mouffe's discourse theory (Billig 1996; Jawroski & Coupland 1999; Wetherell 2001a; Macleod 2002, Philips & Jørgensen 2002a, Van Djik 1993).

broad theoretical framework concerning the nature of discourse and its role in social life' (Potter & Wetherell 1987, p. 175).

The idea of discourse analysis as the 'close study of language in use' (Taylor 2001a, p 5) underpins different discourse analytic orientations but these research traditions differ from each other in terms of more refined research interests. To determine which approach is most applicable for any particular discourse analytic research depends on a number of factors including, for example, 'the type of data one wants to collect, the topic, the academic discipline in which one is working and the discourse tradition which seems most appropriate' (Wetherell 2001c, p. 380). For the purposes of my research, I needed a discourse analytic approach that could be used for pulling out discourses that underpin uses of language as well as corporeal practices. What I needed was an approach that perceived discourses in the broadest possible sense as 'human meaning-making processes' (Wetherell 2001c, p. 390) and made no distinction between linguistic (discursive) and social (extra-discursive) realms. Such distinction is made, for example in conversation analysis and also some scholars in the area of discourse psychology focus merely on conversations (Taylor 2001a; Wetherell 2001c). However, this type of distinction does not hold very easily in a poststructuralist framework such as the Foucauldian research, deconstructionist discourse analysis or Laclau and Mouffe's discourse theory (Carabine 2001; Hall 2001; Macleod 2002; Philips & Jørgensen 2002b; Wetherell 2001c).

Macleod (2002) who has worked to establish a deconstructive mode of discourse analysis points out three methodological and epistemological problems that entail the distinction between 'discursive' (linguistic) and 'extra-discursive' (material):

> Firstly, it denies the central role of discourse in constituting social relations and subjectivity; secondly, it risks sliding into a cause-effect dualism; and thirdly, it creates the untenable position of constantly having to decide what is discursive and what is extra-discursive.
>
> Macleod 2002, p. 19.

Indeed, society is seen from a poststructuralist perspective 'as a vast argumentative texture through which people construct their reality' (Laclau as quoted in Wetherell 2001c, p. 389). Moreover, 'since all social practices entail *meaning*, and meanings shape and influence what we do – our conduct – all practices have a discursive aspect' (Foucault as quoted in Hall 1997, p. 44, emphasis in original). The distinction between 'discursive' and 'extra-discursive' becomes irrelevant in poststructuralist thought because it is argued that all physical objects get their meanings through discourses from the social contexts they are part of (Philips & Jørgensen 2002b).[8]

Thus, without denying the existence of the material body, it can be argued, in line with Foucault (1984c, 1978, 1995), that the body is a target of multiple discourses, made through discursive practices and a 'vehicle' through which discourses act in society. Moreover, the body receives its multiple meanings through the practices it becomes part of and through the culturally available and historically specific discourses that particular situations call forth from what Foucault (1972, 1978) calls the 'archive'. Following this line of discourse analytic thinking, I asked how discourses constructed the dancing bodies of male students and how they operated in and 'spoke' through dance practices in the dance class and in choreographies on stage.

After collecting the data and preparing it for the analysis, reading it through several times helped to identify '*themes*, categories and objects of the discourse' (Carabine 2001, p. 281, original emphasis) in boys' dancing (see Table 4). Techniques of free association were used to explore 'the connotations, allusions and implications' (Parker 1992, p. 7) which the different texts evoked. I marked the topics recognised

---

8   Actually, a poststructuralist view does not have to deny nor affirm the existence of the 'real' including the material body. As Kenneth Gergen suggests, '[w]hatever is, simply is' (1999, p. 222). That is, 'the moment we begin to articulate what there is – what is truly or objectively the case – we enter a world of discourse – and thus a tradition, a way of life, and a set of value preferences … Each commitment to the real eliminates a rich sea of alternatives, and by quieting alternative discourses we limit possibilities of action' (Ibid). From a poststructuralist position, the question whether the material body exists does not require an answer. It would be more significant to ask what are 'the consequences in cultural life of placing such [discursive] terms into motion' (Gergen 1999, p. 225).

on the margins of the photocopied documents, transcripts and choreographic outlines.

Texts in each topic area were subjected to a detailed scrutiny to see how these topics were addressed from various discursive positions. The next step in analysis was to recognise how discourses link to one another. This was done through free association and by drawing various mind-maps. By asking what bodies of knowledge are necessary to produce such statements or acts, I was able to trace discourses in the data. Sometimes discursive underpinnings were easy to pick out through culturally recognisable textual references in individual samples of the data. More often, however, I had to use an interpretative practice to 'tease' out the discourses. Such teasing was done through an intertextual analysis (see below). This analysis provided an illustrative chart of discourses recognised in the texts (see Figure 1).

Topic areas	Topics
Boys	Energy, nature, development, lack of boys in dance education.
Boys' dancing: dance content	African dances, ballet, break dance, improvisation, jazz dance, contemporary dance, tap.
Boys' dancing: other content	Acrobatics, drama, games, martial arts, military training, pop culture, sports training, health & nutrition.
Social psychological concerns	Attitudes, bullying, fear, group, legitimacy, loneliness, normalcy, role models, sexuality, shame, social position of boys in dance, support, tensions, victim, vulnerability, work.
Educational concerns	Authority and discipline, curricular objectives and content, teacher's gender, recruitment of male students.
The male dancer	Athleticism, body, effeminacy, hetero- and homosexuality.
Masculine stereotypes	Athlete, gay, explorer, hero, straight, warrior, patriot.
Dance art	Cultural significance, economy, female realm, male dancing.

Table 4. Recognisable topics in texts on boys' dancing.

The discourses operate in relation to boys' dance education and choreography and Figure 1 displays the dynamic relationship of this intertextuality. The spiral in the figure represents the fluid nature between boys' dance education and different discursive realms. Further, it shows that the relationships between different discourses are not fixed. Yet, certain groupings of discourses appeared around particular masculinities (printed in italics) that these discourses produce and maintain.

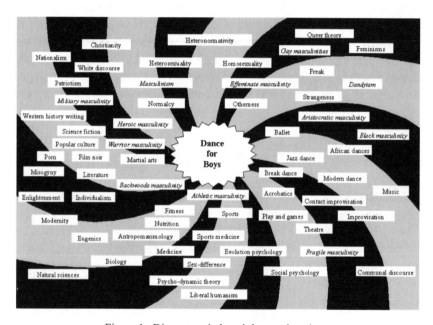

Figure 1. Discourses in boys' dance education.

Following Foucault's (1972, 1978, 1995) idea on discourses as both restrictive and productive and Butler's (1990, 1997) notion of gender as performative, I directed my focus on how gender operated through various discourses in statements on boys' dancing in primary and secondary data. I examined how such discourses were embodied in dance educational practices and in choreography and how they were performed in male students' dancing. I focused also on the limits of the discourses that operated in the examined extracts. I asked what the

66

discourses recognised, enabled or produced, and what they ignored, held back, marginalised or suffocated. In addition, I scrutinised male dance students' accounts to see how they constructed themselves discursively in different ways. While the self-narratives of individual boys who study dance were highly informative, in some cases it was also valuable to include stories of professional male dancers simply because they too have been young dance students once.

As Parker (1992) suggests, one of the key tasks of discourse analysis is to investigate how power operates at two levels: at one level, the objective is to identify which institutions gain and which ones lose when certain discourses are used; at another level, the objective is to see which discourses that are used to position people into different categories are more profitable than others. This involves identifying whose interest is served by endorsing (or suffocating) any particular discourse. Indeed, this final step requires the analyst to elaborate how the texts 'interrelate to give rise to certain tacit assumptions about roles, 'political' effects and social positions' (Parker 1992, 123).

Thus, as my analysis evolved, I moved to consider performances of masculinity that were favoured in the data and the discourses involved in them. In addition, I considered masculine performances that were missing from the data or the ones that were perceived as negative or problematic. This led me to ask questions about which groups would benefit from the use of certain masculine discourses and who gets to be marginalised or silenced. I also speculated about the politics involved in performing certain types of masculinities while other masculinities are rejected. As I followed textual 'threads' that continued through the boundary of a particular extract, or through a collection of extracts, to see how they linked 'with other utterances and other conversations, texts and documents … [that provided] the wider discursive context' (Wetherell 2001c, p. 389), I was able to tease out political meanings of gendered performances in boys' dance education and the discursive underpinnings of these performances.

The next major step was to examine how discursive power operates on personal and institutional levels. By scrutinising boys' accounts from focus groups and some male dance students' self-narratives in their MA dissertations, it was possible to recognise that in a heteronormative society performances of masculinism are more profitable than performances of other masculine discourses.

Intertextuality: Drawing Links between Texts

The juxtaposition of Ludvig Nyholm's (1959) article on dance education with recent texts on males in dance and the intertextual analysis of relationships between these and other relevant texts, made it possible to see performances of heteronormativity as a political means for the field of theatrical dance to fight for its legitimacy in the late 20th century in Finnish society. Intertextuality was also the overarching methodology that made possible the juxtaposition of a vast range of texts from different theoretical contexts, including social constructionist views on the subject, Foucauldian understanding on discursive power, queer theory views on gender as performative and heteronormativity as a culturally dominant discourse, Feminist critique on the Enlightenment and modernity as oppressive discourses and narratives on Finnish cultural and political history.

Following Frow's idea of intertextual analysis as 'an act of interpretation' (1990, p. 46), discursive signifiers, recognised in text extracts from the data, were traced back to other texts which were understood as discursive intertexts. Because 'the intertext is not a real and causative source but a theoretical construct formed by and serving the purpose of a reading' (ibid), there was no need to point out any specific textual works as 'sources' behind the text extracts examined. Rather, it was sufficient to link the extracts to their discursive realms. Some relevant (inter-)texts that belong to these realms were elaborated upon to make the dominant discourses in boys' dance education more visible. The idea was to pin down some of the key tenets of these discourses to underscore some of the consequences of these discourses to boys' dancing.

Deriving from literary theory, 'intertextuality' is a multiply defined term (Allen 2000). In this book the concept is used to refer to both explicit and latent relationships between texts, which is 'the condition of any text' (Barthes 1981, p. 39). Moreover, 'text' is understood in the broadest sense as any meaning-making system.

Frow proposes that a text is constituted from other discursive texts such as social norms, cultural conventions, stereotypes etc., and that

> the concept of intertextuality requires that we understand the concept of text not as a self-contained structure but as differential and historical ... Texts are therefore not structures of presence but traces and tracings of otherness. They are shaped by the repetition and the transformation of other textual structures (1990, p. 45)

Relationships between texts exist because

> the writer is a reader of texts ... before s/he is a creator of texts, and therefore the work of art is inevitably shot through with references, quotations and influences of every kind. (Still & Worton 1990, p. 1)

In addition, they appear to the reader because in the reading process interpretations produced emerge 'due to the cross-fertilisation of the packaged textual material ... by all the texts which the reader brings to it' (Still & Worton 1990, p. 1-2).

Additionally, 'intertextuality' is taken to suggest that people make sense about their lived experiences through culturally available texts. According to Kristeva, the subject, who 'reads' the events of the world as text, is 'composed of discourses, is a signifying system, a text, understood in a dynamic sense' (Still & Worton 1990, p. 16). In that sense, the subject 'is itself an *effect* produced in social context' (Still & Worton 1990. p. 17) and the world, as we know it, is textual fabrication.

This book is written from a social constructionist position. From such a perspective, the researcher-author can be understood as a dynamic structure, an interpretative crux for generating knowledge about various objects through a fabrication of fragmented narratives that discursive power relations in society produce (Foucault 1986, Barthes 1977). The aim was to follow textual traces to juxtapose examined texts on boys' dancing with other texts in order to recognise existing relationships in these texts and to produce interpretations on that basis.

Thus, as the author of this book, I regard my body as a marked site of many discourses. It provided me with a point of access to the discursive texts in the cultural archive, but as for anybody else, its access to this archive was always a limited one. Indeed, from a social constructionist position, it can be argued that the innocence/neutrality/ objectivity of the investigating gaze of the scholar is always blurred by intertextual references and discourses.

Foucault once wrote, 'the only valid tribute to thought such as Nietzsche's is precisely to use it, to deform it, to make it groan and protest' (1980b, p. 53-54). As I scrutinised others' theories and use their concepts from my partial position, I recognise in line with Barthes that

> [a]s soon as a fact is *narrated* no longer with a view to acting directly on reality but intransitively, that is to say, finally outside of any function other than that of the very practice of the symbol itself, this disconnection occurs, the voice loses its origin, the author enters into his own death, writing begins. (1977, p. 142)

Also, following Barthes, I regard 'text' as a fabrication

> of multiple writings, drawn from many cultures and entering into mutual relations of dialogue, parody, contestation, but there is one place where this multiplicity is focused and that place is the reader, not, as was hitherto said, the author. The reader ... is simply that *someone* who holds together in a single field all the traces by which the written text is constituted. (1977, p. 148)

In that sense, as the author of this book, I positioned my reading body as a meeting-ground for texts to mingle and regarded myself as a 'functional principle' that 'limits, excludes and chooses' (Foucault 1984a, p. 119). In the process of looking at dance educational practices, choreographies and dancing bodies, as well as in the process of scrutinising statements on boys in dance, I tried to make sense of what I perceived, through the process of interpretation, by reading dance 'texts' through diverse culturally informed texts. This

70

'violence' was unavoidable for the reason that there is no place for anybody to leap outside the boundaries of discourse (Foucault 1984a). Interpretative acts that require decision-making went on throughout my research process. Yet, such acts did not happen randomly nor were they whirlwinds of the subjective mind. Rather, such acts of decision-making were based on 'interpretative reasoning' (Best 1992). Such reasoning derived from the juxtaposition of different theories in relation to the research questions of the book and in relation to those texts on boys' dancing which were collected as data for the research. I used discourse analytic and dance analytic methods to distance myself from the data in order to scrutinise extracts of the data and to ask what are the theories and concepts that those extracts suggest and call forth. In that sense, I did not arrive at a position that could reveal the 'truth' about Finnish boys' dancing. Rather, I shifted between different positions as these positions emerged from the interplay between me and the text.

There are some limitations to the methodologies applied in this research. First, as Potter and Wetherell suggest, in discourse analysis

> participants' discourse or social texts are approached in *their own right* and not as a secondary route to things 'beyond' the text like attitudes, events or cognitive processes. Discourse is treated as a potent, action-oriented medium, not a transparent information channel. Crucial questions for traditional social psychological research thus cease to be relevant ... The concern is exclusively with talk and writing itself and how it can be read, not with descriptive acuity. (1987, p. 160)

Moreover, dance analysis, as applied in this research, does not aim to reveal the choreographer's or performer's intentions. Likewise, this book does not aim to reveal the 'true' intentions of any individual teacher whose teaching content or methods are described and interpreted below. Rather, the focus is on the surface, on discernable traces in different modes of texts and the relationship of these traces to other cultural texts. What also matters is what these texts and the discourses that operate in and through them accomplish or what they can be thought to accomplish.

Chapter Three
'Boys Will Be Boys'

Characterising Young Males

It is a commonly held belief that

> women and men are different kinds of people, with different abilities and aptitudes, different patterns of personality characteristics, different behaviours and different emotional capacities. (Burr 1998, p. 26)

As a result, gender, defined as 'the social significance of sex' (Burr 1998, p. 11), constitutes a tapestry to our everyday lives as we operate in different arenas of the social world. For example, microcultures in schools, it has been argued, constitute 'key infrastructural mechanisms through which masculinities and femininities are mediated and lived out' (Mac an Ghaill 1994, p. 4).

As the following extract shows, gender matters also in the area of dance education:

> It has been essential that we look at each boy as a boy. Boys have to be perceived primarily as boys and not as children. (Turpeinen as quoted in Saarela 2001b, p. 9)

Dance teacher Isto Turpeinen's statement exemplifies the commonly held view within dance education in Finland about a fixed male core that needs to be considered when dance is taught to boys (Jääskeläinen 1993, Anttila 1994, Turpeinen 1997, Reunamäki 2000, Räsänen 2000a, Bergman 2002). As the differentiation between boys and children shows, the dance educational claim that is put forth in the extract is underpinned by a set of binary oppositions (adult/child, boy/girl, male/female). Boys, as a social group, are located through the notion of otherness outside the position of the child, a position that is left for young females to occupy. This distinction, and the circular claim that boys have to be regarded 'as boys', reveals the essentialist underpinnings of Turpeinen's statement. Hence, it could be argued that an essentialist discourse, a nexus of statements that contribute to the notion about a monolithic core that is embedded in all male subjects, constructs young males unproblematically as a single and unified category. Outside discussion on boys in dance, such a discourse operates, for example, in Robert Stoller's (1968, 1976) work on 'core gender identity'. It also underpins the highly criticised Jungian based work on a 'deep masculine' by Robert Bly (1990).[1] In addition, essentialist discourse underpins much of the so called sex-difference debate.[2] Moreover, it has been pointed out that a belief in 'true masculinity' is shared by the mass media, Christian fundamentalists and essentialist feminists (Connell 1995).

Yet, in the area of masculinity studies the concept of multiple masculinities suggests a more complex view of the male subject (Brittan 2001, Connell 1995, Whitehead 2002). Indeed, as the backgrounds of the interviewed and observed male dance students show, boys who dance are not carved from a single piece of wood. They come from different social and ethnic backgrounds. They also differ from one another in terms of age, body composition, sexuality, interests and so on. Moreover, the poststructuralist argument about the unstable nature of signification (Hutcheon 1989) makes it possible to argue that 'boy' is far from a transparent concept. How young males are turned into objects of meaning-making 'depends upon the structuring of a discursive field' (Laclau and Mouffe 1985, p. 108).

Rather than trying to generalise *what* boys are, this chapter sets out to investigate *how* boys are conceptualised through different

---

1   For critique on Bly's (1990) Iron John, see for example Wolf-Light, P. (1994), Collinson & Hearn (1996) Connell (1995, 2000), Adams & Savran (2002), Whitehead (2002).

2   See Eklund's (1999) extensive review of sex-difference theories.

74

discourses in Finnish discussions on boys and dance.[3] Several questions arise: first, how exactly are boys characterised in the data? Second, what discourses make possible these characterisations? Third, in what rhetoric contexts do these discursive characterisations appear? These questions are addressed by examining the statements of dance teachers and other relevant persons from the data.

The 'Nature' of Boys

The idea that gender represents a relationship of difference explains why maleness and femaleness are often perceived as a set of binary oppositions (de Lauretis 1987, Connell 1995). However, a discourse analytic point of view suggests that there is no neutral position from which to classify such differences. That is, according to Foucault (1994), various discursive preconceptions regulate what can be discerned, how it can be discerned, what is regarded as irrelevant and how the perceived information is interpreted in relation to other existing bits of information. The aim of this section is to show how essentialist accounts about the 'nature' of boys emerge through biology-based discourses in Finnish discussion on dance for boys. In order to do this, this section first places a set of text extracts from focus group material under scrutiny (29.03.2001). Following that, passages from dance teacher Isto Turpeinen's internet homepage (http://www.kolumbus.fi/ isto.turpeinen/index2.htm 15.3.2003) are studied.

---

3   According to Foucault (1984a), our understanding of the 'real' is always constrained by what he calls 'discursive structures'. Elsewhere, he defines discourse as a discerned regularity 'between a number of statements, such as a system of dispersion, ... between objects, types of statement, concepts, or thematic choices' (1972, p. 38). In addition, he sees discourse as an interpretative 'practice which we impose on them [objects of human meaning-making]' (Foucault 1984a, p. 127).

Matt is a middle-aged dance teacher with years of experience in teaching dance for boys and young men at different levels. In the focus group, he explained how, together with his colleagues, he had come to an understanding that male dance students need a male teacher. In addition, he claimed that a dance class for boys needs an educational focus that differs from the objectives of the 'traditional' dance classes that were held for female dance students. His use of the word traditional, in this context, referred to authoritarian modes of teaching. The following three extracts demonstrate the discursive view of boys that underpins Matt's dance educational claim. In the first extract, such a view provides support for the claim that male dance students need a male dance teacher:

Int.:   What was behind that idea?
Matt: Behind the male teacher?
Int.:   Yes
Matt: Well, of course at that time we were thinking about that a great deal particularly in reference to five, six, seven year olds. Again we came to a conclusion, what had come up when teaching in the kindergarten, that one has to, well, sort of strike in time before the attitude of a seven year old boy has changed to that this is a hobby for girls. So that it had to be anticipated, that is, at four years of age it still works, girls and boys go together, but at the age of five it starts to be that boys see themselves as boys (turns to address the interviewer) ... and surely you have some background information on at what phase the boys identity moves to the point that he begins to follow his father and so on.

It could be supposed that the reference to the ability of boys to acknowledge and perform gender stereotypes and other references to their attitudes, identity development and father-son relationship link Matt's reply intertextually with the complex and fragmentary discourse of psychology. It is the discursive framework of psychology, it can be argued, that enables the essentialist idea of boys' need for a male dance teacher:

Matt: We somehow felt that a male would be appropriate in that
       phase for the reason that in the process of creating an identity,
       it influences (the boy) in every way. He kind of automatically
       wants to identify (with a male) and that is why a man is
       important, essential, for the boy.

In the second extract, Matt presents an idea about the identity
development of young males. It is perceived as an automatic and fixed
process that takes place in relation to men. The essentialist
underpinnings of Matt's view become more explicit later in the focus
group when he moves to talk about sex differences as follows:

Matt: And especially the boys are somehow kind of extremely (.)
       well women sure have noticed that a man can be made to
       move when you make them run after something (laughter) that
       is (.) well when you give a ball to a boy he starts running after
       it and kicking it and that energy can be focused to it. A girl
       does not need that medium perhaps quite in the same way. I
       don't know where (.) what brain related difference or genes.

In this extract, Matt speaks about the teaching content of dance
classes. His educational claim is that boys need a different motivation
to move than girls. From a (pro-)feminist queer theory perspective, it
can be noted how women are positioned in this heteronormative and
sexist comment as objects of men's chase.[4] The comment contains an
idea that it is 'natural' for males to run after moving objects just like it
is 'natural' for them to run after women. As the extract shows,

4   Despite certain differences in their theoretical underpinnings, there is an overlap
    in terms of how feminisms and queer theory approach heterosexuality. As
    Jackson suggests, both of these critical stances question the 'naturalness of
    heterosexuality … the common assumption is that neither gender boundaries
    nor the boundary between heterosexuality and homosexuality/lesbianism are
    fixed by nature' (1999, p. 161). Heteronormativity is a concept that has been
    used by feminists and queer theorists to refer to 'the normative status of
    heterosexuality which renders any alternative sexualities "other" and marginal'
    (Jackson 1999, p. 163).

references to genes and the brain structure are used for linking this kind of male behaviour to the male biology. Through this discursive link sex differences, as well as the interests of young males, are constructed in Matt's speech as inevitable and permanently fixed. It is from such biology-based essentialism that the reductionist idea about the 'nature' of boys emerges in his speech. From the same discursive underpinnings Matt's educational claims also emerge.

According to Eklund (1999), sex differences have been explained generally from two distinctive positions: biology-based theories and socio-cultural theories.[5] In the following extract, fragments from Isto Turpeinen's (http://www.kolumbus.fi/isto.turpeinen/index2.htm, 15.3. 2003) article exemplify how discourses of biology-based evolutionary psychology and physical development define young males as 'other' in relation to young females. What emerges is a sex-difference discourse that supports the idea about separate groups for boys and girls in dance education up until 13 years of age:

> Over half of the fertilised egg cells have their sex XY-coded. Consequently, more than half of the babies that are born are boys. On the other hand, this is counterbalanced by the smaller probability for male embryos and born male children to survive – to quote paediatrician Jari Sinkkonen, the boy child is a so called weaker vessel.
>
> The development of boys involves more disorders and as children boys are for example more prone to accidents. Different developmental disorders, such as MBD, dysphasia and Asperger's syndrome, for example, appear distinctly more often particularly among boy children. Also most children and young people who have psychosocial problems are, indeed, boys ... Experience would seem to suggest that boys need to be given an extra year – whereas girls start at the age of 4, learning in a group would seem to work for boys from 5 years on ...
>
> The rapid growth period and the sexual maturing during the early adolescence do not even the situation by any means. Girls grow and mature earlier. When the rapid growth period takes place approximately between years 11 and 14, for girls it takes place earlier than for boys. If the rapid growth period appears most

5   Michael Cole and Sheila R. Cole (1993 as discussed in Ruoppila 1995) make a more detailed distinction by suggesting that in addition to biology-based theories that focus on growing, there are three strands of socio-cultural theories: theories that acknowledge environments influence on learning, universal theories of constructivism and cultural theories.

intensively for a period of 6 months and, at longest, it can take from 1½ – 2 years, the differences between boys and girls in these age groups are significantly large.

It can be seen how in this extract a medical discourse supported by a known medical specialist introduces, through references to chromosomes, embryos, developmental disorders and psychosocial problems, an essentialist bias that underpins the educational claims that are put forth in Turpeinen's text. It constructs the notion of human development around biology-based models in evolutionary psychology that generally focus on explaining how genetic, hormonal and neurological features as well as the brain structure differ between males and females.[6] In this discourse, as the extract shows, the male child is prone to die. He can suffer from different developmental disorders. He also lags behind in physical and social development in relation to girls. In this discourse, the entire development of the male child is 'irretrievably' linked to the Y part of the twenty-third pair of the human chromosomes. From this discursive perspective, the male child is not just different from most girls – he represents the weaker sex.

Hence, biology-based discourses produce essentialist statements on the 'nature' of young males by linking boys' behaviour and interests with male biology. In this discursive framework, young males who stand out as different from what is perceived as the male nature are not taken to undermine the notion of male 'nature'. Rather, as the following extract from Matt's speech demonstrates, such boys are perceived as deviants:

6   The bottom line in these theories tends to be that the twenty-third pair of chromosomes, XX for females or XY for males, produce two lines of physical development that are linked with having a life as a woman or a man (Säävälä 1999). As genes establish the biological layout for human development, it has been suggested, in a biological discourse, that masculine characteristics, personality traits and bodily performance originate from the Y-chromosome, testosterone, or from the small size of men's corpus callosum (Carter 1998).

Matt: Well, there have always been different individuals. I too have started at the age of nine and (.) surely there has been something wr- wrong or (laughs).

Prior to this extract, Matt has been emphasising how due to the male 'nature', a 'traditional' or authoritarian form of dance training does not fit male students. In the extract, he acknowledges the possibility that there can be young males who actually enjoy traditional forms of training. However, they are constructed as exceptions to the rule. By reflecting back on his personal history as a dance student, with laughter and self-irony, Matt includes himself in such group of deviants: boys who had 'something wr- wrong' in them. Further, young males who do not fit into this frame of reference are marginalised as deviants whose relation to the notion of what boys are carries only minor significance.

Hence, it can be argued that biology-based discourses make the 'nature' of boys appear as a permanent quality in male dance students that is irrevocably programmed into their male biology. This enables sweeping generalisations about boys to be made and provides a fertile ground for requests to masculinise dance educational practices. Yet, it would be far too simplistic to argue that biology determines social aspects of life.[7] It would also be far too simple to maintain that essentialist ideas about the 'nature' of boys emerge merely from biology-based discourses. Thus, in the following section the focus turns to other discourses that also provide essentialist views on young males.

7   As Eklund's (1999) extensive review on criticism against biology-based sex difference theories clearly suggests, recent studies regard such theories as overly essentialist.

Heroes and Hunters:
Boys Emerging Through *His*tory and Popular Culture

It has been suggested that popular culture and mass media disseminate some of the most commonly available forms of masculinity (Mosse 1996, Connell 2000, Donald 2001, Dyer 2002). As a discourse, heroic masculinity is familiar from comic books, fiction, Hollywood films and so on practically to every young male. According to Whitehead, the discourse of heroic masculinity is

> captured in the notion of 'man as (lone) hero': the adventurer/explorer/ conqueror trapped in a cycle of return and departure as he exposes himself to new challenges; with a drive to achieve that is not, apparently, of his choosing but comes from 'deep' within his psyche. (2002, p.118)

It could be maintained that Western popular culture constructs its superheroes generally as white, muscular, able-bodied, heterosexual and invincible. They are men who stand against evil. With 'bravery, endurance and self-sacrifice' (Whitehead 2002, p. 122), they help those who are in trouble. For many boys, Superman and Tarzan, the two fantasy characters fabricated by Jerry Siegel, Joe Shuster and Edgar Rice Burroughs, are, no doubt, superheroes *par excellence*.

Interestingly, as the following extract shows, brief references to Superman and Tarzan also appear interwoven in some of the accounts on sex-differences in Turpeinen's text on boys and dance:

> The Y-part in the chromosome of sex operates efficiently and irretrievably, but it constructs a child that is like a "gauzy Superman" ... The physiological differences between growing children are small. Prior to puberty and the rapid period of growth, physical differences do not largely require separated teaching of dance ... Roughness and the directly average "Tarzan-like" quality of boys' physicality are some of the reasons that are worthy of consideration as one is pondering the age to begin with boys in dance education in relation to girls. (http://www.kolumbus.fi/isto. turpeinen/index2.htm 15.3.2003)

In this extract, the two references to superheroes stand out in stark contrast to the surrounding text that is constructed through biology-based discourses. Yet, it could be maintained that it is through these references that the discourse of heroic masculinity amalgamates with the biology based discourse. Together these two discourses introduce the idea of 'roughness' that is used to differentiate boys from girls in Turpeinen's (ibid) text. It could be maintained that the amalgamation of these two radically different discourses is not as unexpected as one might think. That is, stereotypical behavioural patterns of heroic masculinity are made easily recognisable through the wide circulation of images of super heroes in popular culture. Biological essentialism, on the other hand, provides simple explanations for such behaviour by fixing it to the biology of the male body.

Following Dyer, it can be argued that muscularly built and tanned bodies of super heroes are displayed in popular culture 'not as typical but ideal' (2002, p. 265). In addition, however, their armour-like hardness can also be linked to

> a model of white male identity in which anxieties about the integrity and survival of the self are expressed through fantasmic fears of the flooding, invading character of women, the masses and racial inferiors. Only a hard, visibly bounded body can resist being submerged into the horror of femininity and non-whiteness. (ibid.)

Behind the embodied idea of an invincible super hero, there are doubts and uncertainties. Indeed, such see-through and fragile qualities of the brawny fabrication can be detected from the metaphor of 'gauzy superman' that is used for defining boys in the extract from Turpeinen's text. This metaphor can be read to suggest that underneath the gendered performance of the mighty superhero, which is a cultural fabrication and a fantasy, there is a fragile boy, a 'weaker vessel', that requires special attention.

Following Scott (1999), it can be argued that representations from the past participate in constructing our present day understandings of gender. However, it has been suggested that historical texts are not neutral accounts about the past (Jenkins 1995). 'History', as feminists argue, 'has been written from only one point of view, that of the dominant white male' (Brown 1994b, p. 199). Indeed, it is the public domain, the mysterious 'world of men', that appears central to Western history writing. In Middleton's words, 'men's work is a mystery, and mysteries create awe and longing (as many religious leaders have known)' (1992, p. 41). From this perspective, it can be maintained that hunters and experimenters have been given a central position in much of the Western history writing and story-telling simply because they accommodate the mystery of men's public life and the discourse of heroism. Further, this privileged position in turn gives marked prestige for acts of hunting and experimenting.[8] In that sense, it can be argued that narratives on heroic hunters and adventurous experimenters construct a commonly available intertextuality that participates in shaping how socially accountable maleness is understood in Western societies.

Thus, in addition to heroes from popular culture, culturally dominant discourses on men in Western history writing can also participate in shaping how young males are perceived in dance discussions. In the following extract for example, the author elaborates further on the title of her article, which quotes a commonly heard but often unquestioned saying 'boys will be boys', as follows:

Mind of the Hunter
Boys are eternal experimenters, hunters of experiences. Basic elements and motive power of their dance are gliding, flying, speed, strength, skills, courage, bravery, insight and energy. These challenges have to be answered. If the tree of learning is climbed from the wrong end it is not possible to get much further. Those who know the nature of boys also know how dance may capture the entire young man if the echo responds to the young man's call. (Jääskeläinen 1993, p. 4)

8 On one hand, it is common for Western culture to celebrate scientists whose efforts in experimenting have eventually paid off in some form of scientific break through. On the other hand, some Finnish scholars have pointed out how 'killing a sturdy beast' has been regarded as a token of true maleness (Lehtonen 1995) and how many Finnish men still use hunting skills and the ability to fight against nature (and other men) for measuring one's maleness (Virtanen 1996, Lehtola 1998).

As the extract shows, 'hunter', in the caption, as well as 'eternal experimenters' and 'hunters of experiences' in the first line of the extract are concepts that are used in Jääskeläinen's text for characterising the male sex. Hence, a historical discourse on heroism, rather than boys' 'true nature', produces a list of words that are seen as the key essence and the source of motivation of young males' dancing. The genetive form in the caption suggests that hunters have a particular psyche - the 'mind of the hunter'. Based on this, and the explicit reference to the 'nature of boys' later in the extract, it can be argued that Jääskeläinen's text calls forth intertextual traces from the discourses of personality psychology and biology-based essentialism.[9] It is through these discursive underpinnings that a list of words are presented in the text as a collection of fixed personality 'traits' of young males.

Following Foucault's (1972) idea that objects of knowledge are formed by the rules that are embedded in discourses, it can be argued that the discourses that underpin Jääskeläinen's text (1993), regulate effectively what statements can be made about young males in that particular context. The discursive power to convince the reader makes it almost impossible to see that different characterisations could provide a different intertextuality. From such a basis, Jääskeläinen's (ibid) list of young male's 'basic elements and motive power' (ibid) would appear as irretrievably incomplete, perhaps even irrelevant.

This section has investigated some of the ways in which the discourse of heroism participates in constructing the dancing boy through intertextual references from popular culture and Western history writing. Based on the above, it can be argued that the dancing boy emerges through these discursive underpinnings as a rough, physically active superhero whose skilful actions are full of bursting

---

9   Personality psychological theories are used for describing the structures of personality (attitudes, traits, aims and so on), explaining processes in these structures and investigating the individual's behaviour in relation to such processes. As Hakanen (1992) suggests, trait theories that represent one strand of personality psychology are particularly keen to describe the individual's personality as a stable list of characteristics (ibid).

speed and energy. Further, he is curious to confront new challenges as he explores and experiments with things that are new to him. Yet, the heroic dancing boy is a cultural fabrication. As a gendered performance, he appears as a 'gauzy Superman'. Underneath the embodied of heroic masculinity, there is a fragile young male, a 'weaker vessel' that requires special attention.

Finnish Boys and Pressure

The previous section introduced a dancing boy constructed through the discourses of popular culture and history writing as a hero. Yet it also pointed to the fragile young male, the 'weak vessel' that lies hidden under such gendered performance. This section focuses on the notion of fragility of the dancing boy as it emerges through the nexus of nationalist and psychological discourses.

The following extract is from a television documentary *Restless Feet* (YLE1 21.5.2003) that takes as its topic a group of adolescent boys from the Vantaa Dance Institute. In the extract, their dance teacher Isto Turpeinen characterises Finnish boys as follows:

> Again, if we think of the Finnish boy, well, surely he is incredibly reserved. Well, it is a clear fact that one doesn't straightforwardly let out things that are felt inside. One pretty clearly holds on to them. Well, as it has been discussed, boys' expression of emotions has been in a kind of golden cage, and it doesn't come out except in certain, let us say, marginal situations.

In the extract, the underpinning discourse of nationalism enables the act of ascribing a national identity for young males and calling them 'Finnish'. Moreover, the notion of a collectively embodied national identity that is put forth by this discourse makes it possible to perceive a group of boys collectively as a single unified male body, the 'Finnish boy'. In Turpeinen's speech, this discursive rhetoric produces a generalisation that views reservedness through the national male body as a common personality trait in all young Finnish males.[10]

Following Bergman (2002), Turpeinen's concept of 'golden cage' can be defined as an emotional sphere that easily remains closed for young males. In the extract, references to such emotional problems show how the national male body is constructed through a psychodynamic discourse metaphorically as a pressure cooker. The notion that it is merely in exceptional conditions that Finnish boys are willing to open themselves up emerges through Freudian or other psychological theory where the human being is perceived as a hydraulic energy system with innate libidinal forces that seek for gratification. According to such psychodynamic models of energy tension builds up when gratification can not be obtained.[11] Consequently, it has been suggested that this causes anxiety (Hakanen 1992).

Dance teacher Marketta Viitala's (1998, p. 26) book on creative dance exemplifies how psychological pressure can be constructed as a general condition of young Finnish males from a radically different discursive point of view:

> One might argue that boys' modest attendance in dance in Finland depends very much on the attitudes and models that the father, the family, the peers, and the entire community, if not entire society, provide: 'the world belongs to strong men and the dancer is not part of them' ... The basic nature of Finnish boys calls for physical and, through that, spiritual emancipation ... Even a boy has the permission to be *the own sensitive self*...

Also in this extract, the nationalist discourse enables the author to generalise about Finnish boys by linking the notion of pressure to the 'nature' of Finnish young males. However in Viitala's text, Finnish boys are positioned in relation to other social actors, groups and institutions. It could be maintained that within the fragmented

---

10   Historically, this personality trait has been linked back to centuries of solitary lifestyle in Finnish hunting and burnt-over clearing cultures (Ylikangas 1986).

11   As Tavris points out, Freudian and other psychodynamic models of energy have been 'scientifically discredited' (1982, p. 37).

86

discourse of psychology, these kinds of social relations are most commonly covered in the area of social psychology.[12] Thus, it can be argued that the references to interpersonal relationships and to social 'attitudes and models' in Viitala's (ibid.) text emerge through a social psychological discourse that underpins also the notion of social pressure in the extract.

The references about the socially omnipresent attitude that 'the world belongs to strong men' (ibid.) shows that Finnish boys are positioned in Viitala's (ibid.) text in relation to the socially dominant form of masculinity, a discourse of masculinism, that constructs men as strong controllers of the world. Hence, the extract from Viitala's (1998) text can be read to suggest that the discourse of masculinism creates 'outside' pressure, which turns Finnish boys into constrained subjects. A liberated boy's *'own sensitive self'* as the opposite of the constrained boy constitutes a key objective of boys' dance education in Viitala's (ibid.) text.

According to Burr, the concept of the 'free individual' appears at the centre of liberal humanism, which she regards as 'a heavily legitimated discourse in our present-day society' (1995, p. 75). In such a discourse, personhood is perceived

> as a bounded, unique, more or less integrated motivational and cognitive universe, a dynamic centre of awareness, emotion, judgement and action, organized in to a distinctive whole and set contrastively against other such wholes and against a social and natural background. (Geertz as quoted in Sampson 1989, p. 1)

According to Gergen, private experiences also appear central to this discourse, which he calls the *'ideology of the selfcontained individual'* (1999, p. 118, emphasis in original). Hence, in Viitala's (1998) text, the notion about the socially constrained dancing boy can be said to emerge in relation to the liberal humanist concept of the 'free individual'. Further, it can be stated that it is the discourse of liberal

12   According to Helkama, Myllyniemi and Liebkind (1999), a concise definition for social psychology would be that it investigates human interaction and regularities of group processes.

humanism that also underpins the emancipatory idea that young males can be liberated from such constraints.

The extracts introduced here have shown how boys are defined in dance educational contexts, for example, through discourses of biological essentialism, masculinism in popular culture and history writing, nationalism, evolutionary psychology, social psychology as well as liberal humanist discourse of personhood. To shift the focus slightly, the rest of this chapter turns to examine a selection of text extracts in order to illuminate how boys *who dance* are discursively elaborated in different contexts.

The Dancing Freak

The Ballet of the Finnish National Opera lacks good male dancers – especially the 'prince' type, complains dance critic Helena Mäkinen (1959b) in a national Finnish daily newspaper. It is not very helpful that only every sixth student in the Finnish National Opera Ballet School is male, she writes. The fear that boys embody effeminate behaviour in ballet is probably one of the reasons why parents do not put their sons in a ballet class, she continues.[13]

Since the late 1950's the number of boys who dance has increased in the Finnish National Opera Ballet School as well as in some other Finnish dance institutions.[14] Yet, there is a commonly held view that it is rare for Finnish boys to take up theatrical dance (Laakso 1988, Jokela-Nazimov 1991, Lampi 1991, Af Björkensten 1997, Härkönen 1999, Runonen 2001, Hankaniemi 1999). It could be

13   More on Mäkinen's (1959b) article in reference to the fear of effeminacy is found in Chapter Eight.
14   In 1996, one third of the total of 130 students in the Finnish National Opera Ballet School were male (Yli-Sirniö 1996). In 2003, approximately 200 of the total of 1000 students at the Vantaa Dance Institute were male and in the Dancing Boy Residential Course in Kuopio, there were enrolled close to 90 students in June 2003 (Isto Turpeinen 6/9/2003, personal communication).

maintained that these and other statements about the rarity of young males who dance have a tendency to marginalise the dancing boy. The following extract provides an example. It is taken from Anu Hankaniemi's (1999) article on dance education in the western region of Finland.

Well, as presumed, a large number of the students are girls, but also two boys fit in. There is a screaming lack of the dancers of the more handsome sex … also in Kokkola … The lack of male dancers is not a problem just for Kokkola. – Even the school at the Opera takes almost grown-up boys and schools them, says ballet pedagogue Marita Nieminen.

In this extract, the lack of male dance students is presented as a problem not just for the small provincial town but also for the Finnish National Opera Ballet School. It is indeed through the reference to a nationally significant institution of ballet education that the lack of boys is established, in the extract, as a national status quo in dance, or at least in ballet. Further, through the discourse on lack, the two male dance students that are mentioned in the extract are located in two marginal positions. In both cases, these positions are constructed in relation to what is considered as the majority: first, girls in the dance class and, second, the general class of Finnish males, a class that does not dance, according to the article.

Following the French feminist writer Hélène Cixous (1985), it could be maintained that the 'centre-margin' duality is an unequally balanced binary opposition that is commonly used for identifying difference or exclusion. According to Tajfel's (1978) social identity theory, it is common for people to identify their own group in positive terms in opposition to other groups. Hence, it could be argued that the discourse of otherness that emerges through the 'centre-margin' binary opposition and other dualities is often constructed in negative terms. 'Freak' can be considered as one of the negative terms that has been used for identifying otherness. According to a dictionary definition, a freak is 'a person, animal, or plant that is abnormal or deformed … a person who acts or dresses in a markedly unconventional way' (Collins Concise Dictionary 2001, p. 569, sv freak). More generally, it could be suggested that the concept of 'freak' signifies anything that stands out from what is perceived as a conventional norm. As the next extract illuminates, the notion about the dancing boy as a freak emerges though the discourse of otherness:

> When a man is required to display strength, endurance, flexibility and far reaching physical skills all in one and the same performance, the activity in question has to be sports. Truly a man's pursuit.
> When artistic sensitivity as well as abilities to express oneself and put one's soul into it are connected to the same man, the appraisal turns instantaneously to its opposite. Effeminate, womanish, nerd. Commonplace prejudices in Finland in the late 1980s. The male dancer is perpetually a freak, a strange bird that does not fit in to the established conventions. (Laakso 1988)

The above extract from Lauri Laakso's (1988) article 'The Strange Young Birds: The Boys' Dance Course in Kuopio' shows how qualities that are relevant to the sports discourse are linked to men and masculinity while artistic sensitivity and expressed emotions are gendered feminine. Based on this, it can be argued that the act of ascribing feminised characteristics to the male dancer positions him outside the socially dominant masculinist definition of men. This, as the extract clearly shows, labels the male dancer as a 'freak, a strange bird' (ibid.).

Some decades ago when it was rare to see boys in theatrical dance, their marginal position was often defined from the masculinist point of view in negative terms. During the 1990's the increase in some Finnish dance schools has been phenomenal, particularly in the Vantaa Dance Institute where dance is taught for young males from kindergarten age up to late adolescence. One might think that with the increase of boys in theatrical dance the discourse of otherness through which the dancing boy is constructed as a freak would diminish. Yet, as the following extract from the programme notes of the Dancing Boy 2000 gala performance shows, this is not necessarily the case:[15]

---

15 The Dancing Boy 2000–gala performance was held at the Martinus Hall in Vantaa 4 June 2000. The event was organised by the Vantaa Dance Institute.

More than 60 boys on the stage, in a dance performance ... strange, odd. When I started in the business more than thirty years ago, I was more or less the only boy in the ballet school. Throughout my professional career, the small number of boys in dance has been pondered in meetings, gatherings and seminars. And now, more than 60 boys on the stage in a dance performance! What has happened? ... A boy who dances is even today a freak up to the point that in order to cope with the pressure from pals and peers at school, the self [of the boy who dances] has to strengthen to take more than that of others. Then again, a strong self-image harms no one in a contemporary world, through that one can even grow to become an artist once. More than 60 boys on the stage, in a dance performance ... strange, odd ... exceptional, great!

In this extract, Timo Sokura, a former dancer and the Chair of the support association of Vantaa Dance Institute, refers to his years as a dance student and his past career in dance as he tackles the idea of a large crowd of boys dancing on the stage. As Sokura recalls, there were few boys in dance when he entered the field. He also recalls the repeated discussions about the lack of boys in dance. Hence, it could be argued that for Sokura to perceive a large group of boys dancing on stage as 'strange' or 'odd' takes place through the discourse of strangeness that enters into his text through his lived history.

Yet, it could also be maintained that the discourse of strangeness enters into Sokura's text through the commonly held position that boys and girls have different interests.[16] The reference to peer pressure in the extract reminds the reader that schools, playgrounds and streets are all sites where children and young people are constantly patrolling the borders of gender and sexuality.[17] From this perspective, by taking up dance, a boy crosses the discursively constructed boundary that distinguishes between male and female cultural interests. This enters him into a matrix of meaning-making where the discourse of strangeness constructs him as a freak. Hence, the culturally prevalent discourse of masculinism and the social policing of its boundaries

16   Most blatantly, perhaps, such a position is apparent in accounts that juxtapose ballet and ice-hockey. See for example Talvitie (1990) and Janhonen (1996b).
17   On negotiations and patrolling of gender in peer groups, see for example Mac an Ghaill (1994), Nayak & Kehily (1997), Holland et al (1998), Pollack (1998) and Connell (2000).

make the discourse of strangeness still powerful. Until the power of masculinist discourse is strategically undermined, this will eventually continue no matter how much the number of boys increases in the field of theatrical dance. One possible way of doing this would be to highlight and celebrate multiple masculinities and gendered fluidity. Another would be an open confrontation of prejudiced views, as the lecture demonstration discussed below exemplifies.

Drawing from Bogdan (1988) and Adams (2001), a freak show can be defined as the public display of people who stand out from what is considered as a norm in society.[18] It could be suggested that sometimes only a thin line distinguishes a lecture demonstration that is given for educational purposes from a freak show, particularly when the aim of the former is to confront prejudiced views against a socially marginal group by displaying such a group in public. A section from the earlier mentioned television documentary on boys and dance (*Restless Feet*, YLE1 21.5.2003) provides an example of this.

In the documentary, a group of adolescent boys from the Vantaa Dance Institute perform for a group of eight grade students in the auditorium of a local secondary school. Wearing red t-shirts and black trousers, the boys make small hops from side to side with their arms extended to their sides. A backward step is followed by a kick of the left foot and small jumps are accompanied with brushing of feet and pivots around the vertical axis. These steps bear resemblance to Irish folkdance. Yet their sweeping legs, circular arm gestures, double pirouettes as well as lifting and falling of the upper body link their performance to the American and Central-European modern dance traditions. Following their performance, the boys sit quietly on the edge of the stage while their dance teacher Isto Turpeinen stands up to initiate a discussion about boys' dancing with the audience. The following extract from the conversation is printed here in its full length in order give the reader a clear idea not just about the

18   According to Bogdan (1988) and Adams (2001), freak shows were part of the 19th and early 20th century popular culture particularly in America. This cruel form of entertainment included the displaying of bearded ladies, dwarfs, snake charmers, savages and so on to the horrified and amused audiences.

discursive but also rhetoric play that takes place in the conversation as it proceeds:

Isto: How did you, well, when you watched these blokes so what do you think about boys' dancing?

Girl: Others should dare to dance more as well.

Isto: To dare more (.) What do you mean by daring more?

Girl: Well, I mean in a way that [we would] get even more interest, because I think it is great that boys dance and then also because there aren't yet enough of those [male] dancers.

Isto: (Writes the words 'embarrassed man' on the board). Who could tell what's so embarrassing about the dancing of blokes? Who was it, did you say it? Who was it, you? (Giggling in the audience).

Girl: Probably because not so many have it (dance) as a hobby.

Isto: Yeah, there are very few of them, yeah.

Girl: And then in a way, like, because not everybody regards it as kind of so manly that

Isto: Who thinks that if a guy dances, it kind of makes you feel that you wonder whether he'll ever become a man? Hands up. One youn- (.) are you going to raise your hand? Well well. Well well. Who thinks that it makes no difference to the process of growing to be a man whether they dance or not? (A half a dozen hands rise in the auditorium). Okay, we agree on this, right? If we'd talk about your dancing, for example, would that be impossible or possible?

Boy: Impossible. (Mumbles something and then laughs).

Isto: Well, tell us why (.) well come on, tell us. No, I am interested in, I am really interested in, I in a positive mood, we want to hear about it. Do you play football?

Boy: Yeah

Isto: There is a feeling of its own, right (.) in that gang?

Boy: Yeah

Isto: There is, kind of that group. Do you have friends inside that group?

Boy: Yes

Isto: Also outside the time when you have games?

Boy: Well yes.
Isto: Do you also play around outside of the practice sessions?
Boy: Sometimes.
Isto: Sometimes, yeah. (Turns to face the boys on the edge of the stage). Was there something here that is not in dance? That is, mates there inside, there is that group of boys and sometimes you train by yourself. Isn't that exactly the same as in dance? And it is a physical sport that requires some sort of skilled abilities. But then the performances are slightly different.

In this extract, it can be seen how the reference to boys' daring to dance, in the girl's first response, introduces the discourse of embarrassment into the conversation. This takes place despite the fact that she never explicitly uses the words 'embarrassment' or 'embarrassed'. She moves, however, to talk about the lack of male dancers and the idea that it would be nice to see more boys dancing on the stage. Despite her change of direction, Turpeinen has nevertheless captured the idea of the 'embarrassed male' and writes it on the board. Then he confronts this concept with a question. He asks, 'what's so embarrassing about the dancing of blokes?' At first, the girl starts to elaborate this idea by talking about the lack of boys in dance. Soon, however, she introduces the discourse of 'true' maleness into the conversation by suggesting that some people regard dancing unmanly, although this discourse is confronted by Turpeinen. He demands a public confession from those in the audience who perceive dancing as unmanly. Then, by raising his voice, he asks for those who oppose this idea to raise their hands. Finally, he summarises the result of the vote with a rhetoric question 'we agree on this, right'. Hence, the rhetoric game that is played in this conversation is aggressively pushing forward the argument that everyone in the audience agrees that dancing hinders nobody form 'growing to be a man'.

Yet, there is a young male in the audience who openly rejects the idea that he personally could take up dance. Turpeinen confronts this by establishing a common ground between himself and the boy with a reference to football, a socially acceptable sports form that is familiar to most young males. This gives the boy an opportunity to have a dialogue about dance in reference to something that he can relate to. With a set of questions, Turpeinen invites the boy to reflect football as a social practice. Then, by summarising some of the key features of football, he asks a rhetoric question 'was there something here that there is not in dance'. The analogy between dance and football introduces a sports discourse into the dialogue. It is the sports discourse that makes it possible for Turpeinen to define dance as a 'physical sport', which helps him to downplay the embarrassment that is linked to the male dancer. It is through the sports discourse, it can be argued, that the social legitimacy of the dancing boy is reclaimed by renaming him an athlete.

As suggested earlier, there is a thin line between a freak show and the act of placing a socially marginal group, adolescent boys who dance, on display in front of a sneering group of teenagers. However, in reference to the above example, it is important to recognise Turpeinen's strong drive to confront the discourses through which the dancing boy appears as a strange freak and his willingness to offer the means to redefine the dancing boy. These two themes distinguish the above described lecture demonstration from a freak show. In Turpeinen's project, the meaning of the public display is clearly not to exploit the boys who dance but to demystify their dancing. This is done by confronting some of the old myths and deconstructing them in a public debate.

Yet it could be criticised that the performed deconstruction in Turpeinen's rhetoric is not a complete one. It does not dissolve the concept of the dancing boy into an endless play of signifiers that produce multifarious definitions from various discursive positions. Rather, it yields to the discourse of masculinism by replacing a negatively charged definition of the dancing boy with a socially more accountable and legitimate one. Hence, it could be argued that the sports discourse operates in Turpeinen's rhetoric as a textual camouflage, 'a device or expedient designed to conceal or deceive' (Collins Concise Dictionary 2001, p. 213 sv camouflage). In that sense, the deconstruction that is performed in Turpeinen's speech does not confront and resist the oppressive power of the masculinist discourse. Instead, it yields to it and becomes a vehicle for it.

'Normalcy' and 'Supremacy' of Boys Who Dance

Due to the prevalence of the masculinist discourse, it is hardly surprising that those who want to see more boys in dance are willing to downplay negatively charged definitions of the dancing boy. The text extract in the previous section shows how this takes place through the sports discourse. This section continues to explore other rhetoric means to make the dancing boy socially more appealing, accountable and legitimate. The discourse of normalcy is examined first. Then the focus shifts to some examples where the dancing boy is constructed as a supreme physical performer.

Emphasising 'normalcy' in reference to young males who dance can be regarded as an attempt to avoid otherness and the negative connotations that are embedded in a socially marginal position of the dancing boy. This can be exemplified by the following extract from the already mentioned television documentary on boys and dance. It shows how the idea of normalcy emerges in dance teacher Isto Turpeinen's speech through multifarious ascriptions of the dancing boy:

> I don't think one should mystify the dancing boy all that much except that they are entirely ordinary boys. Those boys come from an entirely ordinary group, the entire spectrum, there are tall, wide, choleric, reserved, quiet, loud, peaceful, there are geniuses. Then there are also such lads, who kind of build their life on a sort of narrow and long bridge, but it works out fine even like that. (Turpeinen in *Restless Feet*, TV1. 21.5.2003)

In this extract, it can be seen how the list of various body and personality types puts forth an idea that various kinds of boys take up dance. In that sense, the text highlights the individual differences of boys who dance. This kind of fragmentation quite obviously undermines the notion about the dancing boy as a single unified concept, a negatively defined stereotype: the freak. Further, the idea about multifarious boys who dance and the repeated emphasis on their ordinariness support the notion of normalcy in the extract. In that sense, it can be argued that it is by emphasising multiplicity and ordinariness that the dancing boy emerges, in this extract, through a discourse of normalcy as a 'normal' young male. At the same time, however, it can be seen how the very concept of boy as a single unified embodiment of masculinity becomes eroded. Indeed, as the very last sentence in the extract shows, Turpeinen's account acknowledges multiple masculinities as different, yet equally valid lifestyles.

Within masculinity studies in Finland, there is a common position that argues that competitive sports play a significant part in the constitution of Finnish masculinities (Ylikangas 1986, Knuutila 1992, Härkönen 1995, Puhakainen 1997, Tiihonen 1999). The concept is that the project of winning links competitive sports with the modernist idea of progress (Klemola 1998). The image of the winning athlete excludes, as Lehtonen (1999) argues, any references to homosexuality or femininity. From this perspective, it can be argued that the sports discourse makes it possible for Finnish men to perform the unquestioned 'normalcy' of athletic masculinity as a means to negotiate their social position in relation to the culturally prevalent masculinist discourse. Thus, it is not surprising to find sports discourse providing means to promote the discourse of normalcy in reference to boys who dance.

Constructing the dancing boy as an athlete is relatively common in articles on boys who dance (see for example: Nyholm 1959, Laakso 1988, Tourunen 1988, Bask 1992, Lehtiranta 1993, Harri 1993a). Generally, such discursive rhetoric emphasises the physical condition of male dancers. In the next extract, a quote from ballet teacher Ilkka Lampi in an article on dance and nutrition, the physical condition of male ballet students is discussed as follows:

> On average, dancers from the [Finnish National] ballet have had okay results, but for the boys from the Ballet School of the [Finnish National] Opera who have trained a lot, the percentage that indicates their adipose tissue has been absolutely exceptional. For all of them it has been below 10, for the best ones four, in other words the same as for top athletes. (Lampi as quoted in Bask 1992 p. 31)

Measuring body fat percentage is a commonly acknowledged method for determining the physical condition of athletes.[19] Most top athletes have a relatively low body fat percentage even if its level can vary from sport to sport and on the basis of ethnic and other factors. In this extract, a reference to the fat tissue measurement calls forth a discourse of fitness that establishes an analogy between the male ballet student and the top athlete. It is through this analogy and by referring to numerical data that the dancing boy can be seen constructed as a physically fit top athlete, a socially accountable image that takes distance to the negatively charged stereotype of the male dancer.

As the following quote from a male ballet student exemplifies, the discourse of fitness has significant relevance for distinguishing the dancing boy as different from girls who dance:

> It is commonly thought that ballet is a thing just for girls and that it is merely prancing on toes. The truth is, this is a sport that requires strength. The physical condition of the ballet dancer is better than that of the competing cross country skier. (Nurminen as quoted in Silenius 1991)

In the extract, the emphasis on strength and the comparison between the cross-country skier and the ballet dancer constructs the idea about the ballet dancer's physical supremacy. Moreover, ballet for males is constructed in contrast to 'prancing on toes' as a physically demanding sport. Hence, a discourse of fitness is operating rhetorically in the extract as a means to distance the male ballet students from effeminacy that can be read to stereotypical images of female ballet students.

Lehtiranta's (1993) article takes up ballet dancer Heikki Värtsi's lecture presentation on dance for upper secondary level students in Vantaa, South Finland. Males in dance are constructed in the article as follows:

---

19   Body fat percentage is the calculated amount of adipose tissue in the body that is presented as a percentage of the body's total weight (Rehunen et al 1998).

There is no need to drag boys into the ballet school because the sportslike quality of the field also guarantees the interest of boys ... How is it then for the male dancer to do the military service? Of course he does it. As a matter of fact, he copes there better than other conscripts. He has the strength to run more persistently and also in other physical exercises he stands on a better ground than those who are untrained ... Strength training is part of the male dancer's life. According to Värtsi, ballet has changed during the years. It has gained new elements that require certain sportslike quality. (Lehtiranta 1993)

The male dancer is constructed in the extract as a physically fit athlete who unquestioningly enters the military service. It could be argued that four different discourses operate here: the discourses of sport and fitness construct the male dancer as a physically fit athlete. The military discourse and the discourse of patriotism underpin the notion that the male dancer enters willingly to the military service. It is through the nexus of these four discourses, it can be argued, that the male dancer emerges as a hero, a young male whose physical capability to defend the nation is higher than that of the untrained men.

There is a belief that sports discourse links historically to military training and, particularly in Finnish culture, to national defence work (Puhakainen 1997). In Finland, either a minimum of 180 days military training in the Finnish defence forces or a 395-day non-military civilian service is a compulsory obligation for every male citizen (Finnish Military Defence 2002). Finnish law provides a punishment for conscientious objectors. Also men who choose to do the non-military civilian service are punished with a longer service period than those who serve in the defence forces (The Union of Conscientious Objectors in http://www.aseistakieltaytyja liitto.fi, 23/02/2003). Drawing from Foucault's (1995) argument that penalties, as vehicles of power, carry normative messages, it could be maintained that all Finnish males have to negotiate their social credibility as men in relation to the military institution and military masculinities. Investigating from this perspective how the male dancer is discursively constructed in Lehtiranta's (1993) article, it can be argued that the rhetoric attempt in Lehtiranta's text is to counteract the negative definition of the male dancer by redefining him in a way that

99

is socially accountable for the culturally prevalent discourse of masculinism that perceives athletic, military and patriotic masculinities as a valued norm.

The investigation of text extracts in this section has revealed different discursive and rhetoric acts that construct the dancing boy in ways that escape the negatively charged stereotype of the male dancer. Such acts accommodate the masculinist norm, for example, by constructing the male dance student as a physically fit athlete or a patriot soldier. This type of act tends to reduce the dancing boy into a single concept, which is used rhetorically for renaming the dancing boy. In that sense, it could be argued that the act of renaming works as a means to reclaim the male dancer's lost social position in a society where the masculinist discourse prevails. In contrast to those discursive and rhetoric acts that reduced the dancing boy into a single concept, the act of fragmenting the dancing boy through multifarious ascriptions can be named as another rhetoric means to fight against the negatively charged stereotype of the male dancer. It can be argued that both of these rhetoric strategies, and the discourses that operate in them, are applied in order to contribute to the idea that boys who dance do not stand out negatively from other boys: they are 'normal' young males.

The Need for Support

The marginal position of young males in dance initiates questions about their need for support from other males who dance. This section introduces a selection of text extracts in order to demonstrate how such question is elaborated from different discursive positions. What emerges is a contradictory collection of ideas.

Earlier it was suggested that, in Finnish society, boys are subjected to social pressure by the culturally prevalent discourse of masculinism. There is a common view, not just in Finland but more generally in the West, that boys who dance often need to deal with bullying and other forms of social pressure (Alkins 1994, Rodgers

100

1996, Van Ulzen 1995/96, Grant 1985, Spurgeon 1997). It could be argued that this view, and the idea that boys who dance have to fight against prejudiced views on dance, positions them as victims. Further, such sentiments can be seen to lay the groundwork for therapeutic accounts on boys' need for support from other boys who dance.

Such an idea surfaces in the following extract from one of the focus group interviews. In the extract, two dance teachers, Elliot and Frank, and a music teacher Jeremy, discuss the importance of the dance camp for boys:

Elliot: If I think of education, the reason why I believe this is a good camp, particularly among younger boys, is that compared to the girls of the same age, boys are usually so much behind in ballet. A bit slower (.) on average (.) so what I spoke earlier on, that on average men and boys do not have as good sense and skills as women have. And when there are a huge number of girls who have dance as a hobby, the difference comes also from the process of selection as some of them leave. Well, I don't personally find it like important any longer (.) as I just said, that one should be in a gang of boys and so, but anyhow the situation hasn't changed all that much out in the field perhaps (.) like when there are those (boys) Rick from Turku and Ralf from Lahti and so on from that kind of schools where there are not so many pals, blokes.

Frank: And surely also these meetings (.) well, the situation that there are congenial people together so [it too has] a really big meaning

Elliot: [Yeah surely yeah]

Frank: And in a way it also shows that if one leaves to come here for his own sound will, many most (of the boys) come for their own sound will any number of times again [that is positive].

Elliot: [Yeah, I think so] and that too that it is fun when there are familiar faces here on the camp because for some of them

	they don't have congenial pals at the school, I mean in the comprehensive school.
Jeremy:	And then I also feel that it is important that also on an intellectual and emotional levels (.) boys can be in an all-boys group where they can discuss dance [without having to explain in any way, like what are you some weirdo cause you want to talk about dance] and what kind of feelings and emotions dance awakens and like this.
Elliot:	[Exactly that (.) yeah (.) yeah (.) mmm] (.) Yeah precisely that those who come from schools where there are not that many boys and there is hardly in the comprehensive school or out on the yard that kind of pals with whom it would be possible and then one notices it like (.) that (.) those who have been on the camp more than once like how they from the first day on start to get along with the old pals who they may not have seen for a year...

In the extract, the notion that boys who dance need the like-minded company of other boys who dance can be detected from Elliot's third turn onwards. In his speech, the dance camp for boys is positioned against the comprehensive school. Being set up as binary oppositions, it can be seen how these two social sites are ascribed with contrasting values. The comprehensive school is perceived negatively. Elliot maintains that it does not provide the male dance student with an impartial social environment where he could freely reflect his dance interest. In stark contrast, the all-male dance camp is discussed positively as it supplies 'congenial pals' for boys who dance. It could be maintained that the taken for granted subtext in this extract is that boys who dance have a therapeutic need for a congenial all-male environment where they can air their interest in dance without the fear that such a confession would threaten their social accountability.[20]

---

20 In this context, the word 'therapeutic' is used in the broad sense to refer to any group-processes that help participants to deal with tensions and conflicts by giving them an opportunity to reflect their ideas in a supportive non-threatening social environment.

However, Elliot's first turn in the same extract reveals another rationale that is used for supporting the notion of all-male learning environment. The comparison of ballet skills between boys and girls, the reference to weak 'senses and skills' of males and the remark about the selection process in dance education that produces highly skilled female dance students all exemplify a sex-difference discourse that is also operating in the dialogue. In that sense, it can be argued that in Elliot's speech the notion about male dance students' need for an all-male learning environment emerges not just through the emancipatory therapeutic discourse. Rather, it also emerges through the sex-difference discourse that constructs male students generally as less advanced in reference to either their dance skills or their physical capabilities.

Yet, as the following extract exemplifies, the emancipatory idea that boys who dance need support from other males can also emerge through a discourse on role-learning. This extract comes from a focus group interview where three female dance teachers reflect how their male dance students have coped in an educational environment where most students and many of the staff members are female.

Janet: That [there is] some form of a support group, a background group, whatever this comparison group [is], that one [the boy who dances] does not have to process all those things entirely alone. No matter whether that is a younger man or an older man, it would be good if he could see dance companies where there are men and men attending in training sessions. Well, there is that man's, male-, the male role-model in dance just like the female role model ...

As the extract shows, this passage from Janet's speech has two parts. Her first sentence focuses on communication in the dance class. She expresses her concern about the male dance student's possibility to share his thoughts in an otherwise all-female student group. However, from the second sentence onward, Janet shifts to talk about gendered role-models. Hence, it could be argued that in this extract the discourse of role-learning introduces the idea that boys who dance need other males who can provide them 'the male role-model in dance'.

Yet, taking Janet's first sentence and placing it next to what she and Maggie discussed only a moment earlier in the same focus group interview, an entirely different discursive framework opens up to support the idea that young males who dance need the male company of their kind. That is, earlier in the conversation, Janet brought up the case of Patrick, a dance student who some years ago had left the dance programme without finishing his degree. According to Janet, Patrick had been the only male in his student group. During the course of the programme he had experienced himself as more and more of an outsider in relation to his female student colleagues. Eventually, he resigned from the dance programme for the reason that he wanted to get a job where he could get a guaranteed income in order to support his new family. In addition to economic concerns and the patriarchal idea about the husband as a breadwinner, Janet suggested that there were also other reasons why Patrick resigned:

Janet: Well, I can't remember what they would have been just like this. But I surely know that when women are together and the level of dressing room discussion is more or less, like (.) who is menstruating and all that and how are things going and who is depressed and who is not and yapity yap. It is so different from that what boys have (.)

Maggie: Own

Janet: Own moaning (laughs) yes, but then the thing that someone gets a nervous breakdown and everyone talks about her and gossip and then someone else goes like this and. The group dynamic among girls is so different. Sure they support each other, but then they nevertheless pull the carpet under one's feet because you know all that is there. Well one is so close. Because when you are in that group and you are so close to others training every God damn day, you are in the theory classes, projects, rehearsals, so you almost know from when the other breaths a bit differently what's it all about. So that the entire reflection group around you, around one male, they are all female, and sometimes you get the feeling that (I

104

must get) out (.) And therefore Patrick came to a conclusion that well he established a family and so on. He decided that he would first get a profession where he could make money and then to reconsider dance (.) An entirely respectable decision...

In this extract, it can be seen how Janet puts forth an idea that female dance students tend to reflect their own and their student colleagues' psychic states and bodily phenomena such as menstrual periods. Implicitly this idea can be seen to entail an unquestioned assumption that males do not contribute to such conversations. This idea that is embedded in the discourse about gendered ways of conversing is elaborated further, as the extract shows, in social interaction between the two speakers.

When scrutinised from this perspective, the idea about male dance students' need for a male support group gets a meaning that differs radically from the notion that was put forth through the role-learning discourse in Janet's earlier account. Here the references to gendered ways of reflecting everyday life introduce an essentialist view about the male dance student's difficulties to join in and share what could be tentatively called the 'girl talk' of his female student colleagues. It could be argued that in this discourse the need for a male support group emerges from a notion that without access to the 'girl talk' the male dance student is left in isolation to ponder alone questions about his dancing body, processes of learning, emotional states and so on.

The idea of social isolation is carried further in the following extract, a dialogue between Maggie and Janet a few moments later in the same focus group interview:

Maggie: But it is indeed another interesting question, whether, well I don't have (answer) to that (.) whether it really, that does it help how much the support of even a small community, when there is at least two of them there that form a community in a different way, of course, than if there was only one. That is if we talk about gender that defines that gender defines the forming of that community. It surely is quite interesting, because now in the fourth year there was only this one student who quit. But then on the other hand, there is Sakari, who went through and, that there are also these students who have graduated as the only male in the programme. But I don't know, it might be an interview question to these students, whether they have received support from each other or not. But of course there are also individual differences and friendships are established over and across the gender boundaries and so on. At least I have noticed that there are different kinds of group forming taking place in this group. But gender is certainly one such thing, at least in the dressing rooms.

Janet: Yeah.

Maggie: Dressing room, like the dressing room is a kind of very important kind of forum for forming knowledge for the students. That you also have someone in the dressing room to ponder things with. I'm sure it is a relatively interesting concept, something that one doesn't always realise as a teacher.

Janet: Yeah, and the boys can have some sore thing that the teacher may have said or something, or the other has looked at one in a certain way when the teacher has said something and these issues are generally dealt with once they get into the dressing room.

It can be argued that in Maggie's first account, the reference to friendly relations across sexes inside and outside the dance class undermines the idea about communication difficulties between sexes. This time, however, the idea about the social isolation of male dance students is constructed through the idea about gendered division of social spaces. From this discursive point of view, the idea that male dance students need each other's company emerges from the important insight that reflection and other processes of learning continue informally outside the formal teaching-learning situation. As suggested in the extract, in dance education such informal processes often take place in a socially gendered space: the dressing room.

However, later in the focus group interview Maggie introduces yet another discursive viewpoint that offers a radically alternative way to discuss the male dance students' need for a male support group. This time, she looks at the male dance student's marginal and potentially isolated position positively through the discourse of struggle:

Maggie: That one also extends that male image [and] also kind of the idea of being an artist, when you have this kind of surface of reflection to another man. Surely it is important. Once when I was teaching, not in our study programme but in another one, some young male students cried out loud almost that <u>we have always these powerful, strong, these our women these teachers women they are always women</u> (laughter) <u>they are always women</u> really like that, and <u>why not men why there aren't any men</u>. ... on one hand it may well be that the choreographers who get most publicity are men precisely because they have had to struggle due to these strong dance teachers perhaps, that is, to get their views somewhere else (.) one possibility. In other words, some one way to dance has not penetrated in to the core of that artist, something that can happen also through the education.

In this extract, Maggie introduces a short narrative about a group of boys who study dance in a degree programme and their concern about the dominating presence of women in dance education. Female teachers are described in this narrative as strong and powerful. Male dance teachers are constructed as absent from the everyday dance training of the boys, which makes boys demand more male teachers. It could be maintained that the repeated use of the word 'women' in the narrative, together with the emphasised loud voice, the broken sentence structure and the laughter, as well as the suggestion that these boys had 'cried out loud' their concern, all contribute towards a reading of the dancing boy as a neurotic: a hysteric male worried about his marginal position in dance.

However, as the latter part of the extract shows, the marginal and perhaps also oppressed position of individual boys in dance can also be perceived positively as something productive. Maggie suggests that some male choreographers have perhaps gained their artistic integrity and success precisely through the struggle under the guidance of strong-minded female dance teachers. It could be argued that the 'no pain, no gain' idea of struggle, in Maggie's viewpoint is deeply embedded in the protestant work ethic, which advocates work as an ennobling pursuit. Further, the idea that boys and men need to struggle when overpowered by strong-minded women emerges, no doubt, from a feminist discourse that reads the patriarchal power hierarchy into relationships between women and men.

Based on the analysis of text extracts in this section, it would seem that there is no single and unified rationale that underpins the notion of the male dance students' need for support from other boys who dance. In a therapeutic discourse, where male dance students are perceived as victims of social prejudices, the dancing boy is constructed as a marginalised other. He has a need to share his dance interest with other likeminded young males in an unthreatening social environment. This view is close to the notion that male dance students need each other's company for the sake of gender role learning, an idea that emerges through the role learning discourse.

On the other hand, a sex difference discourse that compares male and female dance students' physical skills and abilities constructs the average male dance student as weaker than his female co-student. This discursive view underpins the idea about the male dance students' need for an all-male learning environment. Yet, a sex-difference discourse also underpins the notion that men and women reflect their lives strikingly differently from one another. These kinds of essentialist ideas can be found, for example, in the writings of some radical feminists (Cixous 1976, Irigaray 1985) and in American pop psychology (Gray 1992). The discourse on communicational differences between the sexes provides a view about the marginalised male dance student who has no access to the conversations of his female co-students. This constructs him as lacking a forum for sharing and reflection unless there are other males around him. A less radical perspective sees functional relationships emerging between the two sexes. This obviously undermines the idea about significant communication differences.

Learning and reflection continues outside the formal teaching-learning situation. In dance education, it could be argued that this takes place most notably in dressing rooms. The fact that dressing rooms in most dance institutions are gendered spaces, there are separate dressing rooms for males and females, excludes the male dance student from an important forum of reflection unless there are other males in the class. In that sense, the male student's need for the company of other males who dance is underpinned by a pedagogical concern that could emerge for example from a constructivist educational discourse.

All these fragmented ideas about the male dance student's need for the company of other like-minded males find their counter-argument from a feminist perspective that perceives the struggle of the marginalised male dance student in an all-female environment as something positively productive. From a feminist perspective that reflects the protestant idea that all major achievements require hard work, it is possible to perceive the marginalised boys in the feminine realm of dance education as struggling future artists. Their artistic integrity and success is eventually produced through this struggle.

Boys as Competitors

In the previous section, most of the presented extracts propose the notion that boys who dance need the company of other like-minded males. The idea about the male dance student's need to reflect his dance interest and share this with others emerges from a number of discursive perspectives. In stark contrast to these ideas that reflect emancipatory, therapeutic and pedagogical concerns, this section introduces a very different aspect to the male to male relationships in the dance class by focusing on the notion of competition.

In the next set of extracts, a section from a focus group interview with three female dance teachers, the interviewees discuss the relationship between two of their male students in a higher level dance programme. The extracts illuminate how the dancing boy emerges from the tense interplay between two highly contrasting discourses: one of competition, the other of comradely support.

Tina: Yet another thing about these boys. There is, well, one kind of competition going on between them in a ballet class. That is, they surely surveil- because of course they keep each other under surveillance. That's it, but anyhow I think they keep it on a relatively healthy basis that [that kind of competing]

In Tina's account, it can be seen how the observation that boys keep an eye on each other in a ballet class is constructed as an act of 'surveillance'. As such, it is interpreted as being part of the competition between the two males. Further, the two male students are constructed as active agents, 'they keep' the competition 'on a relatively healthy basis'. The notion of competition appears implicitly also in Janet's passage that follows, but then the notion of competition becomes more and more contested as the dialogue evolves:

Janet: [Not to mention that they made those solos] then in the repertory. It was such a damn good choice [to make them both do the same]
Tina: [Yee-ah both of them performed both so that it didn't turn into such]
Janet: And also that they were kind of good both of them in it and in a way that both of them took it. But they could still watch each other, how one is doing.

In this extract, Janet introduces an example from the repertory class where the two boys had been made to learn the same solo. This, according to her, was an excellent choice from the teacher. However, it could be maintained that Tina's comment about the way the two students had performed the task begins to question the entire notion of competition: 'it didn't turn into such', she says. Janet picks up from this as she praises the performance of the boys, but turns to use the notion of surveillance as she continues about the relationship between the two boys. This brings the discussion back to competition between the two male students as the following extract shows:

Tina: Yeah, but there really was that kind of small competition kind of going on. And during a ballet class they kind of stay there when women leave just like that to the next class, but they often stay there and together they explore all those jump combinations and (.) and think through how they went and so on but, well, in a healthy kind of way they anyhow want to support each other.

Maggie: Yes (.) kind of each other in a way when people say what is positive about competition, well this exactly, that it helps the other to gain better results. That kind of, I have not seen that competition is a kind of negative thing that [they also compete instead it is a very good thing]

Janet: [I am actually wondering how long that will last] like this, that when does it happen that (twists her hands and makes a squeaking sound)

Maggie: Yeah, well phases phases, each one has kind of better and

Janet: Yeah

Maggie: Surely people always have also worse periods

In this extract, Tina reports how the two male dance students remain in the studio after the ballet class in order to go through what they have just learned in the class. It could be suggested that this kind of social interaction might well emerge from the male students' need to go through the new movement material in order to let it 'sink in'. A stress-free environment, after the class without the surveillance of the teacher and the more advanced female students, is likely to be an optimal place for such reflection. A trusted classmate, giving feedback in a non-hostile manner, is likely to enforce the learning that takes place through such reflection. Yet, in this extract, the discourse of competition that was introduced earlier on by Tina makes the three interviewees see the interaction between the two male dance students as competitive. While the notion of comradely support is also present in the conversation, it is interpreted as a positive aspect of competi-

111

tion. As Maggie puts it, competition 'is a very good thing' because it 'helps the other to gain better results'.

Following Klemola (1998), competition, as an integral part of the project of winning, is built on the notion of imbalance, the distinction between the winner and those who lose. Further, the project of winning establishes itself most notably in the discourses of war, competitive sports and entrepreneurialism that commonly link to men and masculinity. The last two of these are underpinned by the key values of modernity such as directed acceleration, productivity and progress (Eichberg 1987, Collinson & Hearn 2001). Hence, it could be argued that the idea about the competitive 'nature' of male dance students emerges as a discursive idea through the commonly available, culturally constructed notion about men as competitors.

With a continuous flux of media images showing men as competitors in sports, war, business and politics, the omnipresence of the competitive discourse has made the competition between male subjects appear so 'natural' that it is difficult to perceive male-to-male relationships in any other way. Obviously, without the competitive component that the discourse of competition provides, or other means to establish a tension between males, the notion of comradely homosocial bonding might run the risk of collapsing into the notion of homosexual male bonding, a form of male to male relationship that is banned in the discourse of masculinism. Hence, in a heteronormative culture, the discourse of competition can be perceived as a means to avoid the taboo topic of affection and caring in comradely male-to-male relationships.

Extracts examined in this Chapter show how a number of discourses provide generalised and reductionistic statements on young males. In contrast, it is rare to find accounts that celebrate the diversity of boys by perceiving them as an incoherent or fragmentary class even if such accounts exist. How young males are described depends in each case on what the underpinning discursive framework regards as noteworthy. In that sense, different discourses produce various, even contradictory, ways to elaborate on young males. In total, this must be ambivalent and conflicting not least for individual young males who are subjected to these inconsistent statements.

It can be argued that there is not one unified way that young males are characterised in discussions on boys and dance. It is remarkable that even within a single piece of text or within a single focus group interview the definitions can vary. Further, boys are defined in particular contexts through different discursive frameworks that produce rhetorically valid arguments and points of view. Such rhetoric acts tend to boost gender politics that seek means to accommodate the culturally dominant heteronormative discourse of masculinism.

Chapter Four
Discourses in Boys' Dance Education

'Dance for boys' refers to a collection of cultural practices that various speakers and writers regard as particularly appropriate for the teaching of dance to young males. The conceptual complexity of the idea of a special form of dance for boys becomes evident as the accounts and statements that elaborate various topics around this issue are examined as discursively invested texts. 'Dance for boys' as a concept can be considered to be inherently gendered as it stands in relation to what is regarded in different contexts as 'dance for girls'. In this chapter, the claim that dance for boys has to differ from dance education in general leads to a focus on dance for boys as a culturally particular set of dance educational practices.

Following Foucault (1972, 1995) texts on dance education for boys can be examined as discursive frames of reference for the construction of bodily techniques that aim to shape the male dance student's body. When a boy dances, the living flesh and other tissues of the young male are transformed in social interaction through discursively charged dance educational processes into a jumping, turning, arching, sliding, running, kicking, exuberantly moving and complex bodily entity. This is theoretically how the student is gradually, during several years of training, turned into the male dancer. Dance educational practices are guided by objectives, organising principles, methods and frameworks of value that emerge linguistically 'in the context of a particular social and human world' (Adshead 1989, p. 37). Therefore, such principles are never neutral or natural. Rather, they are always discursively invested. It is important to understand that dance practices are never just physical exercising of the body. They are also means for culturally dominant discourses to be disseminated, through the dancing body, in dance institutions and, more generally, in society.

Gender in Formal Dance Educational Discourse

It has been maintained that the gender-neutral orientation of educational politics in Finland constructs official documents where gender and sexuality are erased (Lahelma 1992, Lehtonen 2003). Such gender-neutral language in curriculum guidelines of the extended study programme in the basic arts education in dance, an official document that has been published by the Finnish National Board of Education, can be exemplified with the following extract:

> The content of teaching is such that during her/his early years of study the pupil establishes a basis for the later study of dance. The student's self-esteem and positive self-image as well as physicality and coarse motor skills are developed through basic physical exercise and games. The student investigates by experimenting the movement possibilities of her/his body. During the basic studies, the student practises in a sustained and more profound manner than before as s/he becomes familiar with the basic movement vocabulary of her/his chosen form and other dance vocabulary. The student practises fine motor skills that are typical for dance and understands the difference between coarse motor and fine motor behaviours in her/his own expression. In deepening studies, the student develops her/his dance technique many-sidedly and with increasing complexity. The student develops her/his thinking in terms of dance and her/his understanding of the relationship between technique, expressive form of technique and the narrative content of expression. The student practises clarity in dance. (Opetushallitus 2002, p. 11)

'Pupil', which is a gender-neutral concept, is applied every time in the extract when the text refers to human subject who participates dance education as a learner. Such gender-neutral orientation continues throughout the document.

116

In an official document that provides curricular guidelines for the upper secondary level vocational qualification in dance, the text remains strictly gender-neutral up to a certain point. However, in reference to one particular genre of dance, ballet, there are two passages that require a closer scrutiny:

> The student must have a refined command of the central movement material in ballet and female dancers must have a command of the vital technique on pointe. S/he must be able to perform movement combinations at the barre, both slow and quick movement combinations, that contain different time measures at the centre as well as pirouettes, jumps and combinations that progress. S/he has to know how to develop and maintain adequate mobility and range of movement in order to perform central movement material. (Opetushallitus 2001, p. 47)

As the extract shows, learning ballet is gendered in the document. Performing skills on pointe shoes – an integral part of the ballet tradition – are required only from female students. No explanation is offered why this specific artistic skill that demands extreme control of the body, concentration and stamina is not required from male students. The lack of such explanation shows, it could be argued, that the embodied understanding of pointe work is unquestioningly regarded as an artistic skill for female dancers only. However, several male dancers have deliberately challenged this in performance.[1] In addition some boys like 14 year-old Jaakko in one of the focus group interviews have taken up pointe work in order to improve their body control:

---

1   I am thinking of the travesty that Les Ballets Trockadero de Monte-Carlo performs but also the Belgian dancer Bart De Block in Mark Baldwin's choreography (see Feuchtner 1998) and Mathew Hawkins from the UK, for example, whose re-interpretations of classicism on pointe can be linked more generally with new ballets that shake the gendered conventions that are embedded in ballet as a genre of dance.

Jaakko: During the past few years I have done pointe work ... all exercises that others in our group do ... just for the sake of my balance and in order to develop my ankle. It is rather intriguing (laughs) because not very many boys, usually, do pointe work.

Int: Was it your own, where did this idea come from?

Jaakko: It was my own decision. Well, I have always had lousy balance ... so I decided that I must develop it.

It seems obvious that the gendered biases in reference to pointe work in the document are underpinned by the gendered division of labour in ballet. Hence, it could be maintained that the gendered division of labour is embedded, albeit implicitly, also in the following extract from the same document:

> The student must know how to interpret different types of roles and characters through her/his dance. S/he must have dance technical readiness to perform pas-de-deux tasks from 19th century. (Opetushallitus 2001, p. 54)

As the extract shows, the document demands that students learn particular character roles. In ballet choreographies, such roles are almost always highly gendered. When it comes to partnering, it has been maintained that also such practice in ballet is gendered (Daly 1984, Novack 1993). Hence, the discourses on gender difference and gendered division of labour are embedded in upper secondary level vocational dance education in Finland through the official curriculum guidelines as far as teaching of ballet is concerned. However, in reference to other genres of dance the official document remains gender neutral.

Apart from ballet education, most vocational dance programmes at upper secondary level and dance in higher education remain formally gender-neutral. Modern dance and jazz, folk dances, improvisation, dance composition, dance history, music, movement analysis and other subjects are generally studied in mixed-sex groups. This is not to ignore the gender differentiation that takes place within a mixed-sex class in other ways.

All-male Dancing

Considering the gender-neutral tone in the curricular guidelines for basic arts education in dance, it is thought-provoking that claims about single-sex groups for male students have been made by those who teach at this level (see for example Turpeinen 1997, Bergman 2002, Lampi et al 2002, Nykänen 2003 and http://www.kolumbus.fi/isto. turpeinen/index2.htm 15.3.2003). Two lines of reasoning are used to support the idea about single-sex groups for male students in dance education. The first one emerges through a closed circuit of essentialism that nurtures the view that dance education for male students has to differ from what is taught to females (see Chapter 3). The second line of reasoning emerges from the emancipatory idea that male dance students need to share their experiences in dance with other like-minded males (see Chapter 3).

Not all dance teachers agree on the benefits of single-sex learning. Marketta Viitala (1998), for example, sees that there are far more advantages than disadvantages in co-educational dance. A mixed-sex group is good for the group spirit, she writes and continues that boys bring extra energy into a dance class, which also encourages girls to participate more fully into creative tasks.[2] Yet, even she recognises that in some areas of dance it may be necessary to maintain single-sex groups. In reference to such areas, she mentions gendered division of roles, presumably in the dance repertory class, and certain unspecified dance technical skills that male dancers need to learn.

---

2   In relation to co-educational dance, it is important to keep in mind that in the area of general educational research, studies show that girls are often subjected to bullying in mixed student groups and that co-education tends to strengthen gendered procedures and subjects girls to patriarchy (see Eklund 1999). It has been maintained that a co-educational framework does not guarantee physical, social or motor skills learning in itself. Rather, co-educational practices have to be organised in ways that allow 'the pupils to perform physical activities that will lead to versatile development and equality' (Eklund 1999, p. 396).

Yet, elaborate attempts to provide all-male learning environments through all-male student groups in some dance institutions, as well as the annually held all-male dance camp in Siilinjärvi and the two seminars on dance education for boys in 2001 and 2002 mark the acceptance of the discursively constructed view that dance education for boys requires a content, a structure and teaching methods that differ from other forms of dance education. It is acknowledged that 'even boys love to dance if the teaching corresponds to their needs' (Hietaniemi 1989, p. 61). As the following extract shows, this view is included also in the recently published memo on dance pedagogy for boys (see Lampi et al 2002):

> As a dancer all my life, I could not say that dance did not suit boys or men. Likewise, I could not say that the problem was in boys themselves. Instead, I was, and I am, entirely sure that in the teaching of this [cultural] form, there were once upon a time elements that eliminated boys from the influence of dance. It is likely that one cannot entirely leave out the effect of attitudes. There was nevertheless a reason to have courage to look critically at the teaching of dance, its methods and contents that took place then. It was necessary to ponder whether it would have been possible to develop them so that they would suit better the purpose of teaching boys. (Mäntylä 2002, p. 8)

In the extract, traditional approaches to dance education are positioned against the needs of young males – not against dance per se. Such approaches are perceived negatively and regarded as unsuitable for boys who are placed beyond any criticism. There are certain problems with traditional approaches to dance pedagogy, not least with the authoritarian model (see Smith 1998, Salosaari 2001). Still, the argument in the extract is alarming because it regards changes necessary merely when working with male students rather than arguing for an overall change in dance pedagogy. Indeed, it could be argued that the act of subjecting only males to changes in dance pedagogy signifies the presence of a masculinist bias in the extract.

Moreover, it is striking that no thought is given to the culturally dominant discourse of masculinism and its power to limit what young males can legitimately do (and not do) within the parameters of such discourse. As Mäntylä (2002) argues, it does not make sense to blame young males for not fitting into the culture(s) of theatrical dance. Following Connell (1995, 2000) and Whitehead (2002) it can be seen that the discourse of masculinism is embodied in many young males whose conception of the self is socially constructed in the present Western culture in relation to masculinism. The problems begin when a discourse that is known for its controlling force enters in the dance class as already embodied in young males. From a Foucauldian perspective, attempts to change conventions in dance pedagogy in order to meet masculinist expectations of the boys can be regarded as a way for masculinist discourse to force its way into dance education and to turn it into part of its technology. Considering some of the problems masculinism causes in society and to individual people, its presence in dance education is worth a serious consideration (see Carrigan, Connell & Lee 1985, Brittan 2001, Connell 1995, 2000, Whitehead 2002 and Cranny-Francis et al 2003).

As is shown above, in Finland there is no unanimity about the advantages and disadvantages of single-sex groups in dance education. Yet, several attempts have been made to differentiate dance pedagogy for boys from more traditional conventions of dance education. The recognition that there is an evident masculinist bias in the accounts that support such a distinction, leads into a more detailed examination of the male-oriented dance educational principles and practice.

Teaching Young Males the Way Carpenters Plane Timber

The memo from the task force on dance pedagogy for boys (Lampi et al 2002, see Chapter 2) is an attempt to provide guidelines for those who work with male dance students by linking such a framework to the official aims and the structure of the basic arts education in dance. 'Joy, adventure, pupil-centeredness, basic physical exercising, expression, regularity of training and advancing from the general to the particular' (Lampi et al 2002, p. 2) are some of the special features of dance for boys, the authors suggest. It remains unmentioned, however, why these concepts should be particularly appropriate for dance education for *boys*. Why not for girls or for dance education in general? In reference to core objectives in dance for boys, the authors divide male dance students roughly into two categories as follows:

> The joy of physical exercising and the habit of coming to training classes is the central objective for younger boys. Where the older boys are concerned, it is already possible to talk more precisely about the joy of dance and going to dance training. (Lampi et al 2002, p. 2)

It is telling that dance educational work with younger male students is not defined as dance but more generally as 'physical exercising' in the document. Moreover, the term 'training class' is used in place of 'dance class'. This choice of concepts suggests that dance education for males needs to contain something other than dance during the first few years. Such a view is elaborated for example in the following extract that comes from Isto Turpeinen's interview in Marika Bergman's article:

> But how is it possible in practice to make the boy dance? The boy, who typically smells the danger immediately when the word 'art' is mentioned? By cheating. By concocting a story that we do not actually dance in this class, we boy-dance here; make tricks, have fun. Thus, the boy, suspecting no evil, goes to dance classes for a couple of years, gets friends in his group, experiences pleasant moments, learns to perform cartwheels and suddenly – BAM – he is hooked! He is converted to dance. (2002, p. 82)

The extract demonstrates a commonly held discourse that Finnish males find theatrical dance, and arts more generally, of doubtful value (see for example Laakso 1988, Lampi 1991, Harri 1993, Lipiäinen 1996, Reunamäki 2000, Nykänen 2003, Räty 2003). Hence, rather than starting from dance training that is specific to different genres of dance, dancing is introduced to boys in disguise.

A striking paradox arises when activities that are generally not defined as dance - games, gymnastic exercises and martial arts - are used as teaching content in a dance class to replace some or all of the content that is regarded as dance within more traditional dance contexts. However, the use of non-dance activities in a dance class has been reasoned from a viewpoint that acknowledges social aspects of learning. It has been suggested that the non-dance teaching content helps teachers to turn young male students into a comradely group (Turpeinen 1997, Bergman 2002, Lampi et al 2002). It has been claimed that ideas on 'dance' and 'dance training' can be introduced to boys only after a strong group dynamic has been established and the students have internalised a habit of meeting regularly (ibid). Conscious attempts to keep all-male groups together by emphasising the meaning of group spirit have increased the number of male dance students and kept the dropout-rate remarkably low in at least three dance institutions: the Vantaa Dance Institute, the Finnish National Opera Ballet School and the Dance Theatre of Kajaani (Mäntylä personal information 28.4.2001, Lampi personal information 28.4.2001, Palokangas-Sirkiö, personal information 28.4.2001).

Yet, as the next extract shows, there is also another discursive line of reasoning that supports the presence of non-dance activities in dance classes for boys:

> The different elements in the structure of the class need to be in balance; their variations and developments should constitute an ascending arch, where the progress shifts from basic physical exercising to form-specific exercises. Boys' route to dance is often different from that of girls. Boys can have their own teaching groups from the age of five onwards and they move to study under the extended course at the age of seven. When teaching movement skills, the teacher has to have patience to begin from simple enough skills as well as tolerance to allow for coarse motor behaviour in boys. (Lampi et al 2002, p. 2)

An essentialist discourse can be recognised from the reference to a particular 'coarse' quality of the motor behaviour of young males in the extract. It could be argued that the discourse on rugged quality of male movements calls forth discourses on physical development and motor skills learning. Further, it is through these discourses that the pedagogical principle, which proposes a gradual move from a general physical workout towards more particular dance-specific training, is constructed.

This kind of essentialist view can also be recognized from Turpeinen's dance educational approach called 'a raw timber method' (Räsänen 2000a, Bergman 2002). As Bergman writes, in this method 'a boy is confronted as a boy, as a slightly clumsy and rough mover by his nature' (2002, p. 82). Some of the key principles of this method have been encapsulated as follows:

> One of the principles to teach boys was to advance by hurrying slowly, slowly does it. The boys are given a broad education in the classes. Methods of creative dancing are applied in the beginning in order to create a sense of space and time by moving briskly. As the students grow, physical exercises that are borrowed from sports training are introduced. We play with learned perceptions and create team spirit ... The fact that boys are extremely ready mentally to work towards motivated objectives can be regarded as one of the advantages of hurrying slowly. The mental courage follows from the fact that they have been given enough space for individual experiences and the growth of self-esteem in the education. Fine motor skills have been left in the margin. They have been sneaked gradually into the education. Eventually as the student is willing to perform more openly, has adopted the structure of the dance class and his motivation is high, that is when the results start to show. Once the creative exercises of children's dance and the preparing exercises of free dance are done, boys start to catch up the more finely tuned demands of the curriculum. Hurrying slowly has turned into progressing in a normal speed. (Turpeinen 1997, pp. 13-14)

The extract demonstrates how the discourses of motor skills development, sports training and psychology (cognitive, personal and social) are integrated in a complex way with discourses of creative dance and free dance. It could be argued that some of the key principles of Turpeinen's 'raw timber method' emerge from the nexus of these discourses.

Thus, it can be maintained that two radically different discursive ideas - one that claims boys find dance strange, the other with an essentialist emphasis on male development and motor skills learning - underpin the idea that dance education for boys must start from basic physical exercises rather than from dance exercises.[3] From this dual perspective, the task force on dance pedagogy for boys (Lampi et al 2002) has constructed a three-stage model. In stage one (5 to 8 years of age), young males are brought into contact with dance. In stage two (9 to 12 years of age), their commitment to dance is reinforced. Finally, in stage three (from 13 years of age onwards) the students establish a purposeful orientation to dance (ibid).

In this model, as the pie-diagrams on key areas of emphasis show (see Figure 2), young males are gradually led from more general physical activities towards purposeful study of dance in this model. In stage one, only 25% of the total teaching content is devoted to dance. However, the dance content of the class increases to 40% in stage two and up to 70% in stage three. Meanwhile, in stage one, general physical exercising and gymnastics floor work (rolls, somersaults, cartwheels, flips etc.) cover up to 50% of the total teaching content (see Figures 3 and 4). The remaining 25% is divided between play activities (9%), performance activities (8%) and interdisciplinary work with other art forms such as drama and music (8%). In stage two, the time that is reserved for play activities remains on the same level as in stage one but the time that is allocated to general physical exercising is reduced to 16%. Compared to stage one, in stage two there is slightly less interdisciplinary work with other art forms (5%) and slightly more performance activities (10%). However, significantly more time is allocated to new subjects such as break dance, capoeira, African dances, folkdances, hip hop and so on. In stage three, in addition to the taught dance content, the students are expected to work on their own (12%) as well as in co-educational groups (12%). Even with a strong emphasis on dance subjects in stage three, there is still time reserved for play (6%) (Lampi et al 2002).

---

3   Lampi et al (2002) include various gymnastic exercises that involve the use of equipment (gymnastic mats and mattresses, balls, bean bags, hoops, instruments, sticks, ropes and wall bars) as well as various types of movement games under the concept of 'general physical exercise'.

5 to 8 year-old boys

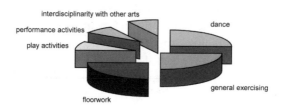

interdisciplinarity with other arts

performance activities

play activities

dance

general exercising

floorwork

9 to 12 year-old boys

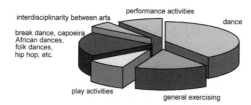

interdisciplinarity between arts

performance activities

break dance, capoeira African dances, folk dances, hip hop, etc.

dance

play activities

general exercising

Boys from 13 years onwards

co-educational activities

play activities

independent work

dance: main subject, subsidiary subject improvisation, choreography body knowledge, dance knowledge, challenging performance activities

Figure 2. Pie-diagrams on the key areas of emphasis in boys' dance education. Redrawn from Lampi et al 2002.

Figure 3. Floor work in Turpeinen's class in the Vantaa Dance Institute.
Video image: Kai Lehikoinen.

Figure 4. Ilkka Lampi teaching acrobatics in the Dance Camp for Boys in
Siilinjärvi in June 2001. Video image: Kai Lehikoinen.

127

The task force argued that dance should be taught for boys in single-sex groups up to stage three. They maintained that it is only after 13 years of age that coeducational classes are realistically possible (ibid). No evidence was given to support these arguments in the memo. However reasonings that emerge through a developmental discourse can be recognised from Turpeinen's interview in Bergman:

> When one is comparing a girl and a boy, both twelve years of age, the difference stands out clearly. The girl's rapid growing period is about to be over, she is starting to develop into a woman for real. The boy, at the same age, is a complete brat as far as bodily control and ability to concentrate are concerned. (2002, p. 84)

In the extract, psychological aspects of male development are placed alongside physical aspects to support the discursive idea that coeducational classes can be organised only once male students have reached a certain age.

In light of these examples, it can be argued that the starting point in dance education for boys is located outside the traditional discourse of dance in the realm of play, games and basic physical workouts. This pedagogical principle is underpinned by two discourses: one that claims boys find dance strange; the other that highlights physical and psychic underdevelopment of young males up until their early teens. From a pedagogical point of view, the idea to progress from more general movement exercises towards more specific dance content seems well argued. This, of course, is not something that should concern just the teaching of male students. More debatable is that the teaching content in dance education is changed in order to accommodate masculinist norms and that cheating is used as a device to get boys involved with dance. These rather pragmatic solutions do not take into account the problems of masculinism. Instead, they turn uncritically into part of the masculinist technology.

How to Handle Nitro-glycerine:
Game Activities and Delirious Boys

Play activities are very much included in the recent memo on dance pedagogy for boys (Lampi et al 2002). In the memo the authors have included an extensive list of different games with brief instructions including: 21 variations on the tag game; 33 variations on single combat; and 38 variations on relay games where the idea is to win as a team. Chapter 6 addresses gendered meanings that are embodied in physical games such as tag. In this section however, tag is studied for some of the reasonings that underpin decisions to include physical games into dance education for young males.

Tag is constructed around the idea of chase. In the basic form of tag, one of the participants is chasing the others who try to escape. The captured participant becomes the new chaser. A variation from this is that the captured player needs to stay still until rescued by one of those who have not been tagged yet (Lampi et al 2002). Another variation is 'sitting tag'— this was played at the beginning of a ballet class for 10 to 12 year-old boys on a dance course for boys in Siilinjärvi during the summer of 2001. In 'sitting tag', the basic idea of catching others remains the same but those who are free can protect themselves by running into the 'base'. Whoever is resting in the 'base' must leave to join the game once someone else enters it (field notes 13.6.2001).

Another vigorous game, 'chain tag', was also introduced during the ballet class (see Figure 5). It is a game where a pair runs hand in hand in order to catch others who run to escape. The ones who are caught have to join at the end of the chain of the capturers. Eventually when all participants are caught, the participants establish a long meandering chain. In the class, dance teacher Ilkka Lampi first used walking tempo to simulate the fast-moving game to ensure that the students had understood the rules. He himself participated whole-heartedly in both games. After about ten minutes of wild running and deafening noise, the game was brought to an end. The boys were called next to a wall for a moment to calm down and to stretch out their inner-thigh muscles. Only then wre they asked to take their places at the ballet barre as their teacher started to demonstrate a plié exercise and talk about the arm-coordination in port-de-bras (field notes 13.6.2001).

Figure 5. Playing 'chain-tag' in Lampi's ballet class.
The Dance Camp for Boys, Siilinjärvi 2001. Video image: Kai Lehikoinen.

It could be maintained that the fast tempo, the sudden changes in the use of directions and levels, and the need to keep senses of sight, hearing and touch open to what is taking place around oneself while moving are some of the typical features of physical games such as tag. In addition, such games are generally based on spontaneous social interaction. It has been argued that physical games contribute to the development of physical agility and coordination as well as social abilities such as team working skills (Lampi, lecture on boys in ballet, Vantaa 29.4. 2001). In addition, it can be suggested that such games can develop relational awareness in time and space more generally.

From the viewpoint of training physiology, one could argue that tag, like other fast moving games, is an exceptional way to start a dance class. Fast spurts and sudden changes of direction in the rigorous game involve the entire body. Such physical action speeds up the respiratory system and the blood circulation. The body becomes quickly warmed up before it is time to focus on more isolated and consciously coordinated use of the body that is typical of traditional ballet training.

More generally, it has been said that physical games provide holistic movement experiences and influence positively on the readiness for learning (Lampi in Räsänen 1986). Further, a many-sided physical basis that can be established by complementing dance training with physical games prepares the dance student to face better professional challenges in dance (Lampi, lecture on boys in ballet, Vantaa 29.4. 2001). In addition, multiple variations of a single game provide a means to include a large amount of repetition in the class content without making it boring for the students (ibid.). It has been suggested that movement games inject fun into the routines of the dance class where an over emphasis on technique training for the name of efficiency can kill the interest of the students (ibid.).

However, as the following extracts show, an essentialist discourse on the 'nature' or the masculine 'core' of young males can also underpin the claim that doses of rigorous movement activity must be included in dance classes for boys:

> One has to be careful when handling the students – the dancing boy is like a glass of nitro-glycerine, so it is not a good idea to let the intensity drop. An explosion on the walls and all over the studio is a consequence of such a drop – unnecessary activity that is away from the experience, from the positive act and above all from learning. (Turpeinen 1998, p. 58)

In this extract, young males who dance are reduced to the concept of 'the dancing boy' who is metaphorically ascribed as 'nitro-glycerine', an easily explosive substance that requires particularly careful handling. The metaphor ascribes an inflammable or volatile quality as an essential feature in young male dance students. This quality is captured rather well in the following description of the young male behaviour in a ballet class at the dance camp in Kuopio during the summer of 2003:

> *Impatient boys* make a couple of cartwheels after the jumps. Someone is making faces at his image in the mirror … Always when Lampi speaks, some boy is hanging upside down, head on the floor. And yet, these boys are experienced practitioners. Seven year-old rascals, first graders at school, are the most difficult ones, according to Lampi. (Nykänen 2003, D7, original emphasis).

As Foucault (1988) points out, this kind of seemingly distracted, random and unfocused corporeal behaviour was interpreted in the classical period to signify 'mania'. This and other forms of 'madness' emerged in relation to the Enlightenment idea of reason as 'unreason' during the course of seventeenth and eighteenth centuries (ibid.). From this discursive perspective,

> the maniac's imagination … is occupied by a perpetual flux of impetuous thoughts … mania deforms all concepts and ideas; either they lose their congruence, or their representative value is falsified; in any case, the totality of thought is disturbed in its essential relation to truth … the cause of the disease is always in the movement of the animal spirits … it is continuous, violent, always capable of piercing new pores in the cerebral matter, and it creates, as the material basis of incoherent thoughts, explosive gestures, continuous words which betray mania. (Foucault 1988, pp. 125-126)

A discourse that takes the Enlightenment standards of the 'rational individual' as the model of mental sanity can be recognised from the following early 21st century account on the unpredictable and unfocused behaviour of young males:

> The class for younger boys contains rolling along the floor as pins and turning a somersault. Concentration shows on the faces but as soon as a short break appears during the change of music, the bodies of boys start to bubble with jokes and bantering. One young man is lost in his thoughts, examining a crawling insect on the floor. Isto has succeeded in relieving boys' concentration problems with physical exercises and games at the beginning of the class. Once extra energy is skimmed off the top, concentration on more refined issues is easier. (Bergman 2002, p. 84)

A non-disciplinary male behaviour in the dance class is constructed in the extract through a psychological discourse as a 'concentration problem' that is located in the young males. The extract exemplifies how disorderly behaviour is psychologised and positioned negatively against orderly disciplinary practice in the educational discourse that is embedded in the Enlightenment ideals of rationality and progress.

Rationality, which is gendered masculine in Enlightenment and the age of modernity, constitutes a narrow framework for socially acceptable behaviour for men (see Chapter Eight). In addition, it has been argued that in a disciplinary system,

> when one wishes to individualise the healthy, normal and law-abiding adult, it is always by asking him how much of the child he has in him, what secret madness lies within him, what fundamental crime he has dreamt of committing. (Foucault 1995, p. 193)

Hence, the disorderly behaviour of young males in Nykänen's (2003) and Bergman's (2002) texts links to 'non-reason' that constructs the young males in relation to 'normal adult men' as 'boys' who have not yet matured enough to control their 'passions'. According to Foucault (1988), the lack of such control constructs them 'mad' in relation what is regarded 'sane' in a discursive legacy of the Enlightenment thinking.

As Foucault (1988) maintains, the body of the person who is thought to be insane becomes the target of various methods of 'cure' during the classical period. Similarly, as the above-discussed extracts show, it is regarded in the 21st century Finnish dance pedagogy for boys that the hyperactive or disorderly behaviour of young males can be cured temporarily with boisterous corporeal tasks. Once hyperactivity is discharged, for example with a round of tag, a momentary state of sanity is achieved, which enables the rational activity of learning. As time passes, some of the young rascals will eventually learn to perform the discourse of sanity (next to the discourse of heterosexuality) through self-control for a more or less sustained period of time, which turns them into legitimate 'men' in the masculinist discourse.

Hence, the idea of including physical games into dance education for boys emerges from two very different discursive underpinnings: on the one hand, the positive influence of such games to the physical and social development of young males is acknowledged through a developmental discourse. On the other hand, vigorous physical games can be argued to emerge as a temporary cure against the 'delirium' of boys through a complex amalgamation of essentialist views on the 'nature' of young males and the Enlightenment model of sanity.

Dance and Sports Training

The discourse of sports training can be understood as a fragmented body of cultural practices that aim to maximise the efficiency of athletes.[4] Usually it also attempts to minimise the risk of injuries and illnesses in training.[5] An examination of articles shows that these objectives also underpin dance education of boys (Räsänen 1986, Bask 1992, Hietaniemi 1992, Jääskeläinen 1993, Harri 1993, Turpeinen 1997, Lampi et al 2002). Yet, as it is argued in this section, sports training discourse operates also as a means to turn dance into a socially accountable cultural practice for boys and men in a cultural climate of masculinism.

---

4   Sports training builds on sports medicine and training physiology, areas of medicine that connect with the clinical and scientific aspects of sports and exercise. For more information, see for example The Research Institute for Olympic Sports (http:// www.kihu.jyu.fi/english/).

5   Recent news about doping, its commonness in competitive sports and the involved health risks exemplify how the health of the athlete is not always central to sports medicine and sports training. I am referring here, for example, to the doping scandal of Finnish skiers in the Lahti Nordic World Ski Championships in February 2001 that gained wide publicity at least in the Finnish media.

Some authors had already proposed the use of sports training in dance education for young males already in the late 1950's (Mäkinen 1959b, Nyholm 1959). Yet, it took close to twenty-five years before such methods were systematically implemented in dance education, first in the Finnish National Opera Ballet School by dance teacher Ilkka Lampi (Räsänen 1986, Bask 1992, Hietaniemi 1992). In this respect, it is justified to maintain that Lampi provided a paradigm shift in the 1980's at least as far as the teaching of male ballet students is concerned. Another person who has eagerly appraised the advantages of sports training methods in dance education for young males is Leena Jääskeläinen, the former Chief Inspector of Physical Education. She worked actively from 1987 until 1999 next to Lampi as a supervisor of the Dance Camp for Boys where sports training methods were utilised (Hietaniemi 1989, Jääskeläinen 1993, the Kuopio Dance Festival – the dance camp for boys brochures 1987-2003).

The sports training discourse can be exemplified with the following extract from Jääskeläinen's article on the dance camp. According to the author,

> Everything in planning and realisation is underpinned by the principles of training. Such principles are carried through in the weekly agenda, the daily rhythm of the schedule as well as in individual training classes and separate exercises. The right ratio between exertion and rest, and the ascending labour that arises from this relationship, establish a foundation. Particular weight is laid on the development of muscle strength and flexibility as well as on the conditioning of the muscles.
> The careers of unnecessarily many dancers have come to an end at their start when the maintenance of one's own instrument has been neglected and one's physical condition has not been cared for. Beginning with a dance technique, when the entire foundation is weak, is like a person who has recently learned to swim attempting to cross the English Channel.
> The principles of muscle conditioning include a warm-up as well as stretching after the class and at the end of the day, strength training as well as other measures that restore the body (sauna, swimming, exercises for oxygen intake and relaxation etc.) (Jääskeläinen 1993, p. 4-5)

The extract refers to 'principles of training' rather than stating explicitly the word 'sports training'. However the presence of the

135

sports training discourse can be recognised from the other use of language: from references to the systematic approach to training and the detailed organisation of the training scheme as well as from the emphasis on the improvement and conditioning of the muscular system. These references are all part of the progress- and result-oriented language of the sports training discourse, it can be argued. Lampi complements ballet training with physical exercises

> that have versatility as their aim. Muscular balance, basic skills and agility are key words when one is aiming to reach a high level of particular skills [in the sport / in ballet – both translations possible] and building preconditions for exercises in dance. (Harri 1993)

Thus, on a field trip to the Dance Camp for Boys in Siilinjärvi in June 2001, I focused, among other topics, on the discursive acts through which the sports training discourse was implemented in dance education during Lampi's ballet classes. The following three extracts describe brief moments from three ballet classes where such acts could be recognised from the practice. The first excerpt describes Lampi teaching a series of three jump exercises to a group of 9 to 12 year old male students who had less than five years of experience of ballet:

> After the warm-up at the barre, the boys move to work on chassé pas de chat en derrière, a cluster of two small jumps, across the diagonal. The step combination is repeated four times during a crossing and there are four crossings before a break. After this, Ilkka invites the students to return to their places in the centre and to stand in a turned-out first position in two lines facing the front. He takes time to explain the arm positions of the first port de bras. The emphasis is on the shapes of the arms and the relationship between the arms and the chest. The students execute the exercise slowly while Ilkka talks through each detail. Then the exercise is repeated three times with the music. Following this, Ilkka commands the boys back on the diagonal. The students return to work on chassé step, but this time in the form of grand pas de chat, a bigger jump that combines a chassé step with a hitch kick. Again there are four repetitions of the step in each crossing. After three crossings on both sides the boys are asked to sit on the floor in a semi circle with legs forward extended. While the group is taking a rest, the boys are asked one at a time to travel by jumping from two

136

feet to two feet over each pair of the legs. One of the aims in this exercise is to understand spatial orientation while travelling with jumps, Ilkka points out to the students. (Field notes 13.6.2001)

The extract shows how the training of ballet jumps is divided into three intensive sections that require each a high capacity of physical performance. The rest periods between the sections allow the students to have a moment of recovery. After the first series of vigorous jumps, new exercises are prescribed for the upper body to keep the class going while the leg muscles receive a well-deserved rest. Similarly, a moment of rest is available after the second series of jumps as the group sits on the floor while the boys perform the third set of jump training one by one (see Figure 6). When the description is read next to the earlier presented extract from Jääskeläinen (1993), it can be seen that one of the key ideas of the sports training discourse, the balance between effort and rest, is being used in the class. From a sports training point of view, it can be maintained that the jump exercises are organised this way in order to maximise the benefits of the training and to minimise the risk of injuries.

Figure 6. Jumping and resting in Lampi's ballet class.
The Dance Camp for Boys, Siilinjärvi 2001. Video image: Kai Lehikoinen.

In the second extract, a group of 12 to 16 year old males who have more than five years of ballet experience are practising the 'cabriolet', a spectacular jump where legs are beaten together during the elevation:

Ilkka teaches cabriolet to the boys by dividing the exercise into three parts. First, he asks the boys to travel in a diagonal by performing a basic chassé that is combined with a hop from two feet to one foot as the free leg performs a grand battement. The step is repeated a number of times on both sides. Following this, Ilkka commands the boys to lie on their backs on the floor. They are asked to rest against their elbows while keeping their legs stretched and turned out in first position with pointed feet. In the exercise, the legs are kicked up one after the other. The second leg that follows is made to beat the calf of the leading leg. The impulse makes the first leg continue its ascent while the second leg returns down. After this, the first leg is also brought down. Ilkka emphasises the quality of movement, which in cabriolet is quick yet relaxed even if the knees are kept extended. Once all this is mastered lying on the floor the students are asked to perform a proper 'chassé cabriolet' diagonally across the room. (Field notes 12.06.2001)

The extract shows, how the training of 'cabriolet' is segmented into three phases: first the steps that travel; then the beating of the legs with the right movement quality; last, the amalgamation of the different elements. There is a moment of rest from jumping and landing between the first and third phase of the exercise as weight is taken off the feet during the second phase that is practised while lying on one's back (see Figure 7). Again it can be argued that the effort/rest relationship that is woven into the exercise emerges through a sports training discourse. Further, the presence of practical knowledge from such a discourse is also embedded in the discursive act of segmenting. That is, the required dance technical task is divided into manageable 'bite-size' exercises that are practised separately before assembling the different elements together for the refined performance of 'chassé cabriolet'.

Figure 7. Exercising cabriolet lying on the back in Lampi's ballet class.
The Dance Camp for Boys, Siilinjärvi 2001. Video image: Kai Lehikoinen.

It has been argued that the craft of jumps, in ballet as well as in other dance forms, requires adequate muscle strength combined with a good use of a plié when the elevation is initiated and also in landing (Teiz 1990). This is particularly true for male dancers in ballet and other theatrical forms of dance where high and complicated jumps are often required from them. Yet, as Lampi (quoted in Räsänen 1986) suggests, it can be difficult for a dance student to develop enough strength into the leg muscles through traditional ballet exercises. According to him,

> correctly practised, classical ballet also develops well all those attributes that are needed in dance but not necessarily far enough – particularly not if the student does not have exceptionally good physical attributes. It is difficult to develop exertion, speed, buoyancy and flexibility, for example, simultaneously

with the demanding ballet technique that presupposes purity from the executed movements. (Lampi in Räsänen 1986)

Thus, the third extract describes how Lampi works with the younger group of boys to gain a better take-off for their hop and to develop the muscle strength in their legs:

Progressing diagonally from the corner, the boys are practising a combination of two steps: a gallop and a step hop. It is a problem for many of them to take-off for a bouncy hop after the gallop. After a moment of unsuccessful attempts, Ilkka asks the boys to follow him onto the staircase in the hallway. He shows them a step hop combination and asks the students to perform it up and down the stairs. This is done repeatedly. Back in the classroom, Ilkka takes five pieces of forty centimetre high hurdles to prepare a track. The hurdles are placed in a line approximately one meter apart from each other. The boys are asked to travel over the hurdles with the step hop –step. Ilkka gives immediate positive feedback to each student who succeeds to perform the task. He is also quick to interrupt a faulty performance in order to give corrective guidance to the students. (Field notes 17.6.2001)

Two exercises are applied: staircase training and a hurdle exercise (see Figures 8 and 9). It could be argued that the fact that one of the drills takes place in the stairs and that the other applies equipment that are used in track events positions these activities outside the traditional discourse of ballet pedagogy. From such a perspective, these activities could seem unorthodox. Yet, similar plyometric exercises are commonly recommended for 'conditioned athletes to increase and develop their jumping, sprinting and explosive power' (http//www.netfit.co.uk/plyometrics_ web.htm).

Hence, as the three above described training practices show, it can be argued that the sports training discourse is operating in dance education for young males where it amalgamates with a discourse of ballet pedagogy. Following Foucault's (1995) idea on 'docile bodies', it can be argued that these exercises operate as part of a technology in the 'micro-physics' of power. Discourses of sports training and sports are brought through these and similar activities into the dance class and implemented in the bodies of male dance students. It is through these and similar discursive activities that benefits of training are maximised to improve the dance students' physical capacity to perform particular physical tasks such as jumping.

Figure 8. Staircase training in Lampi's ballet class.
The Dance Camp for Boys, Siilinjärvi 2001. Video image: Kai Lehikoinen.

Räsänen's (1986) article on dance, health and sports training can be examined as an interface for reflections on sports training, dance education for male students and certain impediments of dance teacher Ilkka Lampi's own body. The following extract presents Lampi's account as it is constructed in the article:

I strained my back because my back and abdominal muscles were too weak for lifting heavy girls and landing from high jumps. This kind of deficiencies can be corrected efficiently with complementary exercises, Ilkka Lampi says.
Not all physical weaknesses come out in ballet school during classes – for that reason, Ilkka Lampi had the students of his highest male class, the boys from the fourth year, tested last summer at the sports institute of Kisakallio under the direction of the well-known sports coach and researcher *Pertti Heliin* … Ilkka Lampi thinks testing is necessary for all students in the future because it is the

141

only way to find out about the deficiencies. The tests make it possible to design individual complementary programmes. (Räsänen 1986)

Figure 9. Hurdle exercising in Lampi's ballet class.
The Dance Camp for Boys, Siilinjärvi 2001. Video image: Kai Lehikoinen.

Further down in the article, Lampi is quoted as follows:

- Skill constitutes the basis even for men's dancing – attributes that can be developed through complementary exercises come next including flexibility, movement range, speed and strength. The dance of males is constituted mainly from these elements.
- I wish to see one of my boys some day as Albrecht from Giselle, for example, and that everything that can be accomplished with a goal-oriented training is embodied in [his] performance: dynamism, energy, strength, complete control of the body, style. (ibid.)

It can be argued that the discourse of sports medicine operates through language as the dancer's body (Lampi's own body and the dance students bodies) is objectified and evaluated in terms of its physical capabilities in the two extracts. The imperfect and defective dancer's body is constructed in relation to a fantasy about the physically fit and smoothly operating perfect body of modernity. As a result, such a fantasy is located in the centre of dance education for young males in this discursive framework. Further, the underpinning discourse also necessitates the examination technologies that are used to detect 'weaknesses' in the dancing body. Moreover, the data that is produced through such technologies enables the implementation of body-corrective practices in the form of 'complimentary exercises'.

The following two extracts provide detailed descriptions of such examination technologies:

- In the middle of 1980's we started to follow the students' fitness with body tissue measures. That is, the measurement of the so-called body fat percentage, a practice that is know from sports medicine. Currently every summer we participate in research that has been undertaken at the University of Kuopio. The research includes three groups: cross country skiers, ballet students and boys who do not participate in any sport or exercise as the third group.
- On average, the ones from ballet have had quite good results but the boys from the ballet school of the opera who have trained a lot got an outstanding figure for body fat percentage. Everyone has had below 10 and the best ones have had four, the same as for top-level athletes. (Lampi as quoted in Bask 1992, p. 31)

The Department of Physiology in the University of Kuopio has tested the physical and motor properties of boys over a number of summer courses ... We have been able to follow the development of the boys' exertion energy, strength in the abdominal and back muscles as well as oxygen intake. Also the body fat percentage has been measured every year.

The results are analysed and the boys are given clear feedback and instructions on what properties should be developed and with what kind of exercises. Many boys have taken the instructions so literally that in the next summer their development has shown not just in their test results but also in their dance ... It tells about the muscular fitness of the boys that we had to set a limit to the test. Once the limit is reached the test can be interrupted. When a young man does 500 crunches and is fine, it tells about the level of endurance that is reached by very few professionals. (Jääskeläinen 1993, p. 5)

The results that are presented from a discursive position of training physiology and sports training are reviewed positively as marks of success in both extracts. The young male dance students who participate in the training regime are compared positively with athletes. Another comparison constructs them positively as more enduring than most of the professional dancers. Moreover, the extracts show that the positive results are used as empirical evidence that speaks in favour of implementing the testing technologies of sports medicine and the regime of sports training into the core of dance education for young males. Hence, the sports training discourse operates in dance education for young males in a circular fashion. Weaknesses in practices that stem from the conventions of dance education are pointed out first. Following this, complementary exercises are introduced from sports training. Next the effects of the implemented discourse are measured repeatedly. Finally, the quantified data is used to argue a legitimate status for the sports training discourse in dance education for young males.

The implementation of the sports training discourse into dance education can be viewed from some perspectives as positive progress. As discussed in Chapters Three and Eight, the sports discourse certainly provides a means for young males who dance to reclaim their social position in a masculinist culture where males in theatrical dance are still very much marginalised. However, a different view emerges when sports training discourse is investigated from perspectives of sports philosophy and sports sociology. Some scholars in these two related areas maintain that the emphasis on progress as well as the technologically oriented and objectifying way to view the 'body as a machine' are some of the key features in the discourse of sports training (Eichberg 1987; Klemola 1998; Puhakainen 1997).

As the discussion above shows, the male dance student's body is constructed in the examined extracts through the sports training discourse as a machine that can be technologically examined and trimmed. The body as a machine is thought to run smoothly unless its maintenance is overlooked. Moreover, it is believed that the negligence in the maintenance of the body destroys also the emerging career. In general, an unfit body is constructed as a problem. In addition, the idea of linear progress that underpins the project of winning in competitive sports can also be recognised from the presented extracts.[6] Hence, discursive acts where sports training methods are used to improve the physical performance of the male dancer's body can be linked to 'citius, altius, fortius' (faster, higher, stronger), the motto of the Olympic Games. Following Eichberg (1987) and Gray (1989), it can be maintained that such aspirations are underpinned by the project of modernity in competitive sports as well as in dance education.[7]

As Puhakainen (1997) argues, the discourse of sports training embodies a significant change in a person's recollection of being in the world as the self-concept is constructed through the 'logic of technology'. In such logic, the self emerges as a calculation of 'cost and profit' in relation to applied training methods (ibid). It can be argued that also the dance student's body can be abstracted through the discourse of sports training into an object of investment that in the Western capitalist discourse can earn its existence only through increased productivity.

Hence, from a Foucauldian position, the extracts that have been presented in this section can be read as a description of how the bodies of male dance students are placed under the scientific gaze of sports medicine, a branch of medical science that is heavily constructed through the discourse of anthropomaximology, the science that aims

6   In a phenomenological thesis on projects of physical education Klemola (1998) distinguishes four such projects: winning, health, expression and self. The discourse of sports training that, according to Eichberg (1987) and Puhakainen (1997), builds heavily on anthropomaximology, the human science of maximised physical performance, can be found to nurture the project of winning in competitive sports where 'victory gives meaning to a contest' (Klemola 1998, p. 126). In the project of winning all training according to Klemola (ibid) focuses on beating the other that is regarded as 'an obstacle that has to be overstepped'.

7   In his socio-historical thesis on exercising bodies Eichberg (1987) argues that the devotion to measuring and linear progress that are central to competitive sports and its training methods can be traced back to the underpinnings of the industrial society. In her book on dance education Gray (1989) shares Eichberg's view by maintaining that the body as a machine metaphor 'reflects our industrial and technological society' (1989, p. 56).

145

to maximise the performance of the human body (see Eichberg 1987). Further, the bodies of male dance students are measured and tested in a number of ways that produces meaningful data for scientific purposes of the research in sports medicine. The complementary exercises that are developed based on the analysis of research data and prescribed individually to each dance student can be interpreted as carefully developed technologies that enable the discourse of anthropomaximology to operate on the bodies of male dance students. Moreover, it can be maintained that these technologies form the bodies of male dance students to correspond to the body-ideal of the discourse of anthropomaximology. Simultaneously they are also formed into bodies that are capable of performing positively for the research purposes. Finally, through these procedures, the bodies of male dance students are harnessed to work primarily for the project of winning and not for the project of art. The argument could be elaborated further by suggesting that the sports training discourse does not necessarily produce exceptionally good male dancers but rather, as the text shows, well operating athletic machines with a high endurance capacity and possibly also an overly performance oriented view of their dancer's body.

Embodying a Dream of Modernity Through Nutrition

While eating is a biological necessity, diets can be regarded as discursive practices through which bodies are shaped (see Kinnunen 2001). It has been maintained that diets have become scientific and that they are constructed around the right/wrong -binary opposition (Gronow 1998, Kinnunen 2001). In reference to theatrical dance, dieting is frequently linked with the light body of the ballerina, young

146

female dance students and anorexia nervosa.[8] In contrast, this section takes one text extract to examine nutrition in reference to dance education for young males.

In Bask's (1992) article on male dance students in the Finnish National Opera Ballet School, Ilkka Lampi is quoted at length on nutrition:

> The boys train five days a week so their nutrition has to have enough of the good type of carbohydrates. Therefore I recommend cereal and roots to them. Typical Finnish food: good bread, potatoes, carrots etc. One lasts a long time on those and they contain trace elements. Ordinary green salad is also part of the healthy diet and fruits as well. However, because one really burns calories in this activity, a popular snack is a banana.
>
> -Adolescents also need proteins, the ones that they have already learnt about at school from the foods groups. It is important to make the students understand that one does not get protein merely from red meat, steaks. Various amino acids are needed daily; one has to have a versatile diet. That includes fish, meat, cheese, milk and the variety of proteins that they provide. My understanding is, however, that access to proteins is guaranteed nowadays and that it is also discussed a lot at school, Ilkka Lampi says. But the dancer also needs energy and that does not come from sweets even if the young boys in the ballet school might sometimes disagree!
>
> It is important to take care of proper liquid intake…
>
> -I have tried to pay attention to the fact that one should drink enough through out the entire workout, and mainly water. When there are longer training periods, I have recommended a drink where half of it is water and the other half juice. A juice-mix is friendlier to teeth than many of the so-called sports drinks that easily turn out too strong. Many athletes in endurance sports, marathon runners for example, also drink juice-water mix for example. (Lampi in Bask 1992, p. 30)

The extract shows, that the discourse of nutrition in dance education for young males operates to construct the male dance student's body by promoting the consumption of certain foods and particular eating habits. The emphasis is on adequate energy intake. Also the consumption of liquids during the training periods is highlighted.

---

8   On anorexia nervosa and female dance students, see for example Braisted et al (1985); le Grange, Tibbis & Noakes (1994); Abraham (1996).

147

Hence, while the male dance student's body is shaped through exercises from sports training, their impact on the body is intensified through a diet. The amalgamation of two discourses, sports training and nutrition, is evident in the extract.

Without denying the connection between nutrition and bodily well being it can be argued that ideas on health and hygiene are not 'neutral' nor 'natural' but indeed loaded with cultural meanings. A diet, such as the one that is recommended in the extract above, is designed to promote health, strength and endurance of the human body, as the extract shows. No doubt, 'longevity' could also be added to this list of benefits of the 'healthy' diet. Yet, it can be argued that these objectives do not come from the project of nature that is in constant move towards decay and death. Instead, it can be argued that they are part of the culturally specific and historically particular objectives that belong to the project of modernity, which celebrates progress and dreams about immortality through a variety of technologies.

Hence, it can be argued that the bodies of male dance students that are constructed through the discourse of nutrition are not neutral or value-free. On the contrary, from a Foucauldian perspective, it can be argued that such bodies are produced through the discourse of modernity and that they operate as mannequins for that discourse. The inability of modernity to deal with the inevitable decay and eventual death of the living material human body can be read from the dance of the diet-controlled and sports-trained bodies that celebrate the maximised performance of the human body. The discourse that operates in such a performance is the same one, it would seem, than the discourse that turns its back on partiality, imperfection, exhaustion, decrepitude and difference in the dream about eternal youth and beauty that is offered to people in Western consumerist culture.

Renaming Ballet

During the 20th century the male dancer has been commonly regarded as an effeminate homosexual (Miettinen 1994b; Burt 1995). This stereotype is often linked to male ballet dancers whose movements embody, as Miettinen (1994b) suggests, aristocratic male virtues - elegance and grace – from the seventeenth and eighteenth centuries. It has been argued that 'hegemonic masculinity' – understood in this book as the 20th century Western masculinist discourse - has rejected both homosexuality and femininity in boys and men (Connell 1995). Hence, positioning oneself as a male dancer or a male dance student in a masculinist culture carries a high risk of losing one's social accountability, as the following extract shows:

> It is not all that easy to perceive ballet immediately as the first fuel for boys to spend their spare time and neither did the Romeo and Juliet of the National Opera make the boys "tick".
> -Noo, utterly terrible, horrible, the boys gasp.
> -I must have slept half of the time, Jaakko Jäppinen confesses.
> The boys explain the reason to leave on the trip, "mother egged".
> ...The boys did not get a spark from Romeo and Juliet to a new and noble hobby in ballet.
> -I rather think not, I don't think I could keep face and, well, surely even mom would have a fright, says Sampsa and shakes his head.
> -I really felt embarrassed on behalf of those men when they were jumping there with balls in their trousers...
> -On the other hand, there could be good-looking women there..., pulls Jaakko back thoughtfully. (Lipiäinen 1996)

This extract is from a newspaper article about a group of culture enthusiasts from Central Finland on a trip to Helsinki to see the performance of *Romeo and Juliet* by the Finnish National Ballet in November 1996. For the article, the reporter interviews three male teenagers from the group. Their responses are in line with some reports about the commonly held view that males and theatrical dance do not mix (Laakso 1988, Nykänen 2003, Pietinen 1997). It can be argued that the extract clearly shows, how embarrassment is expressed

149

'on behalf of' the male ballet dancer. Juha Räty, a former dancer, has described the strictness of masculinist order as follows:

> if a boy makes a mistake and slips from bouncing the ball and playing ice hockey, his masculinity is about to be at stake ... If you mistakenly perform even a single elegant move, you make your masculinity questionable. (2003, p. A5)

It can be argued that, in the extract from Lipiäinen (1996), the male dancer is constructed as an embarrassment because he slips from the masculinist performance of gender and, by doing so, breaks the 'holy' order of the culturally dominant masculinist discourse.

Some dance educational institutions in Finland actively fight against prejudiced views on males in dance.[9] It can be argued that such gender politics include attempts to 'wash' male dancing clean from negative connotations. Hence, the rest of this section examines two discursive and rhetoric means by which such activism operates in dance education for young males.

The rhetoric act of using sports discourse to describe the male dancer provides a gender-political means to construct the male dancer and the male dance student positively in relation to the dominant masculinist discourse (see Chapters Three and Eight). In this light, the implementation of the sports training discourse in dance education can be examined as a means to masculinise dance. Such agenda can be recognised, for example, from the following extract:

> Lampi says that he has always been puzzled and unhappy with the image about the male dancer's effeminacy, which has been linked to ballet and which at present is hopefully a faulty one. He therefore tries to make the training methods seem more comprehensible to the active and sports-oriented boy. A pink dream of tulle cannot motivate boys: performances, stunts and speed come first. (Harri 1993)

9   I am referring most notably to the Vantaa Dance Institute, the Finnish National Opera Ballet School, the Kuopio Dance Festival Dance Camp for Boys, the Dance Theatre of Kajaani and Marketta Viitala's activities in Northern Finland.

Following Sinkkonen (1990), it can be maintained that there are limited options for males to perform their gender in a manner that is socially acceptable in Finland. The discourse of sports provides one of these limited options. That is, it has been pointed out that competitive sport plays a significant part in the constitution of dominant Finnish masculinities (Ylikangas 1989, Tiihonen 1999). In addition, it has been said that sports masculinities have a prestigious position as part of the national defence work (Puhakainen 1997). Hence, it can be argued that in the existing historical and culturally specific conditions, the positively marked sports discourse is used as a means to masculinise dance by redefining it as a sport. With this rhetoric act, dance can be made less threatening for such boys and men whose sense of the social acceptability of the self is depended on masculinist performances of gender.

A similar pattern but a different discourse can be recognised from the following extract that is from one of the focus group interviews:

Matt: Because at first ballet probably sounded to the boys as if nobody would go there, ballet was disguised as foot technique. Would you go to ballet? No. Would you come to a foot technique class? Yes.

In the extract, a male dance teacher explains how in one of the dance educational institutions the staff members had come up with the idea that by renaming ballet as 'foot technique' they could get young males to take up ballet training. It can be argued that in such rhetoric play the new name establishes an intertextuality that provides connotations and images that are more gender-neutral than the stereotypical images of effeminacy that are often linked to the concept of ballet. That is, 'foot technique' appears less distant for a masculinist discourse than ballet that is commonly seen as a feminine practice performed by girls and women. Moreover, 'foot technique' avoids the negative connotations that are commonly attached to the male ballet dancer.

Renaming ballet as 'foot technique' can certainly be advantageous in masculinist culture in the sense that it makes ballet training appear less threatening for young males whose sense of social acceptability depends on masculinist performances of gender. Yet, from a dance educational point of view it can be maintained that there is a major weakness in such a rhetoric play of words. The problem is that the act of renaming ballet removes this arts practice from its cultural and historical framework as a genre of dance. Hence, in a worst-case scenario, selected ballet exercises are drilled merely for the sake of the skilful performance of certain movements, plié, téndu or developé for example, because they are thought to provide a good foundation for dancing. However, ballet has its heritage, its distinctive aesthetic requirements and its techniques that emerge from historically specific cultural contexts that students need to understand in order to appreciate ballet as a genre on its own right.

Renaming ballet as a 'sport' or as 'foot technique' can be a pragmatic solution to the problem of how to get more young males to take up dance or how to get male dance students in ballet to refine their fine motor skills. Such acts of renaming can make ballet appear less effeminate and, hence, ease the tension between ballet and those young males whose sense of self is constructed in relation to others through a dominant masculinist discourse. On the other hand, it can be argued that the rhetoric act of renaming ballet is not radical gender politics because it yields to the dominating power of masculinist discourse rather than fighting against it. Indeed, in dance education for young males, the acts of renaming ballet can be regarded as a small victory for the masculinist discourse over ballet.

Chapter Five
Themes and Practices of Male Dancing

Adventures of the Teaching Content

From classic myths to fiction and film in popular culture adventures are commonly linked to boys, men and masculinity. There is Theseus who entered the labyrinth and killed the Minotaur; Huckleberry Finn's adventures that were first published in 1884 are known to generations of boys and men. In addition, there are Tarzan, Superman, Batman, James Bond, Indiana Jones, Luke Skywalker, The Teenage Mutant Ninja Turtles and so on. The list of male heroes seems endless. Consequently, it is hardly a wonder that the notion of adventure is also commonly linked to dance for boys.

There is a commonly held view in dance educational debate that dance pedagogy for males has to respond to the 'world of boys' (see for example Hietaniemi 1989, Turpeinen 1997, Härkönen 1999, Jääskeläinen 1993, Vuori 1996, Lampi et al 2002). Dance teacher Ilkka Lampi (2002, p. 4) eloquently expresses this view in the memo on dance pedagogy for boys:

What is the teaching of a man made from?
From a little boy's imagination, dreams and fears,
the charm of the great adventure and the danger that is safe,
the memories of one's experiences and forbidden things left undone,
the ecstasy of large jumps and skilful tricks,
the quiet moments and the lovely exhaustion,
the satisfaction of what one has achieved and the right to fail,
the awareness of whose is the last word and the rough-and-tumble that has its time.
From encouragement, praise, words of thanks and acceptance.
From experiences of one's own life as a young man in neon light and when a bit older, from the bitter lessons one learns from his own children.
That is what the teaching of a man is made of.

153

In this poetic elaboration on the teaching of the male student, Lampi rephrases the old English nursery rhyme 'What are little boys made of?' from Feodor Rojankovsky's *The Tall Book of Mother Goose* (1942), or rather its Finnish translation (Kunnas 1954). Such pedagogical practice is constructed in the poem in relation to male fantasies, recollection of lived experiences, masterly control in physical action, accomplishments and failures, encounters with authority, obedience, wild rumpus, urban nightlife, procreation and fatherhood, it can be argued.

The notions of venture and risk that are present in Lampi's poem are open to multiple interpretations and their embodiments in dance education for young males are diverse. On the one hand, a moment of adventure can be incorporated into a dance class situation with the mere use of words. For example, in a ballet repertoire class in the Finnish National Opera Ballet School, Lampi referred to Indiana Jones and his use of the whip as he asked two male students to enter the stage (Field notes 10.5.2001). A reference to 'Batman stickers' glued to the palms is used to help boys to understand how to hold their hands (Nykänen 2003). On the other hand, a moment of adventure can be created with the help of equipment that are organised into a track in the space and giving the track a name that appeals to the imagination of young males.

For example, an illustration in the curriculum that was used in the Vantaa Dance Institute in 2001 shows three training tracks that are designed, according to the illustration, primarily for male students: 'the crocodile track', 'the mutant track' and 'the thunderbirds track'. The illustration shows gymnastics mats, mattresses, ropes and benches arranged in three different ways in the space. In the illustration, the students are marked to move from one location to the next along the marked path in the space. The transitions from one location to the next include, for example, jumps from two feet to two feet, 'free' jumps, climbing, wrestling, striding, somersaults, falls, 'turtle rolls', arm wrestling and so on.

It can be argued that the names of the tracks have an important function in the sense that they are intertextually linked with adventures of certain characters in popular culture that are familiar to young males and, hence, easy to relate to. For example, the reference to crocodiles in the first track can be linked to adventures in motion pictures such as John Weissmuller's fight with crocodiles in the MGM film *Tarzan the Apeman* (1932), Paul Hogan in *Crocodile Dundee* (1986) or even Roger Moore and the fearless leaps over the backs of several crocodiles in the James Bond –film *Live and Let Die* (1973). The references to mutants and turtles in the name of the second track have a capacity to call forth stories about Peter A. Laird and Kevin B. Eastman's creations Leonardo, Donatello, Raphael and Micaelangelo, the four brave teenage mutant ninja turtles that are known to children in different parts of the world (http://www.ninjaturtles.com 08.08.2003). The name of the third track links to *Thunderbirds*: Gerry Anderson's stupendous puppet animations and the story of a family-run rescue team that helps anyone in danger (Bentley 2000).

References to popular culture and the genre of science fiction in film and literature can also be recognised from dance education for young males. For example, space travelling - one of the big dreams of modernity, it can be maintained - constitutes a theme for Isto Turpeinen's *Star Track – the adventure of boys* (1996). The piece was choreographed for eighteen approximately 12 year-old boys out of whom fourteen were engaged with dance and four with youth theatre in Vantaa. The dance performs a story about Captain Kirk who is set to travel in space. An explosion in the energy centre of the research institute interrupts his preparations. Moreover, the new fuel that has been under development at the institute gets stolen by a group of 'dirty vaaders'. The stolen fuel helps the leader of the vaaders to build a portable mass-destruction laser. What follows is a fight between good and evil (Raatikko Dance School and Tikkurila Theatre 1996; Kaikkonen 1996; Tiihonen 1996).

It can be maintained that the name of the choreography and the character of Captain Kirk in the work link quite clearly to the popular American television series *Star Trek* and associated Hollywood films such as *Star Wars*. Moreover, as the following extract points out, it can be argued that the work also refers to other science fiction series:

Tonight, eighteen boys from the dance school of Raatikko and the theatre of Tikkurila leave to conquer the unknown … The boys have prepared themselves for this fast and comic strip kind of adventure for example by studying ways of moving and speaking from the Star Wars trilogy and by reading comics, magazines and albums. (Kaikkonen 1996)

As the extract points out, the process of choreographing *Star Track* involves educational tasks through which the discourse of science fiction is manifested in the dancing bodies of the male students. Elsewhere, Turpeinen explains how

- already in the spring we were practising combat scenes, we watched films and went to exhibitions.
-Based on that, I told the boys, make a solo that fits in that gap. I have then pulled the themes together. (As quoted in Tiihonen 1996)

Figure 10. *True Stories* (2000) with boys from the Vantaa Dance Institute. Photo: Laura Luostarinen. (Courtesy of the Vantaa Dance Institute)

Similarly, it could be argued that Turpeinen's *True Stories* embodies references to popular culture but also to heroic myths (see Figure 10). The large-scale dance theatre work was choreographed in 2000 and directed in collaboration with drama teacher Eija Velander for students of the Vantaa Dance Institute. According to the unpublished production book of *True Stories*, the work is about facing the truth from eye to eye and telling it in the words of young males. Moreover, the work can be said to elaborate the elusive nature of truth. According to the production book,

> the truth is a concept that stretches. In the imagination of a six year-old boy the truth changes and creates new truth. On the other hand, the truth is confused even in the world of us adults: is it always so clear for us what are the facts and what constitutes fiction in the evening news or in the newspaper? The question is about an adventure that embraces the entire world. (Turpeinen 2000)

A page from the production book illuminates the rich intertextual 'mosaic' that emerges during the production process. In the illustration, the different sections of the work are organised vertically inside the large bubbles on the left that connect to a number of associations in the right. In the illustration, *True Stories* emerges through an intertextuality that is constructed by the choreographer. Words in the illustration link to numerous texts in different contexts, which at once become part of the choreography. An attempt to interpret the illustration creates yet another intertextuality. Concepts such as 'earthquake', 'order' and 'chaos' are linked with the 'breaking of the wall'. In the actual performance of *True Stories*, the wall that broke down was made out of numerous cardboard boxes. In addition, the notion of adventure emerges through the intertextuality, which links the story of Theseus in the labyrinth of the Minotaur from Greek mythology together with the heroes of contemporary popular culture including Jedi from *Star Wars* and James Bond. The world of 'action' - detectives, robbers and the police and the entire genre of film noir - emerges into this mosaic of ideas in relation to Bond while Jedi introduces the genre of science fiction, combat forms and the plot of disposing a cannon.

Also, 'fathers and sons' are connected, in Turpeinen's intertextual map, with a number of words that refer to tasks that boys are often taken to do with their fathers: fishing, playing music, whittling wood, wrestling, telling stories and doing sports. In the actual work, in addition to almost seventy boys and three girls, five fathers performed on stage (Saarela 2001a). Thus, fathers and sons can dance together and, through their dancing, make sense about significant life issues. As Saarela and Tossavainen write:

> The entire motto of the performance is that the youngsters in the story live in a town of the size of 100000 inhabitants, where people eat, sleep, are born and die. Life careers and secular acts of fame are always elsewhere. (Saarela 2001a, p. 9)

> Walls are broken down and rebuilt, territories are defended and, beside all that, acquaintance is made with the mystic female sex. Girls represent more powerful and somewhat frightening party, in front of which the young men-to-become are confused. (Tossavainen 2000, p. B2)

Dance critic Auli Räsänen's (2000) description of one of the rehearsal sessions of *True Stories* illuminates how some of the intertextual traces are embodied in the young male dance students. She writes how,

> sixty boys are storming into the training studio at the Vantaa Dance Institute ... The first group dashes into the "fortress", according to the instructions of the teacher, the others are peeking from behind the "wall" ... The space is filled with young male energy that the dance teacher Isto Turpeinen tries to get into some sort of an order. The instructions of Turpeinen echo over the noise, he is the commander of the military troops. Because he is also a choreographer he has all the threads in his hands. "... begins to move now. Leaps and leaps! And dive! The combat begins. Charge!" Turpeinen commands and the boys are getting hold of it.
>   The choreography resembles an action movie. The idea is to move fast, but the groups are still stumbling in the rehearsals, they cannot always remember the direction of the routes of attacks ... The fortresses and the walls are made from cardboard boxes. They are demolished and built up several times during the dance. Turpeinen has constructed the performance so that there is enough action on stage for each group of performers. Otherwise the boys get bored ...

True stories includes spying, fighting and parodying secret agents. Girls are met as well – and poems are read to them. (Räsänen 2000a)

Hence, it can be argued that various 'texts' on adventures enter into dance education for young males through the discourse of popular culture but also from classical myths, activities that fathers and sons do together and from the youth culture that is lived in the streets. Further, a discourse of heroism - the brave male hero who defies death, danger and evil forces in breathtaking attempts to save someone or something – is present in many of these fabrications. It can be argued that such a discourse is embodied through the above presented and other similar dance educational practices in the dancing bodies of young males and performed by them.

The Adventurous Dance Camp

It could be suggested that the notion of adventure is also embedded in the very idea of the dance camp that has been organised annually in Siilinjärvi since 1987. A period of ten to thirteen days in a boarding school environment can certainly count as an adventure for a group of 9 to 16 year old boys, some of who are away from home for the first time for an extended period of time. A daily structured disciplinary schedule (wake-up at 8 am, breakfast, two dance classes - ballet and tap -, lunch, a music class, a class of West-African dances, dinner), new acquaintances and visits to see exotic dance performances can be exhausting but also exciting. Further, the group accommodation on mattresses in empty classrooms, attempts to keep one's belongings in order or to wash some clothes, staying up late against the regulations of the camp and the nightly sneaking in the hallways or outdoors are all conditions that can contribute to the notion of adventure as experienced by young males (Field notes from Siilinjärvi, June 2001).

Figure 11. Studying a West-African male dance with N'Fanly Camara. Boys' dance camp, Siilinjärvi in June 2001. Video image: Kai Lehikoinen.

The dance camp provides introductions to different cultures by including some non-European dance forms in the programme almost every year (Kuopio Dance Festival, Dance Camp for Boys brochures 1987-2003). Learning about different cultures can certainly be adventurous. For example, African dances have been part of the programme of the dance camp in the summers of 1994, 1995 and 2001 (ibid). In the summer of 2001, N'Fanly 'Alya' Camara (Guinea), the artistic director of Wonuwali Dance and Music Company and Outi Kallinen, the choreographer of the company, taught a traditional West-African dance from Sierra Leone to the students of the camp (see Figure 11). In the field notes, I wrote that masculine attributes are brought into the dance by encouraging the young males to perform the dance movements in a larger and stronger manner, lower down in the body and less ornamented than women would normally perform the dance. Hence, it can be argued that the stereotypes of West-African black masculine qualities are embodied in the dancing young males and are performed through broad, deep and strong movements as well as heavy steps and stomps (Field notes from Siilinjärvi, 16.6.2001).

Various combat forms also constitute part of the teaching content of the dance camp for boys. These include, for example warrior aerobics with Henry Smith (USA) in 1989, shaolin-chanquan from China with Ilkka Lampi in 1993 and Brazilian capoeira with Pertti Mäki in 1996 and with Anita Valkeemäki in 1997 and 1998 (Kuopio Dance Festival, Dance Camp for Boys brochures 1987-2003). A warrior masculinity that is embodied and performed in these and other combat forms is closely related with notions of adventure and danger, it can be argued, not least through intertextual references to fight scenes in popular films and comic books that young males tend to consume.[1]

It could be maintained that the discourse of warrior masculinity is closely related to the military discourse. Embodiments of military discourse can be recognised, for example, from a rhythmic drill that took place at the dance camp in Siilinjärvi during the summer of 2001. The exercise was located outdoors in a field where tap-dance teacher Juha Lampi made a group of male dance students run in a circle and sing a call-and-response chant about the superiority of tap-dancers (see Figure 12). The intertextual link between this unconventional method of teaching a steady pulse to dance students and the drilling of military troops in some of the Hollywood films is striking. This is not the only act of introducing military discourse in the form of a tap-dance exercise in the history of the camp. Lampi tells that he also taught a military type of a marching tap number in the camp in the summer of 2000. Once the number was polished, he took the boys to perform it to the officers in the near-by air-force base. In return, the boys got to see a fighter plane flight demonstration (J. Lampi, personal communication 17.6.2001). It can be maintained that these two cases exemplify how an atmosphere of adventure can be created in dance education for boys, by amalgamating the dance discourse with

---

1   For more on combat forms, see Chapter 6.

the military discourse, and by organising a performance opportunity for boys on a masculine site, such as the air-base, to which young males would have no access on their own.

Figure 12. A military-type rhythm drill in Juha Lampi's tap class. Boys' dance camp, Siilinjärvi in June 2001. Video image: Kai Lehikoinen.

Adventures in Teaching Young Males

Teaching young males can itself be an adventurous journey for their teachers. For example, Turpeinen (1998) constructs himself as a 'cowboy' whose 'mission' is to teach dance for young males. For him, the 'mission' is about setting a task in accordance to such objectives that the structures have provided. It is a question about gathering factors of willpower to serve teaching. At the same time, a desire to constitute experiences to the students, and above all to the teacher him/herself, is created. An act constitutes the core in teaching. Simplified, it can be said that an act is a rope with the teacher at one end and the student at the other end. The teacher has to be able create an inner space and, as a consequence to that, the desire to pull the rope emerges in the head of the student. (Turpeinen 1998, p. 56)

As part of the 'mission', the dance teacher has to be flexible in a teaching-learning situation, Turpeinen (ibid) maintains. He notes how the teaching-learning situation is a precarious 'adventure' in the sense that

> boys will be boys. They are all personal, active and peculiar each in his own particular way. The class begins and in the same moment a *tension that is attached to the beginning and the end is set up*. The tension is maintained with a hold that is created in the students on a spiritual level where the stream of emotions and experiences flows. In a way, the emotional aspects are harnessed to serve teaching. (Turpeinen 1998, p. 57)

Figure 13. Pulling out the Joker: boys playing a vigorous game with a bean bag in Turpeinen's class. Video image: Kai Lehikoinen.

Figure 14. Lampi's Joker: a relaxation exercise with a silk scarf.
Boys dance camp, Siilinjärvi 2001. Video image: Kai Lehikoinen.

The ability to adjust flexibly in the dance class and to risk the predetermined class content when something unexpected takes place in teaching-learning situations is seen as a necessary quality in teachers who work with boys. In Turpeinen's words,

> deviating from the prepared course, *pulling the joker out of the sleeve*, can both save the broken act and create a new way to approach the old basic task. One should never play a weak ace nor leave it entirely unused. (1998, p. 58)

The 'joker' can be, for example, a vigorous game or a relaxation exercise (see Figures 13 and 14). Elsewhere Turpeinen defines the concept of the 'joker' as an educational 'tool'. He means with 'using a pack of jokers' that if something in my objectives fails in an acute situation, I have something in my pack that I can use to pull through, so that the class does not flop, the atmosphere does not get ruined and so that I do not lose those students or that individual because of what happened. (Lecture on boys in Vantaa 28.4.2001)

Hence, it can be argued that the teaching-learning situation in dance education for young males is constructed in Turpeinen's accounts as a precarious matter that easily fails. From this position, it can be understood how an all-male dance class appears as an adventure not just to the students but also to the teacher.

In a country where there are not many male dance teachers available, it is not uncommon that female dance teachers have male students in their class (see Viitala 1998, Niiranen 2002). However, as the following extract from a newspaper article on dance education for boys shows, the teaching of male students can be constructed as a precarious adventure and a test for female dance teachers:

according to Lampi, boys in ballet will not train with girls. It is such a different concept. The female teacher has to prove her position in front of the ambitious boys.
"Dancing is for blokes", Turpeinen states. (Nykänen 2003, p. D7)

This view gains support from a female dance teacher Soili Hämä-läinen's autobiographical story that was presented in a seminar on dance pedagogy for boys in Vantaa in the spring of 2001. In the story, Hämäläinen recalls being rejected by her group of male students after they had worked with a male teacher for a period of time. According to her,

after Isto had to leave them due to other work, they would not take me back. They thought only a man can teach a group of boys. It was an unambiguous reply when I told them that, okay, I will get you someone else. (Hämäläinen, panel discussion, Vantaa 28.4.2001)

The notion of being subjected to a test by a male student group can also be recognised from the following autobiographical narrative that was shared by a female ballet teacher in one of the focus group interviews:

165

Jane: I remember how in the beginning I was in suspense because I knew that they had not had a female teacher for a long time … So that made me play. I thought that, well, I guess I have to be a good bloke in order to get their attitude [changed]. And I remember always how (laughs) I had … this shirt where it says Military Academy on it (laughs) … I had been working there in an entertainment squad and received this shirt, but they [the male dance students] did not know it. I wore the shirt the first day … like hi there. And I thought that, why, it all works out, that the boys are really [well behaved].

Jane's narrative shows, how her choice of dance wear for her first all-male ballet class was influenced by what she knew about male 'attitudes' towards women. As an attempt to overcome such 'attitudes' in the all-male dance class, she decides to wear a shirt that embodies a masculine marker, the name of the Military Academy.

As the extract shows, Jane links the masculine marker on her t-shirt with her success in teaching the all-male group. It could be suggested that such experience of success emerges from the fact that the male group behaves well either because of the masculine marker on her shirt or in spite of it. On the other hand, it could be argued that such experience follows from the confidence that Jane gains from the masculine marker. That is, the reference to the Military Academy on her shirt helps her to position herself in relation to young males as someone who is less 'other' than she would be without the masculine marker. It is also possible, it could be argued, that both cases are true and that together they fortify Jane's positive experience. A sceptic could also doubt Jane's story and claim that she makes it up in the presence of two male dance teachers in the focus group interview just to prove that she can work with male students. However important such speculation is, it could be argued, that control is gained (over the students or over oneself) in the teaching-learning situation with an all-male group through the visibly carried masculine marker in Jane's story.

The idea of performing authority is taken up a bit later in the same focus group interview, when Jane recalls how she gained social credibility during her first encounter with the all-male student group. She elaborates it as follows:

Jane: I am pretty good in remembering names ... if I meet someone once I remember the name immediately rather well, like with students even if there are so many of them. So we were doing something. We did the warm-up and of course I had to participate, press hard and do everything even one degree better that the boys so that, <u>hey,</u> if a woman can do it the boys will also start working. Then I received the finest thanks in the world ... when I was just ... putting on a tape or something. I heard something and I said <u>and Petteri shut up,</u> like during the first class (laughs). So I knew [the name] right away when I heard and so on. Then Markku said something like, <u>I guess you are not a blonde after all because you remember our names</u> (laughs). I was just like <u>thanks.</u> I was really like thanks.

The construct here is that a female dance teacher has to prove her social credibility to the male students by showing her physical capability to outdo the young males. It could be argued that with such competitive stance the female dance teacher embodies a masculinist discourse by entering into the game of physical prowess.[2] Jane's story is interesting in that what she regards as a sign of approval from one of the boys is not related to the masculinist marker on her shirt or her masculinist performance of physical abilities. Instead, she receives credit for acknowledging the boys in a disciplinary situation as individuals by remembering the name of one of her students.

This provides her social legitimacy, which is evident in her student's comment where she is positioned opposite to the cultural stereotype of an unintelligent woman, the 'dumb blonde'. It can be argued that the male student's reply is linked to the common patriarchal myth that females are less intelligent than males unless

---

2   On masculinist game of physical prowess, see Chapter Six.

proven otherwise. Further, this myth is embedded deep in the masculinist bias of Western thinking (see Chapter Eight).

The notions of fairness and individual recognition of the students are mentioned by Hannele Niiranen (2002) as some of the keys to success with a male student group. She recalls her encounter with an all-male student group as follows:

> I became a leader of a group in the middle of a term after a popular male teacher, which did not make the situation any easier. The building of confidence took its time but eventually the situation calmed down. Clear rules for the behaviour in the class, consistency and equal recognition of all students furthered the forming of confidence. (Niiranen 2002, pp. 6-7)

Some female teachers like Viitala (1998) and Palokangas-Sirviö (see *Meidän Kajaani*, 5/2001, p. 3) agree with Niiranen that

> womanhood does not hinder the teaching [of male students]. It is important to be present in the situation, to listen and to appreciate the boys' own ideas. In comparison to the world of girls, different creatures habit the world of boys. There is a natural desire to experiment and to experience, a desire to plunge [into action]. At once, even a small idea can turn into a great adventure. (2002, p. 7)

Based on the above discussion, it can be argued that the notion of adventure has different faces in dance education for boys. On the one hand, intertextual references to popular culture call forth adventurous narratives that are incorporated from single dance exercises to entire choreographies. On the other hand, a dance camp and the practices that it involves can be regarded as an adventure for young males. In addition, the idea of confronting a male student group can be constructed from the teacher's point of view as an adventure, which requires readiness to face the unexpected in the dance class and to find ways to gain social accountability and trust from the all-male group.

Adventures of Performing

As Adshead (1981, 1989) maintains, 'performance' can be regarded as an inherent part of the 'act of dancing'. The idea of constructing a performance, defined here as a collection of elements (dancers and their movements, costumes, pieces of scenery, props, lighting, sound and so on) that are given an interrelated structure for a spectator to experience, can be said to underpin all theatrical dance forms (Adshead 1988, Schechner 2002). Hence, various procedures that lead towards a performance, and the act of performing choreography, can be regarded as part of the central practices in dance education.

The place of public performances in dance education for young males was questioned in Turku at a seminar on boys and dance in 1992.[3] At the seminar, assistant professor Lauri Laakso from the Faculty of Sports Sciences in the University of Jyväskylä reported that attitudes towards dance are significantly more negative among Finnish schoolboys than they are among boys in the United States or Italy (Lammassaari 1992). In addition, Laakso suggested that the fear of performing in public is probably one of the reasons why young males do not participate in dance. His view is communicated in *Aamulehti* as follows:

> -The fear of standing out is characteristic to the culture of men. When I went to the army, a mate of mine gave me advice: it will be fine as long as you are not the first one or the last one anywhere, Laakso recalls. Following this logic, 'expression' signifies a rather high threshold for boys. Laakso sees that it would be worth laying less emphasis on performance, in other words performing to others, in dance for boys than is currently done. (Lammassaari 1992)

3   The seminar 'dancing boy – a growing natural resource' was organised by the Board of Dance in the Province of Turku and Pori in the Old Town Hall in Turku 17.10.1992. A performance of male dancing followed later the same day in the Concert Hall of Turku (Lammassaari 1992; Kai Lehikoinen, diary notes).

It can be seen that the absence of young males in dance is explained in the extract in reference to the notion of 'standing out' in a performance situation and what such conspicuousness stands for in the military discourse. In the extract, the reference to the friend's advice on how to behave in the army can be read to suggest that individual conspicuousness is punished with disciplinary actions in the military. Such punishments can be regarded as part of the technologies that are used in the military discourse to hold individual subjects as the easily replaceable property of the state by keeping them anonymous during the period of military training (see Puhakainen 1997). In addition, it can be maintained that disciplinary procedures are often prescribed in the military discourse to humiliate the targeted subject/s in front of the others. Thus, it can be maintained that the presented account in the extract argues that young males perceive a public dance performance as a form of humiliation and punishment. It can be argued that such a theory emerges through a discourse on military discipline and a belief that such discipline is operating also outside the military institution more generally in society among boys and men. The suggestion of cutting down performance activities in dance education for young males emerges as a logical consequence to such theory.

In stark contrast to the theory on the culturally constructed need for young males to avoid standing out in front of others, there is a commonly held view that boys enjoy making dances and performing in public (Af Björkesten 1997, Turpeinen 1997, Viitala 1998, Räsänen 2000a, Hämäläinen and Palokangas-Sirviö panel discussion in Vantaa 28.04.2001). For example, dance teacher Minna Palokangas-Sirviö who works with all-male groups in Kajaani, north of central Finland, describes her work as follows:

> ... it has been a very pleasant but not always so easy if one thinks that I have the background to teach girls in jazz dance and in children's dances ... [I]t has not been entirely clear ... how to begin to use dance with them. We have entered through play and game activities ... combat style, ghost ideas, hip-hop, aliens from space and we have used these ideas to make performances all the time. On the other hand, this [choreographing performances] has been our mutual enthusiasm, I too like the making of dances with them and while I am

thinking of the structure of the class, we are making new performance all the time... (Palokangas-Sirviö, panel discussion in Vantaa 28.4.2001)

The extract shows how a female dance teacher who is uncertain about how to introduce dance for young male students defines choreography as a mutual interest between the boys and herself. It can be argued that the common ground that is established in the practice of making dances helps the teacher to overcome her uncertainties, provides stimulus for the boys and makes the teaching of them a great pleasure for the teacher.

Also Aarne Mäntylä maintains that 'boys want to perform. That motivates them and that is what makes them stay' (as quoted in Af Björkesten 1997). However, 'the programme has to be tailored according to the needs of the lads' (ibid). Turpeinen elaborates this view in his lecture on dance for boys at the Vantaa Dance Institute as follows:

> What started to work in this thing [dance for young males] was that we performed a lot. Like yesterday ... the dance class demonstration contained unfinished pieces ... I am not sure whether I am going to get ... the final performance of the term properly together when we get started ... [T]hese lone wolves made dances that are rugged and raw ... [I]n order to make them meaningful I used dimensions such as, for example, the blokes came on stage wearing rubber boots. Hence, a suggestion was made that those boots are needed for that [the dance] to become something. (28.4.2001)

In contrast to the commonly held view that choreographies need to be refined and danced flawlessly when they are exposed to a public viewing, Turpeinen's account can be said to highlight the idea that in dance education for young males, dancing can be unpolished and choreographies can be presented to the public as 'works in progress'. Further, additional elements can be incorporated in the choreography to make the work 'meaningful' to the spectator or the performers when the performance skills of the students are still lacking masterly brilliance. Such elements can include particular costumes, as it is pointed out in the extract, or the use of voice and various props as it can be seen from some of his works (see Räsänen's description of

171

True Stories above, see also the description of *Seven Brothers* in Chapter Six). In reference to the sound elements, Turpeinen notes that

> voice was used a lot in the performances. They shouted and currently they have spoken lines in almost every piece. We used voice ... in entrances, exits, and standstills. (Lecture on boys in Vantaa 28.4.2001)

In addition, Turpeinen emphasises the importance of letting the students produce movement material on their own. The objective is that

> from the beginning ... they inadvertently start to work on solos plus they have the opportunity to produce their own ideas. In other words [the objective is] to create their movement world through their own bodies... (ibid.)

However, for Turpeinen there is more to solo work than the idea of letting the students establish their individual movement 'voices'. Individual choreographic tasks let him to

> study that bloke. How he relates to music? How he relates to his body? Does he get satisfaction from solo work or should he be coupled up so that he gets a mate to work with... (ibid.)

Thus, the idea of making dances in Turpeinen's pedagogy, the 'raw timber method', is underpinned with an educational objective to acknowledge each student as an individual.

The emphasis on individuality and the making of choreographies take their share from the course plan, which means that less time can be allocated to technical dance training. However, in the 'raw timber method'

> we go forward quietly ... we do not scuffle with the education but, instead, easy does it ... I am not saying that there are no dance exercises, but ... one-third [of what we do] is lost from dance perhaps. But it [what we do] supports our goals ... Once we are further, these elements that have carried the bloke, occupied the dance class and made the case such that they like doing it. They have advanced

in it [and] get an enormous drive through these conditions. These things click with them. After that we can start to take care of the element of dance more forcefully, that is, to catch up within the curricular potpourri. In other words ... gradually the three-year delay is getting less ... and in the final stage we catch up. (ibid.)

As the extract shows, a comparison is made between the 'raw timber method' and some of the more traditional approaches to dance education that emphasise the learning of physical skills that are required in particular dance techniques. Further, within the frame of 'raw timber method' a difference is made between what is regarded as 'dance' and other teaching content that is circumscribed as an educational aid that stimulates the male students and keeps them in the class. This differentiation seems odd if one considers the central position that improvisation, dance compositional tasks as well as building, rehearsing and performing choreographies have in Turpeinen's approach to dance education for young males. Yet, it could be maintained that in the context of his presentation, composing and performing are positioned as aids for dance pedagogy and something that 'gets lost from dance' rather than defining them as central practices to dance as a subject of study.

The assurance about 'catching up' in the extract can be said to signify a concern about the slow pace of mastering the performance of particular dance technical skills in the 'raw timber method'. According to Turpeinen,

the raw timber method has the risk that there are things that are not covered during the critical learning periods. In other words, we don't get them preserved. But these blokes stay here. We have the advantage that with these areas [of teaching content] we create something that makes them committed to this pursuit. (ibid.)

The extract shows two conflicting discourses through which dance education for young males is examined. On the one hand, the reference to 'critical learning periods' points to a developmental discourse on motor skills learning. It can be maintained that this kind of discourse acknowledges that human development takes place in a

173

particular chronological order and sees that critical learning periods are

> the crucial periods in which an attempt needs to be made to acquire fundamental and complex skills. The critical period for any specific sort of learning is that time when maximum sensory, motor, motivation, and psychological capacities are present. (Singer 1980, p. 296)

From this discursive position, it is regarded as crucial to teach particular technical dance skills to the dance students at certain age because it is believed that it is significantly more difficult to learn such skills once the critical period has passed.

On the other hand, it can be argued that the reference to commitment in Turpeinen's extract points to a psychological discourse that is concerned about how to keep the male dance students motivated to continue with their dance interest. As Räsänen writes,

> performing motivates the boys to take up training. According to Turpeinen, the boys have a much stronger desire to show off and perform than the girls have; therefore acrobatic ways of moving and all sort of performing is popular.
> "One fifth of the boys are motivated trainers, however, particularly the younger ones play. I let them perform on stage highly unrefined and receive then the disapproval of my colleagues. (2000a)

It can be seen that the quote from Turpeinen in Räsänen's text lays bare a discourse that underpins more traditional dance educational approaches, which takes the dance student's inept dance technique and unrefined performance to signify that the teacher has failed in his/her work. It can be argued that this kind of unduly technical perfectionism links to professional standards in certain genres of theatrical dance, and ballet particularly. Yet, in dance education, especially at the level of basic arts education, the over-emphasis on such perfectionism can be questioned. Relatively few students from that level move further to actually become professional dancers. Borrowing Turpeinen's words, most of the dance students in basic arts education remain as 'dancers of their own life – and that is fine' (ibid.).

Yet, it could be maintained that an important pointer remains unmentioned in Turpeinen's account. That is, through the emphasis on the art of making dances, and on choreographies that communicate with issues that are relevant to young people, it is possible to bring up dance enthusiasts who are capable of appreciating dances as works of art in their own right rather than seeing dancing merely as physical trickstery. This, I believe, is at least as important a dance educational task as the task of producing dancers and choreographers of high calibre. After all, if there is no audience that appreciates theatrical dance and is eager to see choreographies performed, for whom are we dancing?

Chapter Six
Choreographing Masculinities

Performing Gender

Butler's (1990) notion of gender as 'performative' is central to the understanding of the 'stylisation of the body' within a narrow discursive framework when male dance students' performances of choreography are examined. Performativity is what people do to embody gendered identities and, thus, to become meaningful subjects (ibid). Following Althusser's (1971) idea of 'interpellation', a choreographed male role in a dance can be said to 'hail' the male student to take a position as a recognised gendered subject. It could be argued that his subjectivity is severely compromised if he is repeatedly left in choreographies without a position to inhabit, or if the assigned masculine position does not 'fit', or if it is negatively marked. Dance analytic descriptions of sections from seven choreographies are scrutinised in this Chapter to see which masculine positions are available to male students in dances that are choreographed in dance educational institutions.

Following Foucault, people can be said to be constructed discursively with the help of discipline, that is, a complex embodiment of power and a 'technology' that applies a broad range of 'instruments, techniques, procedures, levels of application, [and] targets' (1995, p. 215). Foucault takes various 'technologies of power' as objects of investigation and identifies three areas where power can be seen to have operated in Western culture at least since the mid-18th century: surveillance, training of people's bodies, and normative judgement. He argues that as far as discipline and coercive acts are concerned, 'technologies of power' are organised by the principle of hierarchic binary oppositions (Foucault 1995).

Foucault's examination of the practices of 'subjectification', or the power relations through which human subjects are constituted, establish a starting point for a Foucauldian analysis of power. He locates the human body in the centre of such analysis. He calls knowledge of how bodies are subjected to power and how these skills are mastered 'the political technology of the body' (1995, p. 26). This technology should not be regarded as a coherent set of understandings. Rather, it is constituted from fragmentary bits of information that form social practices. Neither does it originate from a single institution or state apparatus but is spread throughout society (Foucault 1995).

However, power operates differently in different institutions. Foucault's 'micro-physics of power' (1995, p. 26) is applied to dance education in this chapter with a specific focus on choreography as a form of 'technology' through which dancing bodies are gendered. Bodies do not survive history unmarked. On the contrary, as Foucault argues, power relations act on the human body in a 'political field ... [where they] invest it, mark it, train it, torture it, force it to carry out tasks, to perform ceremonies, to emit signs' (1995, p. 25). The body is

> the inscribed surface of events (traced by language and dissolved by ideas), the locus of a dissociated Self (adopting the illusion of a substantial unity), and a volume in perpetual disintegration. (Foucault 1984a, p. 83)

The presence of different discourses can be read from the dancing bodies. Indeed, as Susan Leigh Foster (1995) argues, the dancing body always writes its discursively constructed history. It is not the dancing subject, the dance student, who is the author of her/his bodily movements. Rather, discursive texts that amalgamate and find an embodied form in the dancing body establish an intertextual tapestry for such movements (Adshead-Lansdale 1999).

In this Chapter, dances that have been choreographed in dance education for all-male and mixed student groups to perform are examined in detail for their embodiments of gender and sexuality. Choreography is investigated as a technology through which discourses of masculinism and heteronormativity are engraved on the bodies of male dance students. These discursively invested bodies become vehicles for discursive power not just in dance institutions but also more generally in society. While a detailed feminist analysis on performances of women and girls falls outside the parameters of this book, females in the choreographies examined are acknowledged in so far that masculinities performed are constructed in relation to them.

Performing Masculinity by Playing Tag

The game of tag is structurally based on a set of binary oppositions such as freedom/constraint and escape/capture. It could be suggested that the idea of freedom and the ability to escape the reaching hands and the control of the other bring so much joy to this game. In that sense, tag can be linked to the discourse of freedom that enters into the modern subject as a desire through the legacy of Enlightenment. As some scholars suggest, such desire is also embedded deep in the history of Finnish masculinities (see Karvonen et al 1998, Tuohinen 1996).

The ethos of 'free will' is particularly well performed in Isto Turpeinen's *Seven Brothers* (2002), a dance theatre piece for more than seventy young male dance students. The libretto for the piece is taken from one of the key works of Finnish literature, Aleksis Kivi's (1834-1872) *Seven Brothers* that was first published in 1870. This picaresque novel is about seven illiterate farm boys whose parents die when the rascals are in their late teens and early twenties. The lads get into trouble with their teacher, a strict parish clerk, and a group of boys from the neighbouring village. Their inability to cope in society, their fear of being punished and the desire to be free out in nature make the brothers rent out their farmhouse and move into the backwoods for a period of ten years. Simple living conditions, misfortune, foolishness, hardship and hard work turn the carefree rascals into honourable men who eventually learn to read, get married - except for one - and make their farm prosper (Kivi 2000).

The idea of leaving to find a solitary place to settle, that is embedded in Kivi's story, reflects an often-repeated pattern in Finnish history (see Ylikangas 1986). The solitary lifestyle links to centuries of hunting and slash-and-burn agriculture that kept the farmers moving from one place to another in forests. It has been argued that such solitude has produced 'muddleheaded hermits' who lack basic social skills (ibid). Using discourse analysis, it could be argued that such a lifestyle and the linguistic means to describe men who live in the backwoods form a discourse of backwoods masculinity. It is within such a discourse that men in the backwoods are constructed as being shy, wishing to keep their distance and having difficulties in communicating (see Ylikangas 1986). Thus, backwoods masculinity as a discourse can be seen to enter into Turpeinen's *Seven Brothers* through its narrative that builds on Kivi's (2000) text.

In Turpeinen's work the notion of freedom and the idea of the tag game can be recognised from section 2 where two women, the mother of the brothers and the old woman of Männistö try, quite unsuccessfully, to hold the young rascals in check. Six of the brothers are harmlessly skipping around. They spin frivolously and perform punching kicks. Flipping their arms makes their bodies turn and a circular movement with their feet leads them into a turn, a hop and a couple of skips that end in a cartwheel. What has been performed in unison dissolves into individual movement patterns: one of the boys runs in circles, the other progresses with a jazzy pas-de-bourrée step, two of the lads skip around while one jumps on the back of another who throws him down. The old woman of Männistö walks determinately after the boys with her fists clenched and upper body forward. She stomps her left foot and lets her focus follow the boy who skips around her. She shouts at him as she continues to stomp her foot. The mother also tries to catch the boys and gather them around her. Suddenly one of the boys jumps on the lap of the old woman of Männistö. She turns around, keeps him in her arms and speaks to him for a moment. A bit later, the youngest of the boys stands beside his mother, holding on to her apron. A group of three boys move around them by skipping, turning and kicking their legs. The young boy runs away from the mother who rushes after him. She carries him back in her lap while he keeps fighting back by kicking fiercely with his legs.

In this section from the choreography, the relaxed quality of skipping and turning steps of the boys as well as their irregular floor patterns can be interpreted as signifying unconcerned and joyful play. The two female figures, the mother and the old woman of Männistö, with their contained upper bodies, bound movement quality, stomping feet, clenched fists and rather direct and restricted use of space can be read to signify authoritative power to the boys. The young rascals, quite clearly, pay no attention to these women's attempts to hold them in check. The brothers escape the women's chastisement. They run away from the reach of their hands and joke around.

The choreography can be seen to contain movement ideas that link to the game of tag. In this tag-like activity, the relationships of gender and age in the two binary roles (catcher/escapee) call forth a particular discourse of masculinity that is performed by young male bodies heedlessly running. It is a gendered performance of young male disobedience where the authoritative power of women is ridiculed and called into question. Hence, from a pro-feminist position, it could be maintained that the performed masculinity in this section is invested in patriarchy.

It should be mentioned, however, that the relationship between the young rascals and their female caretakers in Turpeinen's *Seven Brothers* is more complex than this. It is not just the young males' carefree disrespect towards female authority that is performed in this section. For example, young Eero's firm grip on his mother's apron could be read as an attempt to get love and attention. The mother's apron can be interpreted as a secure and safe place where Eero, the youngest of the seven boys, hides from his bullying brothers. It is also possible to read desire for care and affection into the focus of one of the brothers who is rejected from the lap of the old woman of Männistö. Later, in section 4, when the mother suddenly dies, the helpless cry of a single word 'mother' from the boys can be interpreted as an expression of deep concern. Based on these three and other moments in Turpeinen's choreography, it can be argued that a discourse of masculinity that appreciates women as caretakers who provide motherly nurturing, affection, comfort and security is also performed in the work. When such moments appear in the middle of a tag-like play of power, in section two, a young male psyche that is torn between the desire for freedom and the desire for physical affection can be read from the male dancing bodies in the work.

Playing Combat, Performing Masculinity

In the memo on dance pedagogy for boys, different versions of single combat are included under the category of general physical exercise (Lampi et al 2002). Combat dances can be recognised a basic type of dance because, 'in different ways, masculine combat skills have always been practised through various means of dance' (Lampi as quoted in Tenhunen 1994, p. 8). The common feature in different versions of single combat is to fight for victory. Often these games contain physical contact, pulling, pushing, wrestling, slapping or dragging between the two fighting partners. 'Sailor wrestle' provides a good example. It is a game where the two competitors stand facing each other with their feet lined up left foot behind the right one. The competitors' right feet are placed against one another and their right hands are held together as if shaking hands. The aim is to get the other one to lose his balance and to move his foot by pushing or pulling in any imaginable way (ibid).

Ballet teacher Ilkka Lampi, who is highly experienced in Jiujitsu, a traditional Japanese self-defence system, is known for introducing various martial arts including Chinese Taiji and Shaolin, a Balinese warrior dance, a stick dance from Philippines called Kali and Brazilian Capoeira into dance education for boys (Tenhunen 1994, Räsänen 2000b). It has been suggested that martial arts can benefit dance students in the sense that they develop physical skills (Räsänen 2000b). In addition, martial arts provide exciting choreographic ideas and breath-taking movement material for young male dance students to perform.

The most spectacular fight scene, no doubt, in the history of Finnish theatrical dance is performed at the end of Ilkka Lampi's *General Raiko*, a narrative dance theatre piece that combines Japanese martial arts with high energy gymnastics. It was choreographed to a specially composed Japanese-influenced percussion music by Harri Setälä and performed in 1993 by the students of the Finnish National Opera Ballet School and members of the Helsinki Ju-Jutsu Club. The piece is based on a Japanese legend about the monsters of Oe-Yama

Mountain who abduct a group of young maidens from Kyoto. The maidens are rescued by General Raiko and his samurai warriors (Harri 1993b, Moring 1993, Kangas 1994, Tenhunen 1994). *General Raiko* has been regarded as a successful way to get boys interested in dance. According to the choreographer, 'there are lots of elements that boys like in this. We have succeeded in breaking those preconceptions that regard dance as effeminate' (Lampi as quoted in Kangas 1994). Indeed, the work succeeded in generating even a small-scale 'Raiko-cult' among some young boys who incorporated combat fights with sticks into their games at home after seeing the performance (Tenhunen 1994).

The final fight section begins when the maidens have been let out of the mountain camp while the monsters are asleep. The monsters are taken by surprise by General Raiko and his warriors who suddenly rush in with swords above their heads. The monsters are up and have their swords ready in no time. The combat begins. The samurais and the monsters are slashing around violently with their swords, ramming into their adversaries as well as jumping up and turning in the air to face their next foe (see Figure 15).

A spectacular scene emerges as the fighters chase each other across the stage and along the diagonals performing half flips and cartwheels with no hands followed by high knee kicks, knee pirouettes and 'ukemi', a particular way of falling in Jiujitsu and other Asian martial arts. A sparring scene that follows includes, among other things, various throwing techniques that are at one point performed in slow motion. Culminating in a merciless sword fight, the three monsters are ultimately conquered. When the combat is over, the samurais stand still for a long moment by the three lifeless bodies. In the closing scene, the freed maidens and the samurai warriors travel a lingering path by feet from upstage right corner to downstage suggesting their return to Kyoto.

Figure 15. Lampi as a demon fighting against a samurai warrior in *General Raiko*
(1993). Photo: Kari Hakli. (Courtesy of the photographer and the Finnish National
Opera Archive)

It could be argued that two hierarchical discourses of masculinity
are constructed through the dancing male bodies in Lampi's work.
The monsters are the 'bad guys', constructed as a group of violent
criminals who regard it as their right to harass females in Kyoto. In the
abduction section at the beginning of the work, the women are
shepherded out from the stage like a herd of cattle by the two
monsters while the third one is using his arsenal of kicks, punches and
throws to keep the two guards busy. Eventually they face their violent
death as the 'good guys', General Raiko and his warriors, arrive after
a long journey to rescue the maidens.

The samurais, on the other hand, are constructed throughout the
work in a positive light. They appear as disciplined and loyal as they
gather around their General, follow him and fight next to him. They

are constructed as courageous as they have the guts to confront the three monsters in a far-away place on the mountain. In addition, they show courtesy as they bow to the monk and present him with a gift on their way to the mountain. The act of bowing and handing a gift to the monsters as they enter the mountain camp for the first time in disguise can be read to signify consideration and wit. Moreover, the samurais are constructed as indefatigable through numerous variations of progression as they run, step-hop and move other ways rhythmically through the changing scenery. Of course, the fact that they all survive the violent combat constructs them as unbeatable. Finally, they are constructed as protectors as they lead the maidens back in town. It could be argued that the qualities of the samurais in *General Raiko* are consistent with and constructed through a martial (military) discourse that celebrates heroism. Heroic masculine representations are more commonly known, for example, from numerous Hollywood films from Tarzan to Superman and from James Bond to Indiana Jones where the protagonist's courage and skills are challenged in violent combat scenes.

Turpeinen's *Seven Brothers* (see above) has other spectacular fight scenes. The piece starts with a section where the father of the brothers gets killed in a fight against a group of bears on a hunting trip. More fighting takes place in section 5, which is based on Lauri's dream about the tense relationship between the brothers and some local churchmen in Kivi's (2000) book. In the choreography, the canon, the parish clerk and two of his alter egos threaten the brothers with a punishment in stocks unless they learn the alphabet. They walk in with long wooden sticks in their hands. Juhani, the eldest brother, takes a stick and passes a white puck to the canon who hits it. A game of attack and retreat develops between the two groups. The brothers move towards the clergymen with two jagged steps, take a step back and advance further. With sticks in their hands, they leap forward, pivot quickly and bang their sticks on the ground in front of the four clergymen. Then they turn to retreat as the clergymen repeat the same movement pattern towards them. In a semi-circle, the brothers bang their sticks on the ground (see Figure 16). The clergymen do the same. A quick pivot leads the brothers into a hop on both feet, picking up their knees while holding their sticks on the ground. Immediately the clergymen jump as well. One of the brothers, and one of the parish clerks slam their sticks fiercely together first in the midair and immediately again lower down. The fighting brother swings his adversary's stick around over their heads and brings it heavily down on the ground. With his stick, he picks up the other stick and thrusts it towards the canon who loses his balance and falls back.

Figure 16. Stick fight in *Seven Brothers* (2002). Photo: Isto Turpeinen.
(Courtesy of the photographer and the Vantaa Dance Institute)

The brothers - some of their sticks extended forward, others holding them vertically up – confront the churchmen. The puck is being passed between the two groups. The strongly accentuated organ music stops abruptly. One of the brothers shouts out 'let us move into the forest'. The others shout 'what'. The brothers repeat their charge towards the clergymen after which they retreat. A furious stick fight takes place between four members from both groups. The sticks are whacked forcefully against each other. Standing in wide position with knees slightly bent, the canon and Simeon, one of the brothers, slam their sticks together four times. They pivot quickly and ram together again to repeat the four blows. They pivot once more, this time the canon lifts his stick high up, heading to strike it down on the head of his adversary who defends himself by holding his stick horizontally extended diagonally in front of him. The canon strikes ferociously twice with his stick, then retreats a few steps in order to attack again. He rushes towards Simeon who suddenly kneels down, which makes the canon lose his balance, fall over Simeon's body and roll off the stage. Simeon stands up, collects the canon's stick and retreats a few steps. The music stops. He bangs his stick firmly on the ground and walks off.

Moments later, a fight scene emerges between the two groups where movement material is borrowed from Capoeira, a Brazilian form of martial arts. The basic capoeira step pattern – a well-grounded but light gliding step to the side with knees bent, a soft rocking step back on the free foot that is followed by an immediate weight change back on the front foot and the same to the other side – is performed repeatedly in addition to more spectacular cartwheels, half flips, circularly sweeping kicks and leaps over the back while the body is supported with one hand on the ground.

In Kivi's (2000) original version of the story, the brothers are striking puck with the canon who is playing against them with his spiritual sword. However, the actual physical combat is missing. In Lauri's dream, the canon becomes furious when he realises that the object they are playing with is not a puck but an ABC-book. His curse brings about a storm that rips through them. In Turpeinen's choreography, however, the physical combat between the brothers and the clergymen is constructed explicitly in the work. The combat could be interpreted to represent the tension that builds up between the two groups more generally in Kivi's book. It is only in the second last chapter of the book that such tension dissolves when the old parish clerk and the brothers settle their conflicts. Such reconciliation never takes place in Turpeinen's work. In that sense, it could be argued that the performed discourse of masculinity in the combat section and elsewhere in Turpeinen's work is one that stubbornly resists authoritative power.

Neck wrestling is another form of single combat that is used in Turpeinen's choreography. This first takes place in section 8 where the brothers fight against the boys of Toukola who have mocked them. The second time neck wrestling takes place on Christmas Eve, in section 12, when Juhani wants to test his physical prowess against his brothers. In neck wrestling, the fighters position themselves facing each other in a wide position, knees bent and hands together. The wrestler places his head under his adversary's left arm. The idea is to make the other one lose his balance by pushing or pulling.

Figure 17. *The Newer Quadrille of the Boys from Pyhäjärvi* (1989).
Photo: Kari Liukkunen. (Courtesy of the photographer and Marketta Viitala)

This testing of physical prowess is also included in Marketta Viitala's ironic *The Newer Quadrille of the Boys from Pyhäjärvi*. The work was originally choreographed in 1989 for Young Dance on the Riversides, a group of dance students in Northern Finland, and it was performed by eight 9 to 14 year-old boys and a girl (see the boys in

Figure 17) (personal information Viitala 01.08.2003). The following analysis is based on a later version that was reconstructed for the Dance Theatre of Kajaani in 2000 under the title of *The Newer Quadrille of the Northern Boys* and performed at a seminar on dance pedagogy for boys in Vantaa on 29.4.2001.

In the piece, three boys in traditional sweaters and black trousers set to dance after they have polished their boots. They have serious faces and their eyes are focused down. Their fists are clenched as they march slowly but steadily in a line. Their bodies pull up and sink down. They progress with downward weighted steps and jumps while slapping their thighs. The three dancers gather in a circle with their foreheads touching. They move around in the circle when a group of 5 boys enter marching in double tempo. Taciturnity, stubborn determination and melancholic seriousness that have been said to characterise North-Western Finnish men can be read into these dance movements.

Homosocial bonding can be read from the uniform action: the boys hold each others shoulders as they march cross-step, gallop and jump heavily downward on one foot while brushing the other foot forward. Homosocial bonding also appears in their attempts to show physical prowess. Like fighting bulls, they dance in pairs, foreheads together: a step forward, a step back, three steps forward and reverse while holding their arms slightly bent and fists clenched. Bulging biceps, arm-wrestling, regular wrestling and walking on hands add to this performance of masculine quarrel, persistence and showing of physical prowess.

It can be argued that combat dances come in many forms and they are included in dance education for boys for several reasons constructing varied masculinities. As the analysis of *General Raiko* shows, fighting masculinities can be constructed around the good/evil binary opposition in displays of heroism and delinquency. However, in the fight scene between clergymen and the brothers in *Seven Brothers* fighting masculinity is constructed around the free/ constrained binary opposition that highlights the tension between authoritative power and the Western masculinist dream about the unconstrained man. In *Seven Brothers* the neck wrestling between the brothers as well as the analysis of *The Newer Quadrille of the*

189

Northern Boys point out how fighting can also be a form of homosocial bonding.

In addition, the idea of winning can be recognised as a commonality in the analysed combat scenes. As Klemola (1998) maintains, winning is a project where the objective is not to reach balance but imbalance through the distinction between the winner and the losers. Others are perceived merely as obstacles to be conquered. Hence, fight scenes can also be read as performances of the masculinist practice where males negotiate their social position and accountability as men in relation to other men by showing and challenging physical prowess.

Performing (Hetero)sexuality

Sexuality plays an important part in performances of gender. While sexual desires are manifold and contingent, 'historically sexual identities have been organized into violent hierarchies, where some positions are marked as superior' (Weeks 2000, p. 165). It was earlier argued that hierarchised categories of sexuality (heterosexual/ homosexual) are linked to social positioning. Thus, in society where heteronormative discourse prevails, performing gender in a way that accommodates such discourse can be socially, politically or economically advantageous.

Following the idea that choreographies and other performances can be studied for their embodied sexuality (Franko 1995, Foster 1996, Desmond 2001), this section examines how dancing bodies perform sexuality in dances that have been choreographed for dance students on different levels. Dance examples that demonstrate performances of heterosexuality are taken up first. Following this, the few choreographies that can be said to embody explicit references to male homosexuality or that can be read through queer lenses as performing non-heterosexual relations are discussed towards the end of this section. In the light of these examples, it can be argued that

190

male dance students are subjected to normative heterosexual masculinity in dance education through choreographies that they perform.

Figure 18. *White on White* (1991). Photo: Kari Hakli.
(Courtesy of the photographer and the Finnish National Opera Archive)

Sexuality is often embodied in choreographed sections where two dancers perform as a couple. Jorma Uotinen's *White on White* provides an example. The piece was choreographed for the students of the Finnish National Opera Ballet School in 1991. This impressionistic work of modern dance with a projection of clouds and the sun on a sky-blue backdrop opens with a young male, dressed in white trousers and a white top, circling the stage clockwise with large leaps. As he completes the circle for the second time, a young female, dressed in a white summer dress, joins him in the leap pattern. The opposite sexes as a couple establish a key theme of the work. It can be argued that this theme and its multiple variations – couples spinning, running and jetéing diagonally and horizontally across the stage – establish a recurring heterosexual theme in the work.

Heterosexual relationships are elaborated further in partnering sections. For example, three males enter from stage right with three females sitting on their shoulders. The males move with firm, long, bound and sustained steps horizontally across the stage. As they stop, they turn the females so that they rest their pelvis on the shoulders of the males. The females arch their upper bodies, stretch their legs and open their arms to the sides. Slowly turning on the spot, the females are lowered down and placed on their back on the ground. The males step behind the females, extend their arms up and curve over the female bodies in order to roll over in front of them. The males come up and step back into a plié in a wide turned-out second position as the females climb to stand on the thighs of the male dancers (see Figure 18). Another group of three males enter from the stage right carrying female dancers on their shoulders. They repeat what the first group has just performed.

Meanwhile, the first group of males lower their female partners in front of them and pull them from their hands towards the left upstage corner. They bring the females up and turn them around facing forward. The males support the backs of the female dancers as the females arch their backs and hinge, exposing the front of their bodies and necks. The females are pulled up and placed on the knees of the male dancers and their left arms are brought around the necks of the male dancers. The female dancers walk away from the males, turn back and step into an arabesque. The male dancers pick up the female bodies horizontally and lower them onto their backs, their extended legs folded over their upper bodies. The male dancers sit down behind the females. In the second group, the female dancers who are standing on the thighs of the males are lowered into a horizontal position while the male dancers lean forward. The female dancers arch their backs and glide from back to front between the legs of the male dancers. They are lifted up and placed to sit on the knees of the male dancers. Everything is still.

The three pairs, located stage right, run to exit while each pair is holing each other behind their backs. In the second group, the male dancers lift the female dancers by placing their arms from behind under the arms of the female dancers and locking them behind their necks. They lift the female bodies and exit by turning slowly as the female dancers pedal their legs. The work closes by three male dancers picking up their female partners on the side of their hip as they start turning slowly. A male dancer enters from the stage right, carrying his female partner on the side of his hip. He too starts turning. Another male dancer enters from the down stage right with his female partner sitting on his shoulder. The lights dim out as the music continues playing.

Partnering sections in *White on White* are characterised by active/passive binary oppositions. Male dancers are assigned to the active role. They lead, lift, carry and manipulate female bodies that remain for the most part passive or move from one position to another. These dualities can be examined as imprints of Western 'gender order'. The choreography examined exemplifies how the power relations in the existing 'gender order' of Western societies, or men's dominance and subordination of women, are produced through institutional practices, such as dance education in the Finnish National Opera Ballet School, and how such practices are gendered.[1] Heterosexual bonding is performed in *White on White* in a manner that justifies and naturalises male domination. Hence, it can be maintained that the work is underpinned by masculinism, 'a dominant discourse' (Whitehead 2002, p. 98) that can be defined as

---

1   On 'gender order' see Connell (2000).

the point at which dominant forms of masculinity and heterosexuality meet ideological dynamics, and in the process become reified and legitimized as privileged, unquestioned accounts of gender difference and reality. (Whitehead 2002, p. 97)

Ari Numminen's *People's Celebration* that was choreographed for the final year students of Turku Conservatory in 1998 provides examples of more extreme constructions of heterosexual masculinity that emerge through the discourse of masculinism. In section 4, for example, a male and two females run on stage, line up and bow to the audience. One of the female dancers kneels and starts twitching while the other squats down. The male dancer turns toward the latter, takes hold of her head and bangs his groin repeatedly against her face. He then turns around and kneels behind the other female dancer. Holding her waist, he rams his pelvis against her bottom while the second female dancer fondles his back and buttocks. The group falls into a twitching pile. The dancers moan and pant heavily throughout the section.

It could be argued that heterosexuality is constructed in this dance example through the discourse of the porn industry where women typically appear as sexual servants - oral and vaginal holes that are open for men to enter. Heterosexual sex is displayed as a penetrating act: both women appear as objects of satisfaction for the erect male penis that is signified with the violently thrusting male pelvis. The female body is constructed as submissive; it kneels and gets on all fours. The male body remains on the top, holds the female body still and is actively performing movements that signify penetration.

It could be maintained that embodied dichotomies such as active/passive, taker/giver, top/bottom in the dancing bodies of these upper secondary vocational level dance students maintain the masculinist idea about gendered power relations. The performed masculinity is constructed through the discourse of masculinism that positions men as active, heterosexual, selfish seekers of sexual satisfaction. From a masculinist perspective the sexual act with two female partners can be read to signify masculine prowess, sexual potency, virility and endurance. Following Laura Mulvey's (1975)

194

feminist idea on the 'male gaze', the scene can be suggested to offer a heterosexual male spectator a moment of fantasy to experience a masculinist hype as he identifies with the male character who is having sex with two women. For a male spectator who positions himself outside the discourse of masculinism, as well as for female spectators, the performed non-reciprocal heterosexuality can appear as comical, oppressive, limited or just sad.

Men's access to women's bodies goes unquestioned in the dominant discourse of masculinism and the gendered power relations it maintains. This can be read from Numminen's work, in section 3, which begins with a female dancer lying on her side in front of a flickering light. She is leaning to her elbow and tapping her foot. A male dancer enters. She stays put as he approaches and sits down next to her. The performed polarities of gender order become more apparent when he looks at her, reaches towards her and moves his hand gently upward along her thigh. She pulls her leg away.

The female body is constructed as an object of consumption for men. It is consumed by the gaze of the male dancer, by his touching fingers and even by his sense of smell as he shifts his body close against her back, sniffs her neck and places his hand on her shoulder while letting his fingers run along her neckline. She turns away from him, rolls over her stomach, stops looking at him for a moment and returns to her original position while arranging her dress. She watches the flickering light and smiles. The section ends as he moves closer to her, placing his hand on her pelvis as his fingers shift on her stomach. She grasps his hand and pushes it back. He stands up, looks at her, and walks away and from the distance he turns to say to her in Finnish: 'lehmä' [cow] or 'tyhmä' [stupid]. Looking at the flickering light she slowly stretches up her left arm.

From a (pro-)feminist position the acts of the male dancer can be read as a violation of privacy. The female resistance against male harassment is evident in the work. However, it is difficult to read this section as being sympathetic towards feminist claims about women's right to their own bodies. The man is constructed as a decision-maker who gets up and leaves when he does not get what he wants. Moreover, the man has been given the right to use a derogatory speech act to define who the woman is whereas her right to use speech to define herself or the man has been withheld. Through her self-contained television watching and passivity, the woman is constructed as a weakly resisting passive receiver. In that sense, it could be argued that the performed masculinism in this section is undermining feminist claims about women's right to their own bodies by naming women who resist physical harassment with derogatory speech acts.

Physical violence between heterosexual men and women is also visible in Numminen's work. In section 5, two male dancers hold female dancers horizontal on their chests as they revolve slowly. The males gaze at the females as they lower them down on their feet. The pairs embrace. The male dancers shift their hands on the female bottoms. Their fondling makes the females struggle. A group of five female dancers start banging their shoes on the floor. The two female dancers escape from the males and run to lean against the two walls on down stage corners. The male dancers adjust their clothes, walk on the centre stage and suddenly rush to kick fiercely at the walls on the exact spot where the two female dancers have been standing. The females duck to avoid the violent outburst. As the two males are returning to the centre, the two female dancers run after them and kick them in the back. The blow makes the males to fall into the ground. The group of five women stand up and start running back and forth.

It could be maintained that women's resistance is constructed in this dance section as an instigator of male violence towards women. The masculinist discourse that is embodied in the performance of the male dancers states that men have an unquestioned right to treat women as objects of sexual pleasure. It is left up to women to resist men's groping. Such resistance is met with an outburst of male violence, an act that can be read to question women's right to their own bodies. The commonly known fact that women end up as victims of male violence is acknowledged in the choreography. Yet, in the end of section 5, men are constructed as victims of female violence as the two female dancers attack the two males from behind. The entire section can be interpreted as a display of physical violence that emerges from tensions that gendered power relations and the discourse of masculinism build up between heterosexual men and women in contemporary Western societies.

196

A very different view of the power relations between men and women is performed in Isto Turpeinen's *The Union of Kalamari* and *Seven Brothers*. The former is a dance theatre piece that was choreographed for a group of dance students in 1998. According to programme notes, the piece is about five boys, all named 'Frank', who are eager to grow up. However, in order to become adult men, they have to pass via a road that is governed by a girl named Mari. In addition, there is a group of more mature girls that operate on Mari's street. According to dance critic Jussi Tossavainen (1998),

> Turpeinen's work is understanding and full of insight. Young boys are in a hurry to enter the world of adults but the road there leads through a girl-zone that is both frightening and exciting. Women represent here what they often actually are, the stronger sex. Eventually, through initiation rites the boys get to knock on the door of the men's world. Before then, they have to have courage to spend a night in a forest and what's most terrible – to approach girls. The girls are already waiting seductively for the boys with symbolic apples in their hands.

Based on this reading of Turpeinen's *The Union of Kalamari*, the work can be said to construct males opposite to females as apprehensive. They have to confront females at night in a scary place, a forest. The apples in the hands of the girls call forth biblical references that turn the young males into innocent victims who are subjected to the seductive power of females that leads to destruction, or at least out of a fictive place called paradise. On the other hand, the apples can also refer to fertility, which turns the young males into future fathers, or at least into potential sperm donors. An interesting contradiction in Tossavainen's reading of Turpeinen's work is that confronting the opposite sex is constructed as a necessary rite of passage to adulthood while the idea of getting seduced by the opposite sex is turned into something terrible. It could be maintained that in Tossavainen's reading males do not need females as partners in life for the sake of company. They are not needed for the sake of sexual pleasures either. Rather, females are needed merely for their embodied value in a masculinist game for males to gain social accountability as men.

The theme of growing up and pairing up with a woman is also elaborated upon in the final section of Turpeinen's *Seven Brothers*. The brothers, with the exception of Simeon who remains unmarried in Kivi's (2000) book, pair up with six female dancers who appear in long white dresses and red headscarves. The one who dances with Aapo, makes him perform somersaults, spins him around and rolls him on the ground. The girl who dances with Timo spins him from his arm and neck. The one who dances around Juhani performs rocking movements as if holding a child. She returns later only to throw Juhani onto the ground with an aikido move. Tuomas backs away chased by his female partner. Catching him from the neck, she spins him around, throws him into the ground and remains standing with arms on her hips. Lauri is pushed from his neck, thrusted from his back and also spinned around.

Men, who in the earlier sections of the work have been constructed as resisting authorities, living in the wilderness and fighting rampantly against other men and beasts are suddenly in the final section constructed as truckled to women. Their behaviour is monitored and controlled by women who keep their men 'on a short leash'. Very little joy can be read from the faces of these men. The exception to this is Eero, who dances a short section in unison with his female partner. Even he receives a blow and is left to run after her when, in the middle of their dance, he starts joking around with busy feet. The final section, which from the first viewing can seem as a celebration of heterosexual coupling, opens to a reading about oppressed and unhappy men in heterosexual relationships. The finale is telling: the female dancer who has played master and slave with Lauri by locking his arms over his head and circling him four times at very close distance positions herself in front of him. Pulling his arms around her chest she begins to hum *Our Land,* the national anthem of Finland. She sways gently and smiles. He stands still with an empty expression on his face. The section can be read as a domestication of the brothers into respectable Finnish citizens, which includes that they have to conform to heteronormativity. Compulsory heterosexuality as an embodied discourse in Turpeinen's work can also explain why the character of Simeon, the brother who does not get married, is not assigned any particular tasks in the end of the piece. He is left merely walking in circles.

Like the last chapter of Kivi's (2000) book, Turpeinen's work also highlights women as holders of power. However Turpeinen's choreography leaves unclear that in Kivi's text the power of wives is limited only to the domestic realm. Their husbands, at least some of them, once properly socialised, are assigned to socially accountable public tasks in Kivi's book. In addition, with the exception of Simeon, each of the brothers has a house of his own. In that sense, it could be argued that Turpeinen's interpretation of power relations in the final chapter of Kivi's book is biased. It is lavish in describing how women use power over men but remains quiet about gendered division of labour and property in the story.

The above dance examples demonstrate how more mature dance students in their late teens and early twenties are subjected to normative heterosexual masculinity in dance education through choreographies that they perform. However, as Marketta Viitala's *The Newer Quadrille of the Northern Boys* shows, masculinist rituals of heterosexuality are assigned for dance students to perform prior to their teens. In this choreography a group of boys, age 7 to 9, display their masculine prowess with serious faces. One of the boys remains outside the physical competition and, instead, walks to a girl who has sneaked in during the display. He bows at her, takes a dance hold that is common from ballroom dances and leads her into a whirling dance with long gliding steps. The other boys see the dancing couple, pull out handkerchiefs from their pockets and start to cry. With heavy heads, they exit in line while the dancing couple remains turning in the back.

The gendered power relations that underpin ballroom and many folk dances can be recognised from Viitala's work. The boy is constructed as active. He takes the initiative and leads the dance. The girl is constructed as passive: her task is to follow the boy. Symbolically, the leading role of the boy turns him into a master and the girl into a slave, a piece of property. The dance can be read through Bourdieu's (1985) idea about capital in his field theory. Masculinism, as a discourse, establishes a field where men compete about their social accountability. Valid capital in this game is different forms of prowess including physical strength, skills and the ability to get a girl. In this game, the female body is constructed as a piece of property that guarantees its male owner a winning status. From this perspective the crying of boys can be read to signify their bitter loss. They have failed to get the only available girl in the village, a reality that many heterosexual single men have faced in northern parts of Finland where young females have migrated south after work and education. When the sadness that is performed through the sullen exit of the boys is examined in relation to the happiness of the turning couple, it can be argued that the male who is in a heterosexual relationship is put forth in this work as something positive and worthy in relation to single males.

In dance education social conventions of heterosexual discourse are embodied through learning the above described and other similar dances. It can be maintained that for students whose lifestyles fall in with the commands of the heteronormative discourse these kinds of dances act

> as a constant reinforcement and regulatory mechanism, producing its compliant readers as viable social subjects and regulating any thoughts they might have about alternative gender roles or sexual choices. (Cranny-Francis et al 2003, p. 19)

However, not all dance students are heterosexual and some of them can be quite uncertain about their sexuality. For them, 'compulsory heterosexuality acts as a mechanism of exclusion and oppression, because it consistently constructs them as outsiders, aberrant and bad' (ibid). As a lesbian feminist concept, Adrianne Rich's (1980) 'compulsory heterosexuality' refers to 'the enforcement of heterosexuality' (Humm 1989, p. 34). It is 'the dominant order in which men and women are required or even forced to be heterosexual' (Salih 2002, p. 49). As Humm points out,

> if heterosexuality were not presented as, or perceived to be, *the* 'natural' form of sexual relations then the erotic choices of both women and men and our gender identities would be very different. (1989, p. 34)

There are very few dances that have been choreographed for male dance students or mixed-sex student groups that explicitly or implicitly address male homosexuality. An exception to this is Numminen's *People's Celebration* where a short reference to homosexuality appears in section 9. The section is formed from episodes where different dancers are announced to perform Finnish songs. The fifth song is *At the Sea*, a melancholic love song from Oskar Merikanto that is performed by Jukka Virtala.

Figure 19. Antti Lahti (on the left) and Jukka Virtala in *People's Celebration* (1999). Photo: Markus Lahtinen. (Courtesy of the photographer)

His performance includes swaying, walking in circles with a coat over his head, a collapse, a burst into a run, rolling on the floor, assisted attitude turns and balances, a circular pattern of runs and leaps, bursting into tears, crawling over the seats into the audience and hugging an audience member. The other dancers respond to Jukka's strange behaviour, outburst of hysteria and loss of control by dragging him back on the stage. There is lots of shouting as he is being pushed around. He takes off his jacket, pulls out his shirt and rushes back into the audience. He is pulled back on stage once more. Antti Lahti, the other male dancer grabs Jukka from his hair and shouts at him. Jukka collapses on the floor. He is kissed by a female dancer who is dragged away by another female dancer. He sits on the edge of the stage and plays with pieces of confetti. A female dancer goes to him, kneels down and talks to him. He shakes his head but after a while he agrees to get up, to hold her hand and to follow her. He starts to arrange his clothes.

Homosexuality becomes an issue in Antti's speech act when he walks across the stage to Jukka, points at him with his index finger and says 'you are a fucking homo, I'm going to punch you' (see Figure 19). He takes hold of Jukka's nose. Jukka removes Antti's hand. Antti points at Jukka's face again, gives him a blow on his chest and walks away. He turns to look at Jukka once more, points at him with his index finger and then slowly walks away. Antti's violent speech act and behaviour can be read as a command to behave according to socially accepted norms. The threat of punishment is included in this command. The act of turning back and the pointed index finger enforce the threat and call attention to the social surveillance through which male behaviour is incessantly monitored. Antti's direct focus reminds that in masculinist culture the male gaze operates as a means of social control.

Foucault's theory of panopticon offers a means to read Antti's gaze as a form of masculinist surveillance practice.[2] To gain and to

2   Following Foucault (1997d), panopticism can be defined as any operation of power where constraint and interpersonal surveillance practices are applied in order to create situations of social uncertainty that nurture self-discipline in the subject. The concept owes its name to Jeremy Bentham's architectural composition of a 19th century penitentiary. In Panopticon, prisoners are kept in cells around a central observation tower. The architectural structure creates a condition where the prisoners are aware that their actions can be registered at all

maintain one's credibility in a masculinist context means that a man needs to perform gender in a way that is valid from a masculinist point of view. In a heteronormative society, all males are subjected to the gaze of the male other. The eyes of the other fulfil the function of the observation tower: they do not reveal whether the gaze is a masculinist one or not but they signify about the potential presence of masculinist surveillance. Under such uncertain conditions, the awareness that injurious acts such as hate speech or physical violence can accompany the masculinist gaze instigates self-control in males. Hence, the gaze of the other male can be regarded as a means to implement the power of the masculinist discourse to operate in male subjects as a form of self-control. In the dance example this is demonstrated by Jukka calming down, standing still and sitting down after Antti's violent outburst.

The heteronormative underpinnings of social norms become evident when Antti names Jukka as homosexual. Jukka's behaviour is not explicitly homosexual – whatever that is – nor does he show affection towards Antti. However, he cries and behaves in an otherwise uncontrolled manner. It could be maintained that these behaviours locate Jukka outside the discourse of masculinism and, from a masculinist perspective, outside heterosexuality. This gives Antti an unquestioned right to use violence against him. It could be maintained that violence that is projected towards homosexuality in this dance example does not emerge from homophobia, the fear of homosexuals. Rather, it is evoked through discursively constructed standards of heteronormativity.

Less explicit references to male homosexuality can be read from Katri Soini's *The Last Warning* that was choreographed for the students of the Finnish National Opera Ballet School in 1996. The work has been described as a game between young people that includes sexual relations, crushes and disappointments (Kaiku 1996). Uniformity claims of young people, which can be read from identical costumes and sections of unison dancing, are also characteristic to this

times (for more details, see Foucault 1995). According to Foucault, panopticon forms 'an apparatus of total and circulating mistrust' (1980c, p. 158).

work. One of its six sections constructs a tense relationship between two young males and examines their relationship to a tight group of young people that can be read as a gang.

The section emerges as a cut from a unison group dance. Two young males remain standing up in a wide position opposite to each other as the other members of the group land from a turning attitude-jump into a low level and back towards upstage. After a moment of stillness, they start circling each other, first slowly but then with an increasing tempo as the diameter of the circle diminish. As one of the males slips, the other runs to the group that has established itself in a low level in the left upstage corner. He turns to face the other with his upper-body leaning forward, his arms pulled back and elbows bent. The two run to opposite corners of the stage, turn and rush towards each other. As they meet, the blond boy pushes the dark-haired boy away as this leaps towards him. Up until this point, the relationship of the two boys seems merely tense. Their performance could be read as a competition between the two for their position in the group. However, the relationship grows more complex as the section goes further.

The dark-haired boy makes a non-hostile gesture as he gives his hand to pull up the blond who has after a flip ended up sitting on the floor in front the dark boy. His actions turn violent as he jumps at the blond boy who squats on the ground, kicks him in the lower-back and walks by as the other flips over his shoulder, lands on his stomach. Yet, the blond one runs after the dark boy, touches his shoulder, turns in front of him and lets himself being caught as he falls backward. A moment later, the dark-haired boy runs after the blond boy, puts his hand around his neck and hinges backward in front of him. Moments of letting one's body being caught and held by the other rupture the simplistic idea that the relationship of the two is purely antagonistic even if hatred can be read from the violent acts. It could be maintained that falling backwards to be caught signifies incredible trust as it leaves one's body vulnerable in the hands of the other.

The backward falls and some of the non-hostile runs that the two boys make after each other can also be read as acts of attachment or affection. For example, after the dark-haired boy has approached the blond one in a non-hostile manner by taking hold of his shoulder and jumping up, the blond boy escapes from him. The two can be said to judge each other as they stop to face each, shifting weight from side to side in a wide position. Eventually, the blond boy runs to the members of the group who stand up facing their back towards the two. Hesitantly, the dark boy approaches the group. He runs the last few steps to reach the blond boy who now stands in the group his back turned to the dark boy. As a token of affection, he places his hand in a non-hostile manner on the right shoulder of the blond boy. The token of affection between the two males is met with an instant reaction as the entire group collapses into the ground leaving the dark-haired boy standing up alone.

The section shows the thin line between homosocial and homosexual bonding in male-to-male relationships. It also demonstrates how males who show attachment and affection towards other males are excluded from groups where, through masculinist discourse, male-to-male relationships must be constructed around competition or antagonism. As the reaction of the group shows, affection between two males is believed to have severe consequences. The group collapses, quite as conservatives and religious fundamentalists claimed in Finland during the 1990's that society would collapse if same-sex couples are given the right to register their relationship.[3] It could be argued that with no explicit counter-statements in the work, Soini's choreography does not merely display the dominant heteronormative discourse – it is constructed through it and operates as a vehicle for its politics in dance education.

A relatively similar encounter between two young males, Tuomas Juntunen and Arttu Kangas, is solved very differently in Sari

---

3   See Charpentier 2001 for a detailed analysis of the public debate on the possibility of same-sex marriages in Finland. Charpentier maintains that the heterosexual gender system is constructed as a 'sacred order' in this debate. Further, heteronormativity is produced and maintained as a religion. In English, see Charpentier's article in *Queen: a journal of rhetoric and power*, vol 1.1. Sex & Power: Subjection & Subjectivation available in http://www.ars-rhetorica.net/Queen/Volume 1.../charpentier.htm (15.2.2003).

Hannula's *Reset to Zero - Coincidental Accidents* (2000) that was choreographed for the students of Turku Conservatory. As a whole, the work can be read as a collection of various interpersonal encounters. In this book the examination of Hannula's choreography is limited to a development of a close relationship between two males that establishes a theme for section 4 in the work. However, to contextualise the section briefly, it is useful to know that section 4 emerges from section 3 where a young couple has been dancing. She starts to lose her hold and slips from his grip. He tries to put her arms back around his neck but she collapses. He struggles to keep her from falling but ultimately he has to place her body down. Section 3 constructs an image of a young male (A), performed by Tuomas Juntunen, trying to hold to a female he loves and cares for. Her slipping away can be read as a death or perhaps it is a metaphor for her leaving him. His struggle to keep her embracing him can be read as his attempt to hold on to his object of love. On this basis, he is constructed as a heterosexual young man in love.

Section 4 begins as A mourns next to his female partner's lifeless body. A young male (B), performed by Arttu Kangas, enters with his thumbs tucked into his pockets. Offering comfort, he places his hand on the right shoulder of A who pushes it away, walks downstage and squats down to touch his ear and rub his chin. B walks to him and remains standing with his thumbs in his pockets. In the moments of grief it is often difficult to find an appropriate way to communicate with the one who is in despair. B looks away from A, glances quickly at him, turns his focus down, scratches his forehead and turns his focus back to A. He squats next to A, turns his focus slowly from his hands to A, takes a quick look to his sides and stands up. A stands up slowly and takes a look at B. By tucking his thumbs into his pockets A uses a signifier, which B has embodied at his arrival, to signal his appreciation of B's presence. Encouraged by this, B jerks his knees quickly as if he is making a question. A responds by repeating the same movement. A leading, the two drop down to flip their body over their supporting left arm. They spin on their bottoms, hands and feet as they travel to centre stage. Clearly the two young males have found a common tune from the brisk movements. Sitting on the floor with one knee bent and hands on their chin, they pause to look at each other for a moment.

However, there is also hesitancy between the two. Both men make a sudden flip over their supporting arms to return on their feet. Tension is building up as they are standing in a wide parallel position opposite to each other, pulling their elbows back like two cowboys in a wild-western film. With thumbs tucked in their pockets, the two move closer to each other while keeping their bodies wide open. B walks around A's back to his right side. A shows his mistrust by moving away slightly.

A playful game is initiated as B gives A an impulse with his hip and both collapse down. B gets on his knees as A dives over his back into a cartwheel, turns around and gets on his knees. A shows his trust by leaning his back over B's back and relaxing his body. B's uneasiness in this situation is evident as he takes a quick look to his sides, scratches his forehead and looks again to his side. Metaphorically, there is too much load on his back. He pulls himself from underneath, which makes A fall on his feet. The two look at each other.

B smirks as he suddenly touches A behind his knee. A collapses onto the ground while B dances in front of him with rapid changes of weight and small jumps. Teasing continues. B is about to touch A in his face with his left hand but instead slaps him on the head with his right hand. A arches over his shoulder and falls flat on his stomach. B buzzes around him. As he comes up, B takes A's hand and flips it around, which makes A fall. Continuing his jerky dancing, B gestures A to stand up. More pushing and slapping occurs as B takes the mickey out of A's vulnerability.

A stands up on his shoulder, legs extended up. This way, by being active and introducing a new trick, he gets B to stop teasing him for a moment. B moves right next to A on his all fours. A moves to the other side of B by lowering his legs over B's back. A mutual theme is established as the two pivot around on their bottoms, glide diagonally forward on their legs and dive forward in unison. On the floor, the collaboration between the two continues as A rolls across B's body into a freeze standing on his shoulder. He lowers his legs over the back of B, which leads the two to sit opposite to each other. The reciprocity experienced makes the two males uneasy as both of them leap to opposite directions while maintaining a supporting hand on the ground. They come up, standing in a firm wide parallel position opposite to each other. B solves the tense moment by returning to tease A. In varying ways, he makes A fall down repeatedly as the tempo increases.

A major change takes place when A stops from falling every time B touches him. The two stand opposite to each other. A rubs his nose and looks down. He moves to lift B's hands gently on his shoulders and places his own hands on B's shoulders. As this is an intimate position A has been dancing with his female partner in section 3, used here with a male partner it can signify fluidity of his sexual desire. In this moment of male-to-male physical contact, it could be argued that the line between homosocial and homosexual bonding is eroded. As if asking approval to this new aspect of their relationship, A takes first a look at B's left hand and meets then his eyes. Lifting his palms slightly off from A's shoulders and extending his fingers, B's body signifies modest hesitance. Slowly the two lower their arms and their focus.

Yet the exploration of intimate closeness continues. A grabs B's right hand, pulls it on his shoulder and embraces B for a short moment before he switches his position by placing B's left hand against his shoulder. He moves against B's left arm, pulls out again, takes hold of B's right arm and brings it under his arm around his back, which makes the two embrace. A turns his back against B, holding his arm with both hands over his right shoulder. He turns to take hold of B's left arm and pulls it on his shoulder. As A brings B's arms down, B's palm sweeps across A's stomach. The two embrace. A pulls B's right arm that crosses to his left side and by bending over, he takes a hold behind B's back and lifts him around in wheel plane. It is as if A is uncertain about how to find comfortable ways of being in this close intimate relationship. B turns the exploration of closeness into a game. He pulls A to throw a somersault and moves around him with jerky small weight changes as he comes up. A extends his left arm and points at B with his index finger. B responds jokingly by jerking his knees quickly from side to side while holding his elbows bent, two fingers extended in both hands.

The two move closer to each other. A makes a couple of quick hops while B stands with his thumbs tucked into his pockets. A tries a new approach to his yawning friend. He moves hesitantly to B, takes hold of his right arm, places it around his shoulder and with his left hand takes hold of B behind his back. He spins B around by lifting him with the side of his pelvis. To initiate each lift, B uses his feet to push off the ground while in the lift his knees are pulled up. The lifting sequence is performed repeatedly. Eventually, A throws B off from his neck and turns to face him. Enjoying the vigorous play, the two laugh.

The two establish a common ground in energetic and physically challenging activities. B rushes to A, the two move opposite to each other with small quick, bounding runs and jumps. B throws himself onto the ground. A jumps over B's rolling body and lands with his body horizontally extended on his hands and feet. He rolls towards B who jumps over A and throws himself down. A throws himself horizontally over A's rolling body and rolls back as B skips over him (see Figure 20).

The closeness of the two males is questioned by a female dancer in red dress who enters, stops and stares at the two who continue their game. Another female dancer enters. B rolls himself to A's lap with his head down and legs over A's right shoulder. The woman in red walks to the two and stares at them. Acknowledging the pressure of heteronormativity that is inherent in the situation, A drops B. The two look at the females, stand up, look around and accommodate the heteronormativity by taking some distance from each other. Yet, this is not enough for the woman in red who follows the two and comments on their intimacy by opening and closing her mouth repeatedly. As if challenging the woman and the narrowness of the social norms she represents, the two males look at each other, drop down to leap over the supporting left arm and roll with high tempo on their bottoms, hands and feet. A third female dancer enters.

The two lay open what they have been up to and the reciprocity in their relationship. B bends down on his knees and elbows. A lies on his back on the back of B, letting his arms and neck hang relaxed. The females move gradually towards the two. B throws A from his back and stands up on his hands. A moves to support him from his legs. B drops down and shift to hold A's legs as he stands on his hands and extends his legs horizontally. B jumps in the lap of A. Under the growing social pressure, A first lowers the upper-body of B down and then drops him on his feet as he sees the look on the face of the woman in green dress. The two step nervously as the women approach them. They repeat the drop down, flip over and spin on the bottom sequence in a semi-circular floor pattern as more women enter.

Figure 20. Tuomas Juntunen (below) and Arttu Kangas rehearsing *Reset to Zero - Coincidental Accidents.* Photo: Markus Lahtinen. (Courtesy of the photographer)

A falls to his all fours as B leaps horizontally over his back by holding to his shoulders. He moves behind A to lift him under his arms and whirls him around. As B jumps up, A moves underneath him and picks him up, hanging him over his shoulder. He carries B a few steps and lowers him down. The females get closer to the two males who move downstage with small nervous jumps. The two look at each other and with a sudden run, escape through the group of women between the split in the backdrop. The section ends as the women turn to rush after the males but then stop with their arms and hands half-extended after the two who have disappeared.

Eventually, the sexuality of the two males remains open even if homosexual desire can be read into their homosocial relationship. B's hesitance and repeated attempts to turn male intimacy into a playful joke suggest that he is not gay or that he is still very much in the closet. In addition, A's former relationship with a woman suggest that he is not exactly gay. However, his persistence to find comfortable physical closeness with another male suggests a non-heterosexual desire. He could be bisexual. Yet he clearly has no experience of intimacy with other men. His long hesitance and the clumsy attempt to build an intimate situation with the same bodily signifiers he had used with his female partner suggest that he is exploring new terrain with old tools. A way to speak about the evident shift in his sexuality would be to borrow terms from choreographer, filmmaker and feminist artist Yvonne Rainer and call him 'a provisional heterosexual, or a makeshift hetero … "heterofluxual" or contingent hetero, or *nonessential* hetero' (1999, p. 108).

From a queer perspective, it could be maintained that the significance of Hannula's choreography is that it does not construct male sexuality as something fixed that can be easily located into three categories: gay, bi, hetero. Rather, it leaves open more possibilities for the performers and the spectator to play and identify with the performed male sexuality. It displays the difficulties young males have to face when they negotiate male-to-male relationships in society where the dominant heteronormative discourse is eager to stamp out any signifiers of same-sex closeness and affection. The two males resist the heteronormative discourse as they refuse to compromise their relationship to the heteronormative idea about masculinity.

211

However, to do this, the two need to escape behind the backdrop: the heteronormative message of the work can not get much clearer.

As described in this section, male relationships and sexuality are constructed and performed variously in dances that have been choreographed for all-male and mixed-sex groups of dance students. Different choreographies position males differently in relation to power within the heterosexual gender system. However, heterosexual masculinity is produced through the discourses of heteronormativity and masculinism as the only valid form of masculinity. Affectionate relations between two males are seldom displayed. In the rare cases when such relationships appear, they are constructed negatively in relation to males who are involved in a heterosexual relationship or as something that society disagrees with. Hence, for students who define themselves as non-heterosexual or who are uncertain about their sexuality, heteronormative politics that are produced and maintained in dance education through choreography do not provide positive alternative positions of gender and sexuality to identify with. Making them embody and perform heterosexual conventions can be regarded as a form of heteronormative blindness or as a gender political normalising practice operated by the discourses of heteronormativity and masculinism.

Dance analytical descriptions of choreographies examined in this Chapter suggest that multiple masculinities are constructed and performed in dances that have been choreographed for all-male and mixed-sex groups of dance students. However, based on the prevailing iconography of heroism, physical prowess, combats and heterosexual bonding - and the few examples that display non-heterosexual masculinity negatively - it can be argued that masculinities performed are constructed through the prevalent discourses of masculinism and heteronormativity. As such, they provide limited positions of gender and sexuality for male dance students and for the spectator to identify with.

In addition, it can be argued that gender is discursively invested through choreography into the bodies of dance students. The analysed dance examples show that bodies of male dance students become vehicles for discursive power of masculinism and heteronormativity to operate in dance institutions. Moreover, the fact that some boys include combat games into their play activities after seeing spectacular fight scenes in a dance performance, suggests that choreographies can disseminate discursive views on gender and sexuality in society. Such dissemination also takes place when bodily writing of dancers is read and mediated further in society by media through reviews, press photographs and video-recorded or televised dancing.

Chapter Seven
Negotiating Male Identities in Dance

Gendered Identity as a Construction

The male dance student can be understood from poststructuralist and social constructionist perspectives as a subject who is a reader of discursive texts that are culturally available to him in the social reality that he lives in (Barthes 1997; Foucault 1984d; Worton & Still 1990). His sense of self and his possibilities to act meaningfully (to himself and to others) emerge inside the dance educational context as well as elsewhere in society where he interacts. Thus, his identity can be seen as a dynamic fabrication of fragmented narratives about the self in relation to dance, gender, sexuality, others and so on (Burr 1995; Cox & Lyddon 1997; Davies 2002; Davies and Harré 2001; Foucault 1997a; Hall 1999; Harré 1985; Sampson 1989; Sarbin 1986; Shotter 1997; Gergen 1999).

Following the arguments raised in queer theory, the male dance student's gendered identity can be said to emerge as

> a personal/cultural history of received meanings subject to a set of imitative practices which refer laterally to other imitations and which, jointly construct the illusion of a primary and interior gendered self or parody the mechanism of that construction. (Butler 1990, p. 138)

It can be maintained that people have no gender identity prior the imitative acts that form such identity. Rather, all attempts to position oneself as a gendered and sexualised person emerge from the 'metaphysics of gender substances' (Butler 1990, p. 21) that locate

> the notion of gender under that of identity ... [which then leads] to the conclusion that a person *is* a gender and *is* one in virtue of his or her sex,

215

psychic sense of self, and various expressions of that psychic self, the most salient being that of sexual desire. (Butler 1990, pp. 21-22)

Hence, the male dance student's gendered 'expressions' that, from a traditional humanist perspective, could be perceived as products of identity, are understood in this book through queer theory as being 'performatively constituted' (Butler 1990, p. 25).

In this chapter, self-narratives of Finnish boys in theatrical dance are analysed to show how young males negotiate and perform gendered identities within a cultural practice that is perceived in Finland commonly as a feminine realm. The notion of 'positioning' is central to such analysis. From a social constructionist point of view it has been suggested that people apply categories produced through discursive practices to position themselves in relation to others in their self-narratives (Burr 1995, Davies & Harré 2001, Davies 2002). Social positioning can be 'interactive' in the sense that 'what one person says positions another' (Davies & Harré 2001, p. 264) but it can also be 'reflexive'. That is, 'one positions oneself' (ibid).

The Dancing Self and Significant Other(s)

In Finland, theatrical dance, particularly ballet, is still very much perceived as a hobby for females although one might think that the appearances of male dance artists in the media would undermine this unfounded conception. Moreover, in a Finnish cultural climate boys and men are forced to negotiate their male identity in relation to the culturally dominant heteronormative discourse of masculinism. Therefore, it is hardly surprising that the position of the male dance student is far from neutral.

Some parents, fathers especially, are not always comfortable with the idea that their son studies dance. Yet, there are parents, often mothers but also fathers, who encourage their sons to take up dance. For example, during one of the focus group interviews, a sixteen year-

216

old boy told a story about his mother who, while pregnant with her son and watching a ballet contest on television, decided to introduce her child to ballet regardless of the child's sex. The boy had enrolled in a local ballet school at the age of four and was at the time of the interview seriously planning a career as a professional ballet dancer. A heart-breaking example is a father who was determined to let his nine year-old son participate in dance education despite the oppression the son had experienced due to his dance interest in the religious fundamentalist neighbourhood in the west coast of Finland where they lived. The same father also told a story about his own mother who spat in his face when he, as a young boy, had asked if he could take up ballet. Now in his early forties, the man was perhaps living his danceless childhood through his own son.

As long as socially acceptable or credible ways of performing maleness are constructed merely through the socially dominant masculinist discourse, boys who wish to take up dance in Finland are bound to face reactions in the people around them. As the text extracts that follow show, such reactions have an impact on how male dance students negotiate their identity in relation to dance.

In the first extract, a post-graduate male dance student recalls how he initially got involved in dance:

Risto: Well, I am from East Bothnia, from Kaustinen and it is there that I started [dancing] at primary school age. My mother led a folk dance club and that is how it gradually went on. A very, how would you say, tight group there, a group of mates and that encouraged me to continue there. It is now sixteen years ago when we started there and folk dance has followed me all the time...

Risto comes from a small town in the North-West of Finland that is known from its cultural activities, particularly its famous folk music festival. Before taking up dance at a higher level, Risto danced in the local folk-dance circle where his mother, his sister and many of his friends from school also participated. Positioned in a group that perceives dance positively, it was easy for Risto to take up dance at a higher level without compromising his former identity.

In contrast, it was significantly more difficult for Risto's class-mates Pekka and Lauri to take up dance studies due to their social background. Their self-narratives intermingled in the focus group interview as follows:

Pekka: I should possibly add that I spent seven years in discos because I did not have the sense to go elsewhere [to dance]. We are now getting to the question whether one should take dance classes or not, which has been one of the biggest thresholds [for me] for fifteen years or even longer.

Lauri: Yeah, I too danced in discos as often as I could even if everybody was staring at me like no. Well, particularly in Hanko, it was such a great sin to dance in a disco but, sure enough, I had to dance because I had this incredible frenzy.

Pekka: It was the same for me.

Lauri: So surely one has gained some sort of an education, a small one that is, the foundation is somewhere there at least.

Pekka: Exactly the same for me, that buddies danced, nothing but always going to the disco and eventually … we did not do anything else there, perhaps we shared a beer … but the threshold to go somewhere was big.

Interv: What was that threshold? Why was it?

Pekka: There was no, what would that be, social support of any kind or none of that, well Risto has had some kind of a circle of mates, but [for me] there was no contact what so ever to any, well dance has had its own circles its own world. No, and a kind of own culture, they have the background, cause [for me] from a small-entrepreneur background there are no links to cultural activities. To a large extent, it [my background] has encompassed the technical car sector, very very heavy (laughs)

Others: (laugh)

Pekka comes from Helsinki where there are plenty of dance and other arts activities easily accessible at all times. However, as his family members are not interested in culture, he lacks that significant other who would introduce arts to him. He goes to clubs to dance but organised dance classes had to wait until he became interested in African dances at the age of twenty three when he was already a student in a university. Pekka's growing interest in dance made him leave the university and pursue dance studies first in a folk college and subsequently at a higher level.

Like Pekka, Lauri makes a point about wild dancing in a local disco in a small costal town in South Finland where he comes from. His self-narrative contains an interesting tension between his dance interest and the stringent demands of uniformity that prevails in his peer-group. Moreover, there is a local dance school in his hometown where he could study dance. However, considering the conservative small town atmosphere and the gendered name of the school, The Dance Girls of Soulasmaa, the local dance school is not a realistic choice for Lauri. In his words:

> Lauri: …I think I had it difficult enough so that had I, that is, my brother said at some point after I had taken up dance … that they would have killed you had you danc- had you above everything else also danced, or like this, but that is what my brother said. Yeah, well, that is quite possible, I thought (laughs).

Through the 'voice' of his brother, Lauri positions himself in a tense relationship with the peer-group in his home town. In this narrative, his dance interest is constructed as a marker that marks him negatively to the peers in his home town and makes him a potential victim of bullying. Considering the extreme violence in the narrative that is used to describe Lauri's fantasised life as a dance student in his home town, it makes sense that in real life Lauri never took up dance in his home town. Instead, he moved to study catering in a bigger town, where detached from the social constraints of his home town, he took up modern dance and then applied to study dance at a higher level.

In their everyday life, male dance students often have to deal with prejudiced views on dance and the male dancer. It makes perfect sense that some of them, like Lauri and Pekka in the next extract,

position themselves differently in relation to 'close friends' than they do in relation to 'acquaintances':

Interv: How do your mates react to your dancing?
Lauri: It depends a bit on the circle of mates.
Pekka: Well, at least for me, yes well yes
Lauri: One must, that is, the closest friends surely of course they appreciate and are interested in and curious and come to see performances. Then if we take a grade, kind of acquaintances and mates, sure enough they sometimes wonder what an earth we are doing over here.
Pekka: ... At least I have noticed that, or that I've been thinking that what is their attitude to this ... sometimes I feel that I don't really want them to come to see my work. There is some kind of insecurity ... it would seem that they don't understand or that the change is rather big because I myself have changed incredibly, and then again what the audience sees. If we talk about my mates and not necessarily my friends because friends know how one has changed.
Lauri: Ye-ah, there is a remarkable difference there.

In the extract, 'close friends' are described as people who appreciate one's personal choice to study dance. They acknowledge that such study necessarily entails changes in the person and show genuine interest towards their friend's artistic development. In contrast, people who show no understanding towards one's dance interest or who respond with scepticism are regarded as less intimate friends. The clear distinction that is made between 'friends' and 'acquaintances' suggests that close relationships with those who support the dance interest matter to these young males. Moreover, this distinction can be seen as a means to protect oneself by positioning people that are unsympathetic towards one's dance interest away from the self. On the other hand, people who are sympathetic towards dance are positioned close to the self in order to gain support by perceiving oneself as socially accepted.

From this perspective, it can be maintained that the support of one's parents or other close relatives mean a lot to boys in dance. In

Risto's self-narrative both his mother and his father are supportive towards his dance interest by encouraging him to do 'what you want, but ... try it out first before you quit'. In Lauri's self-narrative, his father does not encourage him to take up dance but he does not object to the idea either. Lauri elaborates this as follows:

Lauri: Well my father has not, he doesn't give a, well now that I am studying here, my father is incredibly happy and pleased that I have sort of found my own field, that this is something where I get along well and I have stayed with this already for two years without taking a hike.

P & R: mmm (smile contentedly)

Lauri: When I was younger, it did not come out of my father's mouth that lets go and dance ... he has been supportive rather than resisting [my choice to take up dance] particularly after I have started to train.

As the first line of the extract shows, Lauri is about to say that his father does not care for his dance interest. He then produces an entirely opposite narrative where his father is constructed as a caring and supportive person. A close reading of the extract shows that in the second narrative it is not Lauri's dance interest that his father is so overwhelmed with. Rather, he is pleased to see that his son has found a meaning to his life and that he has settled down and shows commitment in his chosen field even if that field is dance.

It is a commonly held view that fathers often reject the idea that their sons would take up dance as a hobby or as a career interest (Jääskeläinen 1993, Viitala 1998). Some institutions of dance education, such as the Vantaa Dance Institute, have worked actively to counteract parents' prejudiced views by getting parents, fathers particularly, involved in dance activities. This has included classes that are open for observation, meetings with parents, dance camp for the entire family, recruiting parents to do voluntary work for the dance institution and performances where even some parents appear on stage (Mäntylä, personal information 28.4.2001).

The rise of individualism as a discourse in the 1990's and during the first years of the new millennium has made it more socially

221

acceptable than ever before during the 20th century for young males to take up dance in Finland. The presently prevalent discourse of individualism can be linked to a major shift in the Finnish cultural climate from discourses of uniformity towards discourses in consumer culture that highlight individual choice. Such shifts can be recognised in the diversity that is now available, not just in purchasable goods but also in lifestyles, family forms, sexuality, fashion, hobbies and so on. In the earlier uniform culture it was customary that boys recite masculinist discourse by taking up ice-hockey, soccer or some other team sport. Boys who failed to do so were regarded as an exception to the norm and they were marked negatively as a 'sissy', an effeminate or otherwise 'deviant' male. The present situation is very different. Yet, there are still young males in dance who have to put up with the resistance of their parents, particularly with some of the fathers, who have failed to catch up with the 'Zeitgeist' of the new millennium.

In the following extract from one of the focus group interviews, Jaakko, a fourteen year old boy who took up ballet at the age of seven in a local dance school in South Finland, speaks about the reactions of his parents as he decided to take up dance:

Jaakko: Well, our mom always encouraged me, my sister has practically dragged me to a dance class and (.) well, our father was a bit hesitant. He did not know how to deal with it really. He has calmed down since then.
Int: How did his hesitance show?
Jaakko: Well a bit, kind of like, how come you don't, wouldn't you rather go and play soccer.
Int: Your father would have wanted soccer.
Jaakko: I guess he would have wanted to see me play soccer or ice-hockey, but I have never been a team player, rather, [I] prefer individual performance.
Int: So how does your father currently react?
Jaakko: Well, currently I don't see him very often. He just strolls in late at night when he gets off from work.
Int: Yes.
Jaakko: One gets to see him from seven to eight in the morning.

Int: I suppose that doesn't give you much time to
Jaakko: No, not really.

In the extract, Jaakko is positioned between the conflicting views of his parents. Jaakko's mother is described as an eager supporter of his dance interest. His father is constructed as an opponent who wants Jaakko to stay away from dance and to take up ice-hockey or soccer instead. The father is also described as a distant person against whose wishes Jaakko acts as he chooses a hobby that does not align with the traditional and culturally dominant masculinist discourse. In Jaakko's self-narrative, the father is a person that he meets only randomly at the breakfast table. The communication between the two is rather limited and Jaakko's dance interest is not on the list of discussed topics.

It can be asked whether Jaakko's father is one of those men who turn their back on their children once they fail to turn them, particularly their sons, into masculinist signifiers through which their own social position can be strengthened. That is, a son who performs the masculinist discourse can give a positive lift to his father in fields where masculinism is regarded as valid social capital. By choosing dance rather than ice-hockey, Jaakko fails to perform masculinism. Therefore, from a masculinist perspective, he can be seen as valueless or as a negative currency to his father.

Considering that boys in dance want to be socially accepted and loved by people close to them, it is evident that parental pride matters to them. The idea of seeing oneself negatively as a social strain on one's father can be hard to face. Therefore, as the first two lines in the next extract show, a more positive image of the self as a pride of one's father is constructed in the account. However, the first six words reveal that this construction is a fantasy:

Pekka: I am rather … well, I'm sure that [my father] boasts about
        what I do in his own circles, but there is that [concern]
        about the money, that in what phase, like very clearly it is
        fixed to that work, work and money. And it is precisely the
        same when we go back one more generation. Like my grand-
        dad, with whom I've been arguing more generally about

what I should start doing. It was only yesterday when he came to me and said that have you, do you make money out of it, which is so important to that post-war generation that has rebuilt [the country]. So it [a solid income] has been more than important [for them] straight out to survive. Of course it is like that even today, but anyhow intentions are now somewhat different.

The extract also exemplifies another interesting pointer: the common patriarchal discourse about the male as a breadwinner that is operating through the 'voice' of Pekka's father. Considering that the first major post-war period of prosperity was experienced in Finland as late as in the 1980's, it can be appreciated that the notion of economic survival is particularly important for elderly people who have confronted poverty and shortage in their lived history. Moreover, in Finland, the necessity to rebuild the country after World War II made the commitment to serious work an important nationalist virtue. The large post-war generations created permanent jobs for themselves, which made a solid and steady income an unquestioned norm in Finnish society. However, for those young Finns who woke up to the post-depression new order of the 1990's, unemployment, temporary short-term contracts and poverty were part of the everyday social reality. Educating oneself in a lucrative field no longer guarantees a well-paying job - not even a permanent job. Thus, 'having a life' and enjoying what one does rather than earning money in a 'decent' job seems to be the motto for those who were born after the late 1960's.[1]

From this perspective, what members of the younger generation perceive as an exciting individual career choice or a lifestyle does not necessarily meet the criteria of what counts as 'proper' work for the older generations. Kalle's account below serves as a good example of this:

---

1   See Kauhanen and Lyytinen (eds) (2003), a recent report from SITRA (The Finnish National Fund for Research and Development), for current views of 22 active young Finns (born between 1968 and 1980) on work, life and future.

224

Kalle: Actually, mmm, perhaps ... the only one who has had a very negative or a kind of reserved attitude is my grandfather, well at first. He has been or he is a diploma engineer and he is originally from way out north and, you know, he was so pleased that I was already studying to become a diploma engineer in Helsinki University of Technology and all that. And when he heard that I had kind of changed the field to dance, he was quite unable to speak to me for some time or actually for quite a long time about anything and so on. Only like it's a beautiful weather here today and so on and the interesting pointer here is that my grandmother, his wife, has been a dancer in the Opera. And already when she was dancing there, my grandfather had this attitude that dance is not actually any profession. Like, sure you can work there as a dancer but you had better also work in my office and, well this is how it kind of went.

While Kalle's relationship with his grandfather is otherwise very different from that of Jaakko and his father (see above), the growing distance that is constructed between the boy who takes up dance and his close male relative, father or grandfather, is stunningly similar in the two narratives. In Jaakko's narrative, his father is away for most of the time and the communication between the two is limited to arbitrary encounters. In Kalle's narrative, his grandfather is constructed as a person who is unable to communicate with his grandson after finding out that his grandson has left a study programme in a prestigious technological institution to embark on a career in dance. In addition, in both examples dance is constructed from the perspective of the significant male other as a female practice. In Jaakko's narrative, his father wants him to take up a traditional masculine team sport and in Kalle's narrative dance is, for his grandfather, something that his wife used to do in the Opera. Hence, the two boys position themselves through the perspective of their significant male other into a female realm. The guilt for letting down one's grand/father can be sensed from the two narratives.

Kalle further elaborates upon the relationship with his grandfather as follows:

Kalle: But it is also exciting that although he is what seventy-five or at least closer to eighty that his attitude has kind of changed a bit. It is funny that he has moved to a direction and started asking about our days at school and you know, that it is hard and physical and that it takes long days and even weekends to work. So that in a way through the idea that it is work, it is in a way a real profession, something that you have to study and work and after that it can be accepted.

In the extract, Kalle and his grandfather have been able to rebond after the initial estrangement that took place between the two. The use of the discourse on 'hard work' makes it possible for the grandfather to distance dance from its feminine connotations and to perceive it from a masculinist position as physically demanding. Hence, the discourse on 'hard work' makes dance appear as a socially accepted and legitimate career for a man. This discourse appears frequently in narratives of boys in dance as they describe what dancing is like.[2]

Boys in dance are often forced to cope with the conflict between their interest in dance and what others think is socially acceptable because dance, as seen through the culturally prevalent lens of masculinism, is commonly perceived as a feminine activity that does not provide a 'proper' occupation for a man. The responses of the significant others – family members and peers – bear importance to boys in dance. Young males who dance hope that their commitment to dance is respected. Moreover, they wish to get support for their artistic development from people who are close to them. They also hope to make their parents proud. Estrangement between the boy who dances and his significant other(s) can take place if the two are unable to apply a discourse that makes dance appear positively for both parties. Rebonding between the two is possible through such a discourse. Moreover, as discussed in the next section, a conflicting position can

2   For interviews on boys in dance where the discourse of hard work is present see for example Innanen (1997), Sarjas (1995), Sairo (1990), Hietalahti (1996), Silenius (1991) and Leinonen (1994).

cause significant tension for a young male in dance, particularly if his social background and his dance interest clash.

Dance and the Conflicting Selves

As Bronwyn Davies points out from a poststructuralist point of view,

> contrary to much of our experience, a consistent thread running through our discursive practices is the idea of each person as unitary, coherent, non-contradictory and as fixed in certain ways. (2002, p. 281)

In relation to this, a thought-provoking self-narrative is interwoven in Tuomo Luhtanen's (1998) MA dissertation, which elucidates how dance studies in Theatre Academy influenced the author's male identity. In the dissertation, Luhtanen refers to his rural background, 'traditional' upbringing, military service and a job in a factory to construct his identity prior to his dance studies. In the following extract he locates his new position as a dance student in higher education against the backdrop of his former identity:

> In my previous studies and jobs where the work atmosphere had been male-dominant, I was used to taking orders from a man. Lunch breaks were filled with dirty jokes and chat about car maintenance. When I came to Theatre Academy, these moments of chat between classmates were naturally missing. I don't say I miss that. I'm only trying to say that it was a rather big change. (Luhtanen 1998, p. 17)

The references to male supervision in the author's school and work history, sexist humour and 'car-talk' locate the author's former identity within a working class masculinist context. The realm where his dance studies take place is constructed as radically different from this context. Thus, there is a major gap between the author's social background and his new position as a student within an urban academic and artistic dance context, which is generally considered as a feminine realm. The following extract where Luhtanen writes about dance from the perspective of his former identity exemplifies such gap:

> If in those days someone had claimed that dance too is work, I would not have believed it. I was a boy from the countryside whose dream since childhood had been to become an actor. Dance had entered the picture only a few years before the theatre school started. I knew very little about dance and the names in Finnish contemporary dance were unfamiliar to me. Among dancers I was in an entirely strange world. (Luhtanen 1998, p. 15)

From the rural working class perspective dance, unlike theatre, is located outside the occupational realm in the extract. In addition, from this outside perspective the author sees himself located in the alien realm of dance.

As the next extract shows, the author's social position and the discourses through which dance is perceived in that position make it difficult for the author to negotiate his identity as a dance student:

> It was rather sad to notice that before the school started none of my friends was interested in my dance hobby. Dancing was not men's work. As [the programme in] Theatre Academy started, people's interest increased remarkably. I had been accepted in a place that made a certain impression just with its name. I was happy. (ibid.)

In this extract, dance constitutes a tense relationship between the author and his close peers who have very little or no knowledge to maintain an informed discussion on theatrical dance. From a masculinist perspective, they perceive dance as an improper occupation for males. For these reasons, talking about dance has little or no value as a legitimate form of social capital to them, which shows in their lack of interest.

However, it is remarkable that in Luhtanen's narrative his connection to a formal institution in higher arts education brings him social credibility in the eyes of his peers. It can be argued that the name of the Theatre Academy carries a certain masculinist marker that was attached during Jouko Turkka's period as a principal of the school in the 1980's. Turkka is a well-known Finnish theatre director whose shaven head, intense focus, high physicality, loud voice and straight-

228

forward attitude can be easily interpreted as ragingly masculine, even aggressive. Following Bourdieu (1985), it can be argued that the discourse of masculinism that links to the name of the Theatre Academy through Turkka operates as a form of social capital that has validity within a masculinist culture. Hence, the Theatre Academy, as an established institution that is marked masculine, helps the author to favourably re-position himself as a dance student in relation to his peers and to gain social credibility within his peer-group.

Yet, as the following extract shows, the tension between a masculinist discourse and Luhtanen's dance interest remains unsolved in the self-narrative:

> I had to change my conception about myself as a person. Earlier, it had always been easy to be a man because I had never had to suspect my own maleness ... My doubts emerged already after the first year [in the Theatre Academy]. I tried to prop up my maleness by force. I was afraid that I was taken for being gay if I was not masculine enough. Emphasising one's masculinity must have looked pretty stupid, I am sure. When I performed, I was very serious and overly dramatic. I acted determined and was afraid of softness. Yet, I had no other means at my disposal because my upbringing and what I had learned were located [in the Theatre Academy] in an environment that was different and new to me. The idea that someone might take me for something that I was not was scary, although I myself did not really know who I was. In that point, my self-assertion was still missing. The school [the Theatre Academy] had led my mind into a very chaotic state. (Luhtanen 1998, p. 15)

The extract describes how the author's earlier unquestioned conception of the self as a heterosexual man starts to disintegrate in the new position as he enters the dance programme in the Theatre Academy. A fantasised 'other' that judges the gendered performance of the author and makes authoritative statements about his sexuality is constructed in the self-narrative. Being labelled as gay marks the author negatively in relation to the fantasised other whose hetero-normative position is never questioned. The label of homosexuality also marks him negatively in relation to the masculinist discourse. Hence, doubts about one's social credibility as a marked man lead the author to perform masculinity in excess to counteract the socially negative mark of homosexuality. In Foucauldian terms it can be said that the discourse of heteronormativity operates on the author-subject through fantasised technologies of social surveillance and normative judgement. As the author-subject submits to the power of hetero-normativity, his body turns into a 'vehicle' for the heteronormative masculinist discourse that the body embodies and performs (see Foucault 1995).

Luhtanen (1998) blames the institution where he studies for his 'identity crisis' as follows:

> I would have needed more male teachers for my support at school because from them I would have received the necessary model of the male dancer's being. At least I would have been able to make comparisons. Because women dominate the entire field, I had little chance to identify with them [male dance teachers] … Me stumbling with my maleness was very much caused by the fact that the teaching of female teachers did not bring me closer to masculinity but, rather, away from it. Women, of course, teach only from the female point of view … I think the difficulty with everything was that the education was dominated by women. I had nothing against women, on the contrary. Few men get to spend their days with attractive young women. (Luhtanen 1998, p. 17)

In the extract, the self as a male dance student is positioned in relation to fantasised others, the absent male dance teachers, that the author constructs as desired role models for himself. These fantasised men are constructed as holders of certain knowledge about male dancing that the author lacks. Dominant women in the dance programme are constructed as obstacles between the author and his desire and they are blamed for hindering the author's attempt to find the 'Holy Grail' of male dancing. They are constructed as sirens that lead the author away from his masculine mission into bewilderment over his identity. Further, their knowledge on dance and teaching of dance is constructed as feminine knowledge. That is, their teaching emerges from a single 'female' perspective that does not help the author to become a 'man' in dance.

A 'disclaimer', 'a verbal device which is used to ward off potentially obnoxious attributions' (Potter and Wetherell 1987, p. 48), can be recognised from the second last sentence in the extract. In this particular context the author's claim that he has 'nothing against women' can be interpreted as an attempt to protect the author from attributions of sexism. What follows the disclaimer is particularly striking. The last sentence of the extract can be read in two ways: on one hand, it can be interpreted as a compliment to female beauty; on the other hand, it can be taken as an act of bragging through which the author affirms his heterosexual orientation as he boasts with his exclusive position as a 'cock in a hen-house'. In both of these readings women are positioned as objects for the heterosexual male gaze. Hence, a clear masculinist sexist discourse can be recognised to be operating in the extract. Women are constructed as unfit dance teachers for the author but they serve well as objects of consumption.

There is a curious bias in Luhtanen's (1998) self-narrative. He blames the female teachers in the institution where he studies for making him confused over his male identity. He also maintains that his social and cultural background provides him with the means to cope in the environment of dance that is new to him. He overlooks, however, the effect of the heteronormative masculinist discourse that operates through his social and cultural background. It can be argued that the confusion over his male identity emerges precisely because his means to cope are embedded in a heteronormative masculinist discourse. The overwhelming power of such a discourse makes it difficult for him to reconcile his identity in relation to the two social groups: one where he identifies himself as a heterosexual working class country boy; the other where he positions himself a male dance student in a terrain that is dominated by women.

As Foucault (1995) claims, discursive practices shape the body. In dance education such practices do not only bring out a metamorphosis in the flesh, they also introduce new ways of moving and perceiving one's corporeality. Luhtanen describes the changes in his body as follows:

> The teaching methods aimed to deconstruct the attitude I had learned. We made meditative journeys into the self and tried to listen to our inner voice. It was inevitable that the teaching changed my understanding about life. The psyche also transformed as the body was shaped. I could sense and discern the three-dimensional space around me. I learned to move in a new way and my entire body-awareness expanded rapidly. As my body and movements got free, I myself got uninhibited. My attitude towards life in general became wider and more tolerant. Old principles had to give space to new ideas. The workers appearance grew supple. My palms got soft and they embodied graceful

features and gestures. The man of one posture who had become livelier had more shades. It was not even possible any longer to be the same person I had been when I entered the school a year earlier. There was no longing for being the same person either. (1998, p. 16)

In the extract, soft hands, gracious gestures, liveliness and subtlety that are constructed in contrast to the male worker's posture result from one year of dance studies. The more liberal self is linked interestingly with the more relaxed way of 'being in the body'. As the next passage shows, the author is also tolerant towards himself in this new and less inhibited position:

> The purpose of this transformation was to make me understand my situation. A lot would still need to happen in order for me to understand myself. I realised that maleness was not dependent on external matters. On the other hand, it was easy to be any kind of a person at school because there was no permanent connection to the outside world. All time was school time. (ibid.)

A cultural boundary is perceived between society and the institution where the author studies dance. The dance programme is seen as if it was detached from the rest of society. It is constructed as a place with its own liberal value system where more fluidity can be permitted to construct oneself as a man. For example, the self is freed from the compulsory need to display masculine markers on the body in the realm of dance. However, this freedom is limited inside the realm of dance only.

Elsewhere, such freedom is not a self-evident privilege and, as the next extract shows, the author is driven to live a double-life:

> During the first year at weekends, I tried to get outside the dance world. I escaped to another town to my former mates. There I could have a safe life because they knew who I was. (ibid.)

The tension between the two 'worlds' is evident in the extract. The author flees the world of dance to his 'mates' in his former life where life is 'safe' because he can re-embody the familiar masculinist identity with no questions asked. This 'outside world' is constructed positively in relation to the world of dance that belongs to women and femininity. It is surprising that the author remains committed to dance despite the cumbersome double-life and the confusion that the 'dance world' has brought over his identity. He explains the solution as follows:

> My double-life started to get too burdensome and eventually I gave up. I did not want to run away any longer. Instead, I wanted to face my problems. I started to understand my maleness through other things than dance. It was a big enough cake to understand dance that it created big crises in my life. I obtained my balance primarily through life outside school. A relationship provided a more solid ground to my life. Having a woman beside me, I was able to carry out my maleness in a natural way. (Luhtanen 1998, pp. 16-17)

Following Butler (1990) and Davies (2002), it can be argued that the author's dilemma arises from a discursive illusion that makes him see himself as a single coherent entity in terms of his biological sex, self-concept and acts that are believed to 'express' his 'inner self'. Living in the two distinctive 'worlds', the author becomes aware of his two contrasting selves, or two identities, that cannot be successfully amalgamated. The belief that the 'self' has to be a non-contradictory whole makes it hard for him to embody multiple and diverse masculinities. Dance remains constructed as something negative that has turned the author's life into a crisis by making available to him masculine discourses that are incoherent with his working class masculinism. The link to the 'outside world' and the familiar heteronormative masculinist culture are constructed as a balancing factor, something familiar that brings order into chaos.

As the author suggests, his relationship with a woman balances out his life. The relationship provides him with a 'natural' way to perform masculinity and sexuality in the sense that it lets him carry on in a coherent fashion with the familiar heteronormative masculinist discourse. The female companion marks the author's sexuality for him and, more importantly, for others in society, for example at school as well as among family and friends. As a heterosexual marker, she wards off any doubts about the sexuality of the author as a male dance student. Despite his involvement with theatrical dance the author is no longer labelled as gay because in our culture a close male-female relationship is interpreted from a dominant heteronormative perspective unquestioningly as a heterosexual relationship.

This example shows that males with a strong heteronormative masculinist background can have difficulties in solving a conflict between a masculinist identity that is constructed through their background and the more flexible and open-ended possibility to live one's maleness in a more liberal environment than a dance programme can provide. This is not to say that diversity and multiple embodiments of identity are given space in all dance educational practices across the field of theatrical dance.[3] Rather, as argued next, dance educational practices can enable or limit the embodiment and performance of multiple identities.

Dance Practices that Enable and Limit the Performance of Diverse Identities

Unlike Luhtanen (1998), not all male dance students claim that female dance teachers limit the 'development' of their identity. However, dance practices in different institutions of dance education can be perceived by the students as either enabling or limiting the embodiment and performance of multiple and diverse identity constructions. This argument gains support from the self-narratives of two male post-graduate dance students that are examined next.

In his MA dissertation on lived corporeality, Joona Halonen questions the biology-based categorisation of people into two groups, men and women, as he claims that

> our bodies are multiple in the same way that we mean when we speak about multiple identities. I think there is not only a single sex in people. Femininity

---

3   See Chapters Six and Eight. See also Risner's (2002a) article on heterosexism and homosexual abuse in dance education in America.

and masculinity are present in all bodies. It is up to each and everyone to consider whether to use them or not. (2000, p. 17)

In the extract, gender is defined as a possibility, something that is available for everyone as a resource - much like a wardrobe full of various garments that can be worn on different occasions according to one's personal liking or choice. For Halonen, this open-ended indeterminacy is not constructed as a threat but as a pleasurable opportunity to be playful through dance. In his words:

> Contemporary dance is for me a jigsaw puzzle of masculinity and femininity. In my work as a dancer, it brings me pleasure that I can combine different sides of me. I see, for example, the use of strength, jumps and acrobatics as masculine characteristics. I have experienced the encounter with feminine softness and elasticity as well as dance-like sustained movement combinations as a challenge. Just in the exploration of new movement qualities, through physical difficulties, I need to face mental knots. As a psycho-physical entity, I find dance and movement are great opportunities to carry out and bring forth humanity, the creature that is real, honest and fragile. For me, it is not a man or a woman but a bit of both. (Halonen 2000, p.17-18)

The author constructs himself as a multifaceted being in the extract. Masculinity and femininity are seen as different facets that can be incorporated in different ways. In that sense, gender is constructed as a playful fluidity rather than something that is essentially fixed. Dance is perceived as a pleasurable site that makes the embodiment and performance of multiple gendered discourses possible. The value of such play is evident as it enables the deconstruction of fixed concepts, or what the author calls 'mental knots'. It helps the author reach beyond the strict division of binary categories man-/woman and see such division as 'heterosexist' (Halonen 2000, p. 17). Yet, even as a gender hybrid, the dancing subject, as described in Halonen (ibid), is unable to dissolve the binary opposition through which gender is perceived. It is merely left to mix and blend characteristics of masculinity and femininity that themselves are cultural constructions.

Like Halonen, Carl Knif (2000) also provides a self-narrative where dancing is constructed as an important means to embody and perform diverse identities. However, for him such embodiments and

235

performances reach way beyond gender. Well before school age, influenced by dance on television, Knif created homemade ballet performances that enabled him to live through his fantasies. In his MA dissertation on improvisation and its meaning to the search of his own dance, he describes this delightfully as follows:

> As a child, I copied all the dance that I saw, mainly classical ballet on television. I sucked all impulses into myself: visual, musical and physical. I was most mesmerised by the incredibly beautiful costumes and the virtuoso utmost graceful movements, the world that all the elements of ballet contributed to in order to mediate it. My dance was born out of the characters I embodied. On my own, I created a homemade ballet. Toothbrush jugs turned into pointe shoes and from diverse covers and textiles I created stage costumes. The costumes and the role characters inspired my dancing; I could be a man or a woman, a child or a grown-up, an animal or a spirit. One at a time or all of them simultaneously in a mix. Sometimes I did not dance at all, just the process of turning into something else was satisfying for me, I expressed one side of my personality and played with it. The process of turning into someone else mesmerised me entirely. I could plan and prepare my outfit for hours and I did not give up until I had found exactly the right way of using for example a sheet in order to create the illusion I was looking for. The moment I observed myself from the mirror, I understood that that was not I but a part of me that had expanded and become incredibly alike. It was not only my appearance that had changed but also my way to observe and to experience. I was not scared; on the contrary, being secure, I knew exactly what I should do. I found my self in a form of ecstasy where the characters totally mesmerised me. Dance made me happy, not just the movements but also the music, the songs, my entire being. (Knif 2000, pp. 18-19)

The desire for the freedom to construct the self in multiple ways is central to Knif's self-narrative. Homemade dances are constructed as a site of exploration. These dances are described as a means for Knif to identify with, embody, perform and dissolve a spectrum of identities: human, animal, spiritual and gendered. The author's experiences of embodying multiple identities are constructed in his self-narrative as joyful and inspirational metamorphoses where a number of elements - costumes, props, music, movements and images (perceived and imagined) - amalgamate. In contrast, Knif describes his first encounter with organised dance education as follows:

Dance was there, and so was music, when my parents took me to a newly established ballet school. I found the movements and music in ballet, but the roles were too narrow for me to fit in more than just a very small part of me. I got to play with my own creativity and expression elsewhere. (2000, p. 19)

Movements and music are also mentioned as central in this dance experience. However, the organised dance activities in a ballet school are constructed as limiting in terms of embodiments and performances of multiple identities. Learning ballet gives space only to a fraction of that creativity and fantasy that is embodied in Knif's homemade dances. Knif's words highlight that gender operates as a limiting power in and through social institutions as he recalls that

I may have never been as courageous as then ... After that I started in the elementary school and turned into a coward; it is not suitable for a boy to be foppish. (2000, p. 18)

In this section, it has been pointed out that different dance educational practices – and, indeed, different genres of dance – can enable or limit the male dance student's embodiment and performance of identity (gendered and otherwise). As Chapters Six and Eight argue, heteronormative masculinism in dance education is a key discourse that limits the male dance student's performance of gender and sexuality. However, as Knif's (2000) account above points out, boys who dance are also subjected to gendered discourses at school.

Dance, Bullying and Heteronormativity

Boys whose acts do not fit within the dominant heteronormative masculinist discourse in peer groups, particularly at school, are often subjected to hate speech and bullying (Scraton 1995, Kehily & Nayak 1997, Dunning 1999, Lehtonen 2003). Because theatrical dance is an unusual interest for males, this makes boys who dance potential targets of bullying in their peer group outside the dance community.

237

Bullying can be particularly problematic for young male dance students before their self-concept becomes less dependent on their peers' views in their late teens or early twenties. Bullying was discussed in one of the focus group interviews with four thirteen to sixteen year old boys on the dance camp for boys in Siilinjärvi in the summer of 2001. The interviewed boys came from different parts of Finland and they all had taken up ballet at an early age: one at the age of four, the others around seven and eight years of age.

In the interview, the question about bullying followed a discussion about group dynamics and hierarchic relations within the group of boys in the camp. In the camp, the large group of students was divided into smaller groupings of four to seven boys. Informal rules that were intrinsic to the group determined how these units were formed. One's position in the camp depended, according to one of the older boys on

Teemu: how much you have trained, how many camps you have attended and how well you know the older ones or those who have attended more times…

Some bullying took place across the smaller groupings, the boys reported. Particularly some older boys took advantage of their age and size outside the scheduled activities in order to get what they want. One of the older boys commented on this as follows:

Mikko: Well, it works like this, using the power of the elderly [one says that] you don't take that computer or I'll hit you (laughter).

Yet there was also resistance. According to Mikko, 'the younger ones fight back just like the ones who are a bit older'. Minor scuffles among the boys in the camp were not seen as something particularly problematic. On the contrary, despite some scuffles, the boys were generally on good and close terms with each other. In Mikko's words, 'everyone kind of looks after one another'. Moreover, it was appreciated that in the camp 'no one can call you names because you

238

dance ballet' (Mikko). Still, bullying in dance can be seen as part of the tough competition, particularly in institutions that produce professional dancers. As a 12-year-old male ballet student points out:

> There are also swinish persons in the dance gang and one has to be hard-headed to fight against these arrogant blokes. But it would be cowardliness and giving up if one yielded and quit dancing due to the oppressing competition. This is a form that requires grit. (Mäki, K. as quoted in Innanen 1997)

However, bullying that focuses on the male dance student's dance interest and takes place in a peer-group outside the dance context, particularly at school, bothered some of the boys as the following extracts from the focus group interview show:

Int: Have you been called names or bullied?
Eero: Yeah … particularly from such guys who have not been my friends and who are kind of … I have been able to say to them that okay get lost … I really have no interest to see you. Or like those who are perhaps weaker than I am … and also those who have tried to get others to involved because I dance, that I am this kind of girlish (a deep breath) homo who (a deep breath) and … .

In Eero's account, bullying outside the dance community takes place in the form of speech acts that aim to injure the target of these acts. In such speech acts males who are interested in dance are linked with femininity and homosexuality. In addition, such harassment involves more than just the bully and the victim. As Eero's account suggests, the bully encourages others to also participate in bullying.

There are two linguistic coping strategies that are used in Eero's account to discuss bullying. First, he distances the bullies by acknowledging that they are unimportant to him because they are not his friends. Second, he constructs the bullies as physically weaker than what he himself is. Hence, linguistic strategies through which the self is positively distanced from the bully are used to cope with the idea of bullying. As the next extracts show, there are also other such strategies.

Mikko: Well, that calling dancing or ballet names goes really so around the corner (.) … it really has nothing to do with ballet when you are being called with names.

Eero: Mmm.

Mikko: Instead, what they try to do is to injure you in some way.

Eero: Mmm.

Mikko: Well, even if you did not dance ballet, they would find some other way to hurt you.

Eero: Well yeah.

Mikko: So it really does not matter whether you dance ballet or not.

It is denied in this short dialogue that dancing per se has anything to do with bullying. Instead, Mikko is pressing an argument that the bully is first and foremost interested in the act of bullying. Such a person continues harassing others no matter what. The act of constructing the bully as an inevitable problem serves as a linguistic strategy that has great significance to these boys because it relieves the speakers from perceiving themselves and their dance interest as something negative that causes bullying. Moreover, this argumentative strategy guards against the idea that one should give up dance to avoid being bullied because the cause of bullying is located in the bully and not in one's own dance interest.

The idea of confronting the bully or those who use hate speech against males in dance is introduced in the focus group interview by Teemu as follows:

Teemu: Well but, one has to say back [to the bully] … go to see a performance somewhere so that you'd get a better idea about this [art] form. That's what one can say straight at them.

Eero: Yeah, it would be nice [to say it] like that, that one could.

Teemu: But they don't take it into consideration at all.

Jaakko: Because they would be like, I'm sure I'll go to see something.

It could be maintained that confronting the bully requires significant courage that not all victims of bullying have. As the extract shows, it is difficult for the boys to speak about such 'weakness'. Eero's reference to the lack of courage to confront the bully is left uncommented. Instead, both Teemu and Jaakko are ready to propose that a confrontation would not produce positive results. That is, confrontation is constructed as an unnecessary act.

As the conversation continues, Eero plays an imaginary game where he positions himself and the other boys in dance into a position of a non-dancer as follows.

Eero: But ... what if ... one had never taken ballet, that is, if one knew no more about ballet than what I just said about these cartoons where there are precisely these girls who move around with a skirt on ... what kind of a concept would we have on ballet had we seen something similar (.) [Perhaps we would not have called others by names because our personality is such (.) yes, yes, but perhaps we would not call them by names].... .

Mikko: But it depe[nds so much on the personality. Well, I have such friends who].

Teemu: Yeah, about personality.

Mikko: Because I have such mates who know nothing about ballet but it is still kind of okay, a cool form as such [(.) so it is then again quite obvious].

Eero: [Yeah, right but (.) yeah like] some of my mates also think it is a totally okay form because ... they know nothing about it but still because it is my hobby they appreciate it to a certain extent (.) and they would not go to someone and say that it is a stupid form.

As the extract shows, a discourse on personality characteristics that is presented by Mikko is put into immediate use by Eero. He suggests that he and the other boys in the focus group interview have such personalities that even if they knew nothing about ballet they would not speak badly about boys in dance. Thus, a discourse on personality is applied to position bullies as people who have problematic personality characteristics unlike boys in dance. This construction gains additional reinforcement from Teemu's short comment and from

Mikko's reminder that he has peers who know very little about dance and yet think it is okay. Eero points out the same as he introduces a discourse on friendship in the conversation: his friends do not speak badly about ballet because they know him and his dance interest.

As the next extract shows, the discourse of friendship that enters in the conversation directs Teemu and Mikko to talk about the importance of having close friends around if targeted by the bully:

Teemu: Yeah, and if another lonely guy starts to make trouble, there is possibly some other mate nearby who, in principle, can support you.

Mikko: Well, at least for me it has been very [useful], after all, I am rather popular in our school ... so I have such a large circle of friends at school that there are very few who start to call names, and there are friends next to me saying you can't really be serious. It is very useful.

A theme on 'self-esteem' is introduced next in the focus group interview as Mikko takes up the idea that one can change schools if one is bullied:

Mikko: I don't even know whether it would do any good to change school all the time.

Teemu: Schoolwork would no doubt go really

Jaakko: It would get worse all the time and that would make it feel like

Teemu: You sure have a really bad self-esteem if you change school all the time.

Mikko: Yeah, if you can't take what others think about you the last thing you should do is take up dance...

Jaakko: Yeah, it doesn't work out if one is like, that person said something nasty, I quit this hobby, I can never do anything at all.

Mikko: Yeah well, and the point is that if you live your life the way others want you to do it, what kind of a person would you be.

242

As the extract shows, escaping bullying is linked in the focus group interview with low 'self-esteem' that limits one's possibilities to act in the world. In addition, the interviewees suggest that such escapism can damage one's schoolwork. Hence, a victim of bullying who escapes rather than faces the harassment is constructed negatively in the interview. In comparison, good self-esteem is linked with individual decision-making and constructed as a necessary requirement for boys in dance. The last line of Mikko's speech that repudiates those who cannot resist social pressure is rather telling. It points out that a discourse of individualism is strongly present in the conversation and that it is through such a discourse that justification is sought for one's dance interest.

In relation to the discussion on bullying in school, the following reference is made in the focus group interview to the commonly held false belief that all males in dance are gay:

Jaakko: But there is still that stereotype. That is, these narrow-minded people think immediately that, you know, you dance ballet you fucking queer.
Mikko: Yeah, well that is how it is, but they don't understand.

Jaakko's account points out that being marked as gay is not something neutral for boys in dance. As the words 'fucking queer' show, such label bears highly negative connotations in society. Moreover, Jaakko's account embodies a linguistic strategy that is used to confront hate speech. That is, people who use hate speech are constructed negatively as 'narrow-minded' homophobes. Later in the focus group interview, Mikko suddenly moves to ponder about the stereotype of the male dancer as homosexual and, as the following extract shows, this instigates an ardent discussion between the boys:

Mikko: But I really don't understand why ballet dancers are called gay. I don't, I would once like to hear how someone calls [male dancers] gay and substantiates the argument. How do they substantiate it? Think about some ice-hockey team (.) a group, only men in there.

Eero: Mm[m]

Jaakko: [Yes] really

Mikko: And then one boy and twenty girls (.) what, a homo, what.

Jaakko: What's the difference.

Mikko: A homo, how come (.) mm like really not a homo.

Jaakko: Yeah like really (.) ee in ballet it is not a herd of men playing on some field and then they (.) rush to take a shower together.

Eero: [Mmm]

Mikko: [Yeah exactly] but that's precisely it, that on a trip to a performance with girls (.) twenty girls so I can't understand how they can call them gay, perhaps they really (.) are envious.

Eero: Mmm, well, you know, perhaps they think it is a hobby for girls (.) [and if we kind of] think that it is not a hobby for girls.

Jaakko: [Because there are those twenty girls there]

Mikko: Well, sure sure.

Eero: And when (.) one starts to think that they see it as a hobby for girls and if some boys want to try it out (.) they try to be something that they are not (.) then, or well (.) it may occur to someone that such boys are gay.

The extract shows three interesting rhetoric strategies through which homosexuality claims are distanced from the male dancers and also from the speakers themselves: first, the taken for granted heterosexuality of male ice-hockey players is put into question in Mikko's account in the beginning of the extract. The idea is carried further in Jaakko's third passage where some homosocial bonding in ice-hockey, such as showering together, is constructed as potentially homoerotic; second, heterosexual markers are attached to boys in dance in Mikko's later accounts. The male dancer is constructed as a 'cock in a henhouse', a single male with a large number of females around. Heterosexual orientation is underlined with rhetoric questions by asking how can a male in such position be gay; third, a patriarchal discourse is used to claim that boys and men who use hate speech towards males in dance are 'envious' of them because they cannot access women the way males in dance can.

In the extract, Eero presents a different interpretation of the reasons for hate speech. Dance is seen as a feminine practice and for that reason those males who take up dance are positioned through difference. They are perceived as males in a female realm, which makes them unquestioningly gay. Later in the focus group interview, the boys question the negative connotations that are often linked to gays by pointing out that homosexuality can be perceived from different viewpoints:

Eero: On the other hand, if they think that, if one thinks that being gay is like okay
Teemu: A lifestyle
Eero: Okay, it can be that I am not, but just, just if some guy is gay so so what. It's quite different if you think that it is an illness, then you start looking at everybody with a kind of strange gaze, like okay is that guy over there gay or, should I talk to him.
Jaakko: Like, is he looking at me into my eyes, what does he mean, stay away from me.
Eero: Well, that's how the stupid reaction towards them [gays] gets started.

The extract shows that the boys in the focus group find that homosexuality, as an acceptable lifestyle, is nothing outrageous. However, they acknowledge that some people perceive homosexuality as an illness. They link homophobic behaviour to such a discursive view and see it as a product of such a view.

Hence, boys in dance face bullying that has to do with hierarchical peer-relations and competition within the dance community. The bullying that boys in dance are subjected to outside the dance context takes place in peer-groups particularly at school. Boys in dance use various linguistic strategies to talk about bullying. It can be interpreted as ignorance or envy, or the bully can be seen as a problematic personality to avoid seeing one's own dance interest as the cause of bullying. The boys acknowledge that some people see dance as a feminine practice and males in dance as gay. As femininity and homosexuality read negatively in a heteronormative masculinist culture some boys in dance use linguistic strategies to construct the male dancer and themselves to the world as heterosexual. The excessive need for some of the boys to underline the male dancer's heterosexual orientation in the conversation shows the compelling power of the heteronormative discourse. However, such a discourse is unable to silence deconstructive voices that in the examined focus group interview also shed light on the discursive underpinnings of the negativity that embraces the stereotypical notion of the male dancer as gay.

On the basis of the analysis presented in this chapter, it can be argued that boys in dance negotiate and perform their identities in self-narratives that they tell to themselves and to others. In such narratives, they position themselves in relation to other people inside and outside the dance context. In addition, they construct themselves in relation to the culturally prevalent heteronormative masculinist discourse that operates in self-narratives often as an oppressive power through imagined or real 'voices' of the other.

Bullying is identified as another oppressive practice that outside the dance context focuses on the dance interest of boys in dance. In the act of bullying, dance is constructed through the culturally prevalent discourse of masculinism as a feminine practice and the male dancer as gay. In everyday contexts where the discourse of masculinism prevails these discursive interpretations mark down the social credibility of boys who dance. Such negative marking exemplifies quite clearly that femininity, homosexuality and dance are oppressed categories in Finnish society. To avoid carrying a negative mark, some boys in dance protect themselves with discursive rhetoric and performances of heterosexuality. At the same time, such self-protective practices produce and sustain heteronormative social order.

246

Positioning the 'self' as a male in dance can be problematic because such positioning is subject to what Shotter (1985, 1989) calls 'social accountability'. That is,

> we *must* talk [and perform also otherwise] only in certain already established ways, in order to meet the demands placed upon us by our need to sustain our status as responsible members of our society, where the 'must' involved is a moral must. For, even as adults, our status is a morally tenuous one, and if we fail to perform in both an intelligible and legitimate manner, we will be sanctioned by those around us. (Shotter 1989: 140-141)

Following Shotter, to avoid negative stigma or punishment, boys in dance are forced to perform gender for others in a way that is socially acceptable. This makes many of them stick to a constructed reality that they share with others in heteronormative society and use 'the *already established* ways' (Shotter 1989, p. 141, original emphasis) to perform masculinity that is imposed on them in dance education and elsewhere in society. As examples in Chapter Seven show, male dance students use culturally dominant discursive resources to position themselves in relation to others by calculating what kind of responses their performance of gender instigates in others. Following Shotter (1989), their 'anticipated responses' can be seen crucially as part of their 'self-consciousness'.

Thence, boys in dance do not access culturally dominant discourses habitually but because there is a socially prevalent moral code and because they want to have a recognised position and a 'voice' in society. In that sense, the 'freedom' of these boys to perform gender and sexuality is limited by the discourses that are culturally available to them but also by the discourses that are considered as valid social capital within the groups they interact. In this light dance for boys appears as a site of oppression where distance is taken from women, effeminacy and homosexuality to maintain social accountability.

Chapter Eight
The Fear of Dancing 'Queerly'

Heteronormative Masculinism: A Doxa in Dance for Boys

On the basis of what has been recognised in previous chapters, it can be argued that heteronormative masculinism operates as a 'doxa' in boys' dance education.[1] As a key discourse, it oppresses boys in dance by restricting their embodiment and performance of gender and sexuality. As Worton and Still suggest, 'relations of production and the socio-political context ... [can] be included within a broad definition of *text*' (1990, p. 1). Thus, when culturally dominant discourses, such as heteronormativity, operate in these vast textual fabrications they also powerfully influence texts on boys' dancing. In addition, they induce social practices and, also, acting subjects inside and outside the dance educational context. It is crucial to understand that meanings attached to male dancing through the 'doxa' of heteronormativity are biased rather than 'neutral' or 'natural'. The intertextual analysis presented in this chapter aims to 'unsettle' such doxa by explicating culturally prevalent discourses that force boys in dance to embody masculinism and perform maleness in a narrow heteronormative register.

The focus of this Chapter is effeminacy and homosexuality: two negatively marked signifiers in male dancing. The relationship between texts from Western Enlightenment, Finnish political and

---

1   Following Barthes, 'doxa' can be defined as "a stereotypical meaning, a fragment from the intertextual environment of the social text, constituted by established discourses, by the already written and the already read. But *doxa* expresses the already written as if it were literal, representational, denotative and, thus, as if it were natural" (Allen 2000, p. 91).

cultural history, queer theory of the late 20th century and accounts on boys and dance from dance teachers and other authorities in Finnish theatrical dance from mid to late 20th century are examined to provide a broader interpretation about the emergence of such negative marking. The way the threads are drawn across and between various discourses and the way different texts are juxtaposed with each other is an intertextual interpretation from the perspective of the author of this book.

Clean Finnish Dancing

The first all-male dance class was established in the Finnish National Opera Ballet School in the autumn of 1959. The same year, public discussion on male dancers and boys in ballet was particularly active. Dance teacher Airi Säilä questioned 'our prevalent preconception that ballet does not suit boys' by defining male dancing 'to a great extent as a sport' (Mäkinen 1959b, p. 16). Explicit reference was made to Bryan Ashbridge, a dancer from the Royal Ballet, who happened to be in Finland at the time partnering Svetlana Beriosova at the international ballet festival organised by the Finnish National Opera. In another article, Ashbridge was introduced as 'an athlete prince' and 'a sports star' (*Helsingin Sanomat* 22. 5. 1959, p. 14). The New Zealander had been playing cricket and football in his home country and coached high jump in the UK before his ballet studies in the Sadler's Wells Ballet School at the age of 21. According to the article 'the muscle coordination he had learned from the sports together with excellent training established the ground for his rapid rising' (ibid). Ashbridge had been offered a contract as a ballet dancer after only one year of ballet training, the article points out.

It is likely that Ashbridge's visit to Finland gave dance critic Helena Mäkinen an idea that sports training should underpin dance for Finnish boys. A few months after the first all-male dance class had started in the Finnish National Opera Ballet School, she writes on boys in dance in a national newspaper as follows:

> For some reason, Finnish boys in ballet have an inclination to become slightly feminine, too delicate, and almost coquettish. Indeed, the fear of such an outcome is probably the reason why so few boys are sent to ballet school. In this group, which had both new boys and boys who were in their second year of study, one could already see posing that is not at all required from ballet boys; 'the prince' should surely not be effeminate. (Mäkinen 1959b, p. 6)

The narrow construction of the male dancer as 'the prince' is problematic. Clearly, the aristocratic male is not the only character that men in dance perform – not even in ballet. Yet, this stereotype makes it possible for the author to treat effeminacy as an inappropriate characteristic of the male dancer. Effeminate behaviour in boys is criticised and effeminacy is constructed almost as a disease that young males catch in a ballet class. By naming the nationality of boys in the Finnish National Opera Ballet School, Mäkinen suggests that turning effeminate in ballet is a particular feature of Finnish boys. Metaphorically speaking, effeminacy is seen as an encapsulated virus like herpes, for example, that lies latent in the body but marks its carrier with a painfully flourishing shame when provoked. From this perspective, effeminacy is constructed not only as a shameful mark on men but also as a 'latent weakness' in young Finnish males. For the virus of effeminacy to become activated, the boys need just a few classes of ballet and 'ta-dah-poof' the undesired 'posing' emerges.

Mäkinen's article provoked a strong response on male dancing and dance education for boys from Ludvig Nyholm, a dancer in the Finnish National Opera and the chairman of the Union of Finnish Dance Artists in his article that was published later the same year (see Nyholm 1959). How the general public perceives the male dancer is not a trivial matter for Nyholm. On the contrary, as the title of his article suggests, it is regarded as a 'problem' that needs to be dealt with. In his words,

> we must eliminate the perception deeply rooted in the rank and file of our nation that, to put it mildly, 'only effeminate men take an interest in dance art'. Where does this perverted idea come from? First and foremost, I would like to

seriously emphasise that it would be highly desirable that the leading arts institution and other ballet schools of our country should as soon as possible receive also real male pedagogues to take care of the teaching of our male dancers on a pertinent and sound basis. (Nyholm 1959, p. 4)

Nyholm's position in the field of theatrical dance in Finland and the strategic place where the article was published, a journal of the Union of Finnish Dance Artists, makes his text an important historical document. The fact that questions about the male dancer and the teaching of ballet for boys was discussed in the media in this manner suggests that representations of gender had become a burning question in relation to the male dancer, perhaps even a potential threat to the field of Finnish theatrical dance in the late 1950's. In addition, Nyholm's (ibid) article is also a useful text for this research from a discourse analytic point of view. It links explicitly to some culturally prevalent conceptions through which homophobic and misogynist discourses operate even in more recent texts on male dancing. Thus, extracts from his article are used in this chapter to draw out textual traces that link to socially dominant discourses and also to recent texts on boys and dance to demonstrate relationships that exist between these texts.

Nyholm's (ibid) text presents a tense relationship between gendered performances of some male dance teachers and what is seen as the idealised male dancer in Finland in the late 1950's. This becomes evident from his use of the words 'also real' in the above presented extract. It is not enough for him to wish that there were more male teachers in dance education, but more specifically these men have to be 'real'. Thus, he seems to ignore the efforts of his male contemporaries who were teaching ballet and other dance forms in Helsinki and elsewhere at the time.[2] It leaves very little room to doubt what kind of men and masculinities are rejected when he writes that

in ballet, the experience of perfect beauty often remains out of reach of the general public only because of the unpleasant posing and wiggling of hips that

2   Repo (1989) points out how a number of ballet schools emerged around the country in the 1950's when the first ballet dancers retired from the Finnish National Opera.

252

can be seen among the earlier mentioned (male) dancers. The (so far) young and healthy Finnish mentality does not tolerate this. (Nyholm 1959, p. 4)

An abstract nationalist concept, the 'Finnish mentality', constructed as innocent and incorrupt, is used to repudiate male performances of effeminacy. The reference to such collective mentality shows that the discourse of nationalism is operating in Nyholm's text. As the next extract shows, the period of war is blamed for bringing this kind of 'corruption' into Finnish dance:

> The attachment and the rationality of the human being collided during the war However, thinking and sound reason woke up the sleeping truth and goodness in us and helps us to carry out the 'nature'. This means that our admirable humanity has re-awakened. (ibid.)

The extract is open to multiple interpretations. It can be seen as a critique against the irrationality of war but it can also be read as a comment on the bonding that went on between men at war, far away from home and women. The references to the restoration of 'rationality' and 'sound reason' construct what went on during the war and immediately after it as irrational and unhealthy. These references show threads of Enlightenment thinking running in Nyholm's text. Such discursive underpinnings can also be recognised in the following extract:

> Our Finnish dance art should not fall back into the state from which it has once risen and changed its character towards a better direction in the eyes of the general public. We must develop and look forward … so that the triumphs, which we are proud of, may remain indomitable. (Nyholm 1959, p. 10)

A strong belief in progress is another notion that illuminates Western Enlightenment. For example in Hegel's writing, history is perceived as a linear progress from past to present as the world moves towards its perfection (Saarinen 1985). This view has been sustained up to present day by some historians who, as Jenkins quoting Carr suggests, perceive that the past was moving, that it was moving in the right direction, and that this right direction consisted of a movement from 'the worse to the better, from the lower to the higher'. (1995, p. 55)

This kind of discursive view on the development of theatrical dance in Finland is evident in Nyholm's (1959) text. This becomes particularly visible in the concern expressed about the possible regression of Finnish dance art. In addition, the announced imperative to 'focus forward' and the command to organise dance education of male students in a way that does not bring down the level of dance achieved show indisputably how the discourse on progress operates as rhetoric in Nyholm's writing. Hence, optimistic belief in progress in dance links Nyholm's text with the Enlightenment notion of accumulation of knowledge. This kind of optimism has been recognised as a central tenet in the discourse of modernity:

> Since the eighteenth century there has been a prominent assumption that increasing rationality is conducive to the promotion of order and control, achievement of enhanced levels of social understanding, moral progress, justice, and human happiness. The pursuit of order, promotion of calculability, fabrication and celebration of the 'new', and faith in 'progress' have been identified as pivotal features of modernity. (Smart 1993, p. 91)

The concern about progress in theatrical dance amalgamates with the concern about national progress in Nyholm's (1959) text. In modernity, such concern is embedded in the Enlightenment idea of the nation state. As the emphasis shifts, particularly in Hegel's writing, from the individual to a more general level, the value of an individual citizen becomes recognised merely as a contributing member of the state. Freedom, which is the ultimate goal for Hegel, cannot be attained without discipline. Therefore it is attainable only under state control that, for Hegel, resonates with the universal reason (Russell 1996; Saarinen 1985; Lloyd 2000). From this discursive position, progress becomes constructed as a public achievement that contributes to the growth of the nation state. This way, in the discourse of modernity, it is possible to see that acts of public persons, such as politicians, scientists, philosophers and artists, represent 'the very embodiment of rational, self-knowing will of the nation' (Connor

254

1997, p. 61). In modernity, such acts are taken to represent progress, an attained level of civilization in contrast to 'barbarism' or 'savagery' (Williams 1988; Foucault 2003). Hence, the notion of cultural progress is constructed in the discourse of modernity, through the Enlightenment spirit, on the idea that '[a]s individuals grow in knowledge, so does the state gain in efficacy' (Gergen 1999, p. 7).

The emphasis on national progress in Nyholm's article becomes particularly interesting if we follow an argument that Finns do not constitute a homogenous group of people and that the notion of Finnish 'cultural unity' is a myth (Lehtonen, M. 1999; Saukkonen 2002). It has been suggested that discursive talk about national characteristics of Finns has been used as a means to level down cultural differences and to unite people in order to make them loyal to a Finnish national identity (ibid). Frequently there have been ideological or political objectives behind such projects.[3] It is likely that this kind of rhetoric was needed in the 1950's when Finland was still recovering from the war. The people had to be brought together to rebuild the country. Also the political position of Finland was more than precarious during the cold war (Jacobson 2001). The historical situation of Finland enhanced the use of 'integral nationalist' rhetoric that historian Jyrki Smolander (2001) recognises, for example, in president Kekkonen's social-political view.[4, 5]

---

3   After the Finnish Civil War (1918), for example, when the Whites had defeated the revolutionary Reds, nationalist rhetoric was used as a means to reunite the nation (Ahonen 2000; Sevänen 1994). A bourgeois-patriotic discourse, the so-called 'white ideology', was applied for this purpose (ibid). The key values of such discourse can be encapsulated as 'home, religion, and the fatherland'; the slogan that even today decorates much of the conservative liturgy. In addition to emphasizing family values, religious virtues, patriotism and nationalism, which can be explicitly read from the slogan, it has been suggested that the white ideology supports an agrarian spirit and military defence (Sevänen 1994) as well as patriarchy and eugenics (Ahonen 2000). It could be added that white discourse is also heavily heteronormative.

4   Smolander (2001) defines 'integral nationalism' as a form of 'organic nationalism'. That is, the nation is perceived as an organism, a body, which is constructed from a number of parts. In organic nationalism, the welfare of the nation goes before aspirations of its individual citizens. Thus, one of the key

The political climate of the late 1950's can be sensed, for example, from Kekkonen's speech to academics in May 1959. He states that 'as a small nation we have no large international tasks' (*Helsingin Sanomat* 31.5.1959, p. 18) and that Finland 'should concentrate on internal affairs' (ibid). He emphasises that cultural progress is a paramount asset to Finland. In his words,

> the rightly handled tasks of the Finnish nation have always taken place in the field of culture. It is now, more purposefully than ever before, that we must gather our strengths to restore our cultural life without forgetting any of its fields. This has to be done fully conscious of the fact that precisely that may be the rescue. Precisely that can return the trust to the free future of the nation, the bright tomorrow of our fatherland... (ibid.)

As the extract shows, Finnish politicians had started to practise a form of self-censorship to deal with the large and powerful U.S.S.R. as a neighbour.[6] Focus was shifted from international tasks to domestic ones. Moreover, the national progress that is highlighted in Kekkonen's speech is underpinned by the discourse of modernity and some of the earlier mentioned key ideas that the Enlightenment philosophy has contributed to the Western way of conceptualising the nation state and its cultural progress. Eventually, the foundations for the Arts Council of Finland and for eleven Regional Arts Councils that were established by the Promotion of the Arts Act in 1967 were laid in the early 1960's (Komiteamietintö 1965, Repo 1989, Karhunen 1990). Kekkonen's emphasis that all areas of culture should be revived must have been good news to Finnish dance artists because

objectives of this type of nationalism is to integrate the people. See also Patrick Hall (2000).

5   Urho Kekkonen was Finland's president from 1956 to 1981.
6   Max Jakobson writes about the political climate of Finland in the late 1950's. He notes that 'Kekkonen's conception of the relations between Finland and the U.S.S.R. was contradictory in so far as, on the one hand, he spoke genuinely about the friendly relations between the two countries, on the other hand, he demanded Finns to treat the eastern neighbour as it was an implacable Moloch that might get angry from the smallest indiscretion or incautious remark' Jakobson 2001, p. 261.

the status of theatrical dance was still unstable in the 1950's (Repo 1989). The revival project made it possible for dance to fight for its legitimacy as a recognised part of Finnish 'high' culture.[7]

In this light, Nyholm's (1959) article can be interpreted as an attempt to construct theatrical dance as socially accountable so that it would qualify as 'high' culture. In the above extract from his article, the marker of nationality and the possessive pronoun 'our' operate as a means to generalise and homogenize. This rhetoric strategy of a nationalist discourse bundles together different practices of composing, performing and teaching dance and turns their products into national property. Following this, theatrical dance, in its role of enhancing national coherence, is said to embody a level of cultural progress that reflects the status of national achievement in terms of human intellectual development.

It can be argued that the project of reviving Finnish culture in the late 1950's involved the use of nationalist rhetoric that influenced how men were understood. A masculinist discourse provided the only socially acceptable mode for men to perform gender in public in this socio-historical context. As is elaborated further in the next section, in order for dance to gain a place next to more established art forms it had to demonstrate its accountability as a pertinent and pure cultural form. For this reason the male dancer's performance of gender and dance education for boys were subjected to criticism and stringent control.

Sanitation, 'the study and use of practical measures for the preservation of public health' (Collins Concise English Dictionary 1992, p. 1191) is part of the social regulating system that Foucault (2003) calls 'biopolitics': a mechanism of power that deals with the

---

7   The Central Arts Council of Finland did not establish the National Council for Dance, however, before 1983. From 1968 to 1982 only one seat was reserved for a representative of dance in the National Council for Theatre (Repo 1989). This speaks clearly about political reluctance towards dance as art even if the Ballet of the Finnish Opera that was established in 1922 succeeded in gaining a more stable position, after several threats to be closed, gradually from the late 1950's onwards (Repo 1989, Suhonen 1997, Vienola-Lindfors 1997, Räsänen 1997, Ahonen 2000).

'increasing organisation of population and welfare for the sake of increased force and productivity' (Dreyfus & Rabinow 1986, p. 8). Biopolitics emerged in Western societies gradually from late 18th century onwards with an objective to make people healthier, stronger and long-lived (Foucault 2003). This makes social sanitation part of modernity and eugenics, 'the planned breeding of the best in society' (Weeks 2003, p. 33), as an example of such project. Paradoxically social sanitation also destroys life. According to Foucault (2003), themes of evolutionism have justified the regulation of population as well as rejection, expulsion, mutilation or even killing of people for improved heredity, longevity and economic profit.[8]

In Nyholm's (1959) article, there is a peculiar link between the discourse on cultural progress and the notion of 'health'. That is, contrary to a more recent concept about fragmented audiences and segmented markets (see Strinati 1995, for example), Nyholm is writing about Finnish audiences, the 'general public', as a mass of people who have something in common: they are 'healthy' people. Moreover, Finnish dance education needs to be on 'a pertinent and sound basis' Nyholm (1959, p 4) claims because 'we must ... guide our young male dancers on a healthy and inspiring path of the dance art' (1959, p. 19). While 'healthy' as an adjective is open to a number of meanings in different discourses, its meaning emerges, in this particular context, through a nationalist discourse of social hygiene and refers to an unsoiled moral purity that is perceived as an indisputable quality of Finnish people.

8   20th century Western history is full of examples of national sanitation projects including prenatal testing, forced castrations of socially 'unfit' and the holocaust (see for example Eräsaari 1997, Foucault 2003, Weeks 2003).

The Trouble with the Feminine

Effeminate performances of boys and men are the key concern of Nyholm's (1959) article. Such performances are constructed in relation to the purity of the collective mind of Finnish people when he claims that 'the Finnish mentality that is (in so far) young and healthy does not tolerate' (Nyholm 1959, p. 4) effeminacy in males. A strong masculinist position that rejects the notion of gender-bending is evident in the extract. From that position, femininity is constructed as a marker that marks men who carry it negatively as something that is not 'sound' or 'healthy'. This raises a question about what makes feminine markers negative to the masculinist discourse.

There have been occasions in Finnish history when masculinist discourse has played a significant part in discussions of the national or ethnic characteristics and virtues of the Finns (Lehtonen, M. 1995 and 1999). Women and qualities thought of as feminine have been excluded almost entirely from such discussions (ibid). However, devaluation of women and the feminine is not just a Finnish phenomenon: it is embedded in Western thinking more generally (Beauvoir 1999, Lloyd 1993). In Treusch-Dieter's words:

> Within Western discourses – from antiquity to modernity – woman has circulated as 'a mutilated little man' (Aristotle) or 'stunted creature' (Freud). Woman is nothing unless she is signified by the Male. She exists only within the male production of significance, which she has to reproduce. According to François Lyotard, 'civilised women are either dead or men'. (1998, p. 15)

From a feminist perspective, it has been argued that Western philosophy that is written predominantly by men is in general preoccupied with two 'fundamental categories ... separation and domination' (Humm 1989, p. 164). From Plato to Aquinas and from Descartes to Hegel, Western thinking is embedded in a patriarchal tradition that subordinates women and disparages the feminine in relation to men and masculinity (Lloyd 1993). Organised around the principle of reason, the discourse of modernity links men and masculinity with reason while women and femininity are associated with emotional qualities. This, as Lloyd (1993) suggests, is reflected in the sexual division as it appears in modern day Western society. The pre-eminence of reason in Western philosophy has participated in constructing the sexual division in the social order, she argues.

As Seidler (1994) points out, the dichotomy between reason and nature and the privileged position of reason in the Enlightenment philosophy are significant to the sexual division and to how masculinity gets constructed as a privileged gender in opposition to the feminine in the discourse of modernity. He notes how in the Enlightenment it was believed that

> through reason alone we can guide and control our lives ... [and therefore] reason comes to define our humanity and that our humanity is cast *in opposition* to our 'animal' natures. (Seidler 1994, p. 1, original emphasis)

Women were generally positioned closer to nature than men in the Enlightenment thinking. Following this distinction, Descartes positioned women as the source of comfort and reinvigoration for men who were occupied in the search for pure reason. Further, Rousseau constructed the feminine as an immature state of consciousness and women as a potential source of disorder. Moreover, Schopenhauer perceived women as immature children (Lloyd 1993).

The rejection of the feminine, that is so prevalent in the discourse of modernity, links to how the Enlightenment constructed women as 'driven by their passions', less capable of rational thinking and therefore unfit to operate towards the common good of the public. Thus, in modernity, signs of effeminacy have been read to signify immaturity or inadequate rationality. Further, emotional signs, or signs of 'passion', that have also been linked with women in the discourse of modernity have been feared as a potential threat to the state. In modernity, feminine signs have not logically belonged to the realm of public affairs that is constructed as a site for strategic action, competition, fight, victory and progress. This is one of the key reasons, it can be argued, why women's contribution to the arts, for example, has been ignored to a great extent or belittled in the history of Western arts.

In Western misogynist society that so entirely mistrusts and, hence, marginalises women, performing femininity is considered a weakness. Hence, in such a society, social performances of dominant masculine discourse can be considered in Bourdieu's terms as 'cultural capital'. In society where

> the man's world, male values and male lifestyles have become the common aims of all, everyone stands to gain from enhanced assessment (both by oneself and others) if they conduct themselves in line with these aims. But they lose once they abandon these objectives – when a man presents himself as a woman. As long as the man is regarded as the superior being, he gives up something if he appears as a woman. (Merz 1998, p. 11)

This links back to the social constructionist notion of positioning through social accountability and the way men use rhetoric to negotiate their social position in a heteronormative masculinist culture.

Effeminate features in the male dancer can be read to suggest softness, playfulness, silliness, and even vulnerability. These qualities can be seen to contradict the politically constructed and publicly distributed image of the ideal male of the 1950's: the celebrated soldier who defends the country, the strong, hardworking, serious and rational man who rebuilds the country and the athlete whose competing body symbolises the determination and the winning spirit of the nation. 'Sisu', the Finnish word for grit or persistency, is a quality that links these three representations of men together. It is also a common word in everyday language to describe the particular tough and determined quality of the Finns. In the climate of the post-war reviving project, it was probably regarded as inappropriate, possibly even unpatriotic, for men to show feminine qualities or playfulness. In this light, male dancing was also at stake.

Hence, the serious demand to discard markers of effeminacy on male dancers emerges in Nyholm's (1959) article through the discourse of masculinism that operates in modernity by marginalizing women and signs of femininity (except as objects of heterosexual male gaze). Such markers are perceived from a masculinist position as signs of weakness or inadequacy, which is a reason to locate females and those men who perform effeminately outside the public realm - the realm of reason that forms the nation state and its achievements of

261

'high' culture. What follows is that theatrical dance has a very small chance of being positioned as 'high' art in this kind of discursive framework unless 'real' men provide it social accountability through performances of masculinism, just like Nyholm (ibid) insists.

Homophobic Discourses and the Male Dancer

While it has been acknowledged that homosexuality can not be linked to any single set of physical or psychological characteristics, it is common for people to make implicit references to homosexuality by explicit references about effeminate characteristics or behaviour of (gay) men (Dollimore 1991, Weeks 2003). Stigmatisation of homo-sexuals links to 'homophobia'. As the second part of the term indi-cates, homophobia has often been conceptualised as an internal state of human psyche, a fear of homosexuality or homosexuals. An attempt to read homophobia merely through the discourse of psychosexuality may, however, fail to see the complexity of this cultural phenomenon and end up oversimplifying it as psychopathology in the heterosexual. As Dollimore suggests,

> we must understand a much longer history wherein homophobia intersects with, for instance, misogyny, xenophobia, and racism. In short the obsession with homosexuality is always about much more than homosexuality. (1991, p. 29)

A way to conceptualise homophobia is to investigate how it has been produced discursively in different historical contexts. In the discourse of Christianity, for example, homophobia has been often constructed through 'an old persecutory view that homosexuality is wicked and unnatural (against God and nature)' (Dollimore 1991, p. 93). Sexology, a scientific discourse on sexuality, contested this con-ception in the late 19th century by constructing homosexuality as an 'anomaly', an 'illness' or a 'perversion' (Dollimore 1991, Weeks 2003). These discursive views were (ab)used in eugenics and in the discourse of nationalism that aimed to protect the nation state, its borders, people, race and culture from 'weak blood'.[9]

Thus, from a discourse analytic perspective, homophobia can be understood as a web of discursive texts where interacting ideas constitute a body of knowledge that subordinates gays and lesbians from heterosexual people. Heteronormative texts that are 'encoded in language, in institutional practices and the encounters of everyday life', as Epstein and Johnson (quoted in Nayak & Kehily 1997, p. 139) note, constitute a significant part of this intertextuality.[10] This discursively produced knowledge can be said to instigate social practices that subjugate non-heterosexual people to oppression, social positioning and violence.[11]

In Finland, these late 19th and early 20th century conceptions remained as the prevalent 'truth' on homosexuality up until the late 20th century. As Juvonen (2002) points out, the 'third sex' was perceived in the Finnish media as a form of 'degeneration' and a 'contagious disease' that was spreading from Sweden in the 1950's and 1960's. Officially homosexuality was lifted from the psychiatric disease classification in Finland in 1981 but this does not mean that the influence of a psychiatric discourse has vanished from everyday articulations on homosexuality (Stålström 1997; Juvonen 2002; Parkkinen 2003). In addition, homosexuality was criminalized in Finland up until 1971. It was only in 1988 that a review was undertaken in the country to reform the penal code that stems from 1889. The anti-discrimination legislation, including discrimination on grounds of sexual orientation, came into force in 1995 and it was only in 1999 that the censorship law against measures that encourage homosexuality was lifted (Hiltunen 1998, Parkkinen 2003). The law

9   See Plant's summary (quoted in Dollimore 1991, p. 93) of some of the nationalist responses to Doctor Magnus Hirschfeld's attempt in 1898 to change the general view on homosexuality in Germany.

10   Following Jackson, heteronormativity is defined here as 'the normative status of heterosexuality which renders any alternative sexualities "other" and marginal' (1999, p. 163).

11   On oppression of gays and lesbians, see, for example, Sinfield (1993) and Connell (1995).

regarding the registration right for same sex couples came into force no earlier than the spring of 2002 while the question about adoption rights for same sex couples is still not possible. In this context, it is hardly surprising that the notion of 'good citizenship' has embodied heteronormative requirements in Finnish culture (see Gordon & Lahelma 1998, Lehtonen 2003).

From this perspective, it can be seen that there is more than just performance of effeminacy in male dancing that concern Nyholm:

> The worst problem in our ballet is the few numbers of male dancers. I dare suggest that this is mainly due to the common conception among parents of small boys that earlier in our dance art, there appeared unhealthy currencies and tendencies pointing toward degeneracy. Consequently, there is the prejudice that male dancers in general suffer from a perverted mental life. As children intending to become dancers must start training at the age from eight to ten, parents simply do not dare sacrifice the future of their sons for a career in which the morals of their sons face the risk of falling into decay. It is only when we are able to do away with these prejudices, when we can eliminate these tendencies on stage, in ballet schools and other educational institutions, when there is no more prancing and wiggling of the pelvis in male dancing but vigour, power and agility that the large and sound public longs for and demands, only then we can expect to see more male dancers join our few ranks. We must be honest despite the fact that we have our personal likings. (1959, p. 5)

It can be recognised that the then prevalent prejudiced view on the male dancer's 'perverted' personality is constructed in the extract through a homophobic discourse that is common to the 1950's media accounts on homosexuality. A curious paradox emerges in the last sentence of the extract where it is emphasised that despite individual (sexual) preferences male dancing has to be 'honest'. It can be asked whether the text suggests that non-heterosexual male dancers should restrain from performing their sexuality in public. Nyholm's urge to eliminate signifiers that link homosexuality to the male dancer, embodied effeminacy being regarded as the most visible of such markers, shows that this is precisely what is requested in the text. Thus, 'honesty', in this context, means performing masculinity in a way that accommodates the socially prevalent heteronormative ideal despite one's sexual identification.

264

To sum up, partially due to historically prevalent discourses that devalue and oppress women and non-heterosexual men, and partially due to the political climate, there was an urgent need to rectify how the general public saw the male dancer in the late 1950's. In a context where male performances of effeminacy were interpreted as signs of homosexuality and linked with degeneracy, mental illness and criminality, it was politically dangerous for theatrical dance, which lacked a legitimate status as 'high art', to let males to perform in an 'unmanly' way in public. The effeminate male dancer could potentially damage the legitimacy of the dance art by marking it as a degenerate and morally corrupt form of culture. Hence, non-heterosexual men and male behaviour that did not accommodate the masculinist norm must have presented a serious economic threat to institutions of dance including the Ballet of the Finnish National Opera and the Union of Finnish Dance Artists. This explains the urgent tone in Nyholm's text as he claims that dance education of boys must be organised on a 'pertinent basis'.

Citius, Altius, Fortius

The project of winning that is deeply embedded in modern competitive sports can be linked to the idea of progress in modernity (Eichberg 1987, Klemola 1998). In addition, political and ideological uses of sport are widely acknowledged (see for example Brohm 1989, Cahsmore 1990, Puhakainen 2001). The role of competitive sports has been highly significant in creating national spirit in Finland during the 20th century (Tiihonen 1999, Puhakainen 2001, Tervo 2003, Heikkala et al 2003). It has been commonly discussed that males who do or are committed to sports are seen to signify national spirit and to produce that spirit (see Tiihonen 1999). Moreover, sports in Finland can be seen as part of the national defence work (Puhakainen 1997). This links the project of masculinity in the sports to that in the military. Thus, the idea about the importance of male athletes to Finnish society can be seen to emerge through the interplay of nationalist and military discourses.

Thus, in Nyholm's (1959) article, agile and powerful performances of male dancing are favoured and effeminate ones repudiated. By quoting dance critic Mäkinen at length, he openly welcomes her idea on sports training for male dance students:

> Sports training provides generally the best basis for male dancers. It would be more than necessary that boys in ballet took up athletics and sports vigorously as well ... It would be desirable, of course, that boys got their ballet training from a male teacher who was a true example to them as well as a qualified pedagogue. (Mäkinen as quoted in Nyholm 1959, p. 5, 10)

The sports discourse suits Nyholm's wish to 'wash out' 'degeneracy' from dance because, as Mikko Lehtonen (1999) says, the image of the winning athlete is such that it by definition excludes any references to homosexuality or femininity.

Hence, a gender political strategy emerges through the interplay of discourses of modernity, eugenics, psychiatry and nationalism in Nyholm's article during a period in Finnish history when the infrastructure of arts is about to be reconstructed. By de-feminising male dancing and constructing the male dancer as an athlete the objective of this strategy is to make dance socially accountable: to make 'the popular front ... understand and love our dance art as respectable national property' (1959, p. 5).

Resonance in Recent Accounts

In Finnish dance discussions on males in dance, Mäkinen's (1959b) and Nyholm's (1959) articles are far from single and outdated examples of accounts that devalue feminine or are underpinned by homophobic ideas. For example, in a publication on dance at school that was produced by a task force of Finnish National Board of Education in 1991, dance teacher Ilkka Lampi writes:

266

> One wishes that boys' interest in dancing would become more common and that the level of their teaching would increase, because without boys, dance as an art form is poorer and does not waken wide interest. (1991, p. 12)

If theatrical dance is choreographed and performed by female dance artists only, then, of course, the embodied perspectives are somewhat limited: male viewpoints are missing. It is hard to see, however, that dance would be less valued or less interesting just because it is performed by females and not by males. It can be seen that the embodied view in Lampi's text belittles or undervalues the work of female dance artists. The idea to get more males in dance through dance education is a corrective through which theatrical dance is hoped to gain a more recognised status as an art form in Finnish society. In that sense, Lampi's text resonates with Nyholm's text even if it lacks the homophobic string of social sanitation. However, such a string is attached to other recent 'texts' on male dancing.

Heated public debates on same-sex marriages and adoption rights of lesbians and gays provide indisputable evidence on the continuing homophobia in the late 20th century Finnish society.[12] In such debates those who object to equal rights for lesbians and gays legitimise heteronormativity, for example, by 'referring to Christian vocabulary, to common sense understanding of psychoanalytic terms or to biology and "nature"' (Charpentier 2000). Moreover, 'that which is about to subvert or threaten the heteronormative order … is believed to threaten also the Finnish society' (ibid). Hence, culturally prevalent homophobic discourses also underpin recent discussions on the male dancer.

For example, a psychoanalytic discourse that underpins homophobic concerns on male dance students' 'personality' and mental

---

12   For example, Sari Charpentier's (2000) research on letters to the editor in six Finnish newspapers published during the heated debate on same-sex marriages in 1996 shows the continuing prevalence of homophobic discourses in Finnish society. According to Charpentier, heterosexual gender system is published in 'the writings that *oppose* same-sex marriages and adoptions … as a *sacred order*' (ibid) in the sense that it is considered '*inviolable* [and] guarded by unquestionable authority and continuous control of its integrity' (ibid.).

development is embodied in the following extract from an interview that was aired on the radio network of Finland's public service broadcasting company (YLE) a few years ago. In the report lecturer Eija Jokela from Savonia Polytechnic is interviewed about the dance camp for boys at the Kuopio Dance and Music Festival. She speaks about the importance of parental support to boys' dance interest and continues as follows:

> Surely, the su- support for the hobby comes primarily from home. And also that you understand that dance is not just something that somehow distorts your personality, or that, if a boy does dancing, that he has therefore (.) kind of grown to a certain direction. (Jokela in YLE 1, 13.6.2001)

The discourse about the fear of boys growing 'bent', as used in this extract as well as in Nyholm's (1959) article, explains why parents hesitate to let their male children take up dance as a hobby. Nyholm's article exemplifies how the discourse on moral degeneracy constructs the idea that parents fear risking the future of the male child in dance training for the reason that they believe theatrical dance is a minefield of immorality. Similarly Jokela suggests that parents often have the wrong idea about the influence of dance on boys. This view is expressed also in an article in *Helsingin Sanomat* where three male dance teachers are interviewed:

> According to Lampi teachers acknowledge that men who dance are still in Finland easily regarded as homosexuals. In the world of dance this thing [male dancer's sexuality] has no meaning, but sometimes one needs to talk about it with fathers. "I remind them that not all handball players turn into Finnish Swedes either".
> Most of the men who dance are ordinary fathers with a family, just like Lampi, Turpeinen and Mäntylä. (Nykänen 2003, p. D7)

A prejudiced view on the male dancer's sexuality and the idea that a male child might 'turn' gay in dance is put forth as a fatherly concern in the article. This apprehension, which resonates the homophobic discourse on homosexuality as 'contagious', is confronted in the text with a reference to three dance teachers as family men to assure the reader that 'most' men in dance are heterosexual.[13] Hence, discourse on fatherhood and family are used to fix married male dancers with children unquestioningly as 100 percent 'straight'.

Since the beginning of the HIV/AIDS epidemic in the 1980's,

> the attempt to reaffirm discrete categories of gender/erotic identity has been framed in a discourse of contamination, seepage and quarantine. That this should be so is unsurprising: once HIV was (misleadingly) perceived as a disease *of* homosexuality then it became imperative (for misinformed, paranoid non-homosexuals) to maintain distance not only from homosexuals, but from homosexuality. (Wilton 1996, p. 128)

The discourse of contamination is one of the interpretative frameworks through which gays are constructed in the public discussions in the late 20th century Finland (Charpentier 2000). Such discourse is visible also in dancer, choreographer and dance teacher Ari Numminen's speech in the following extract from Rauhamaa's (1994) documentary on Finnish men in dance. Numminen speaks about his work at school as follows:

> They [boys] always get this kind of (.) I can see it in them that, at first, they are terribly prejudiced. Their first lines are usually "Can you get AIDS in here?" or the sort. Of course, that's because we have these encumbrances as male dancers.

As the reference to Acquired Immune Deficiency Syndrome shows, getting contaminated with a lethal virus is constructed as the primary concern of schoolboys when they enter a dance class. Considering the fact that the HIV/AIDS epidemic has been commonly described as a 'gay plague' (see Weeks 2003), it is obvious that the reference to male dancers' 'encumbrances' refers, in this context, to the prejudiced view that males in dance are gay. In addition, however, because homo-

---

13 There are no statistics available on non-heterosexual males in dance in Finland. However, in the United States, Hamilton's (1998, 1999) survey findings suggest that approximately half of males in dance are bisexual or gay. See also Risner (2002c).

sexuals are constructed as a source of disease, the 'gay' male dancer becomes 'a metaphor for dirt, disorder and decay' (Weeks 2003, p. 102). The stigmata of malady and corruption, which male dancing carries through a link to homosexuality in Finnish culture, are put forth, in Numminen's speech, as the reason why schoolboys are sceptical about dance education. This kind of reasoning constructs schoolboys unquestioningly as heterosexual and homophobic. Moreover, homosexuality is put forth narrowly and in negative light.

In the same documentary, a homophobic discourse operates in choreographer Alpo Aaltokoski's speech as he describes male dancing in ballet as follows:

> Roughly one could say that dance has been seen as something in which men are nebulous oddballs and sort of "homo ballet princes" and the like so, well, this image has somehow, it is not like that any more. Today they do not prance in white tights any longer but do other things instead, and somehow the works are closer to people, to this society and our present life situations.

Binary oppositions operate in the extract to differentiate two types of male dancers: past and present. The past one, which is marked with references to homosexuality, aristocracy and effeminacy, refers to the ballet dancer whose artistic performance is belittled by calling it merely as 'prancing'. In addition, 'white tights', an unusual piece of clothing for contemporary men, are mentioned as the only garment of men in ballet. Moreover, this narrow stereotype of the male ballet dancer, the romantic prince, is ridiculed and nullified by calling him a 'nebulous oddball' and by claiming that this type of representation of maleness has no relevance to people in the present. The references to effeminacy and homosexuality make this construction obnoxious to heteronormative masculinism and, therefore, undermine its social accountability. In stark contrast, the 'other things' that present day male dancers do are constructed as culturally more relevant, or more accessible, to contemporary audiences than the performances of the ballet dancer.

In both extracts a particular rhetoric is used to distance the 'self' from the negative stereotype of the male dancer as gay. In Numminen's account, the pronoun 'we' is used to position the 'self'

270

among other male dancers. By taking up the stereotype of the male dancer as gay, and marking homosexuality negatively with references to schoolboys' comments on AIDS, this stereotype is constructed as a burden to all male dancers. Thus, the act of positioning the 'self' and other males in dance as victims of homophobia can be seen as an attempt to distance the 'self' from the negative stereotype of the male dancer. In Aaltokoski's account, a position is carved out for the contemporary male dancer, which the speaker identifies with, by marking the male ballet dancer negatively with references to effeminacy and homosexuality. This provides a position that is not constrained by the negative stereotype of the male dancer as gay. Hence, the extracts can be seen as examples of publicly occurring speech where men in theatrical dance perform heterosexuality to negotiate a socially accountable position in a heteronormative society.

Stepping 'Queerly'

The analysis presented in this chapter shows that texts on male dancing from the 1990s and early 2000 resonate with the late 1950's view that pertinaciously rejects homosexuality and male performances of effeminacy as damaging. The rejection of effeminacy in male dancing can be understood as a body politic that is embedded deep in the history of Western thinking. Such a politic strives towards maintaining a consistent masculine identity because women and femininity are seen, in Western thinking, as inferior to men and masculinity. Moreover,

> femininity becomes located in women, who then become the bearers of and come to signify all that is threatening to masculine identity. (Burr 1998, p. 111)

Femininity comes to represent something contagious that 'must be constantly kept under control, constantly supervised' (ibid). Thus, rejecting femininity and endorsing masculinity in everyday perform-

271

ances of gender can help men to 'feel that their own bodies are safe from contamination by femininity' (ibid.).

In a similar way, homophobia can be seen as a practice of drawing boundaries around what constitutes 'real' masculinity (Connell 1995, Burr 1998). However, as the extracts examined in this chapter show, 'the boundary between straight and gay is blurred with the boundary between masculinity and femininity' (Connell 1995, p. 40). That is, being gay is linked with femininity and markers that are seen to mark effeminacy in male dancing are taken to signify homosexuality of the male dancer. Moreover, the same boundary is blurred between healthy and unhealthy, progress and degeneracy, patriotism and disloyalty. Through various heteronormative discourses homosexuality and male performances of effeminacy come to represent something negative, something that stigmatises males in dance and constitutes a 'problem' for educational programmes in dance for boys.

A questionable reason to argue for 'straight' performance in dance is the fear that 'queer' steps can make dance art fall backward in terms of cultural progress. Due to the prevalence of heteronormative politics in the 20th century and the discourses these politics have brought to undermine homosexuality, stepping 'queerly' – male performances that clash with masculinism – has been carrying a negative marker. Flagging 'queer' has been seen as politically dangerous for theatrical dance in Finland because it refuses to conform to the heterosexist order and therefore undermines the taken for granted position of heterosexuality as 'normal, good, worthwhile, true, [and] pure' (Cranny-Francis et al 2003, p. 75). In that sense, performing 'queerly' threatened the art of dancing with a marker of corruption, which risked theatrical dance its position as 'high' art in Finnish culture in the late 1950's.

In the liberal climate of current arts politics, there is no reason to suggest that dancing which confronts heteronormative embodiments of gender threatens the status of theatrical dance in Finland. On the contrary, choreographers and companies that enhance the Finnish art scene with such performances have been well funded. In that sense, the recent funding structure speaks highly of democratic values that underpin public arts funding in Finland. However, funding of dance institutions in basic arts education is almost entirely dependent on the tuition fees that people pay. Therefore it is significantly more risky for these institutions, in comparison to publicly funded choreographers and companies, to produce dance that clashes with prevalent hetero-sexist norms of society. Hence, the urge in dance education for boys, in the area of basic arts education, to form educational practices and choreograph dances that accommodate the culturally prevalent masculinist discourse.

For many males in dance the constructed stigma of homo-sexuality is an often-faced unnecessary constraint. Young boys can been subjected to bullying because their dance interest collides with what is from a narrow, yet culturally prevalent, masculinist perspec-tive seen as masculine. 'Straight' males can face difficulties in reconciling their dancer identity with their identification outside the dance community.[14]

Also the enforced masculinism in dance education is oppressive, not least to non-heterosexual male students who can find it difficult to accommodate their performances of gender to 'compulsory' heterosexuality. Yet, the stigma of 'queer' dancing is equally oppressive to them because the identity position of an effeminate homosexual that is attributed with negative discursive connotations from sin to sickness and from insanity to infidelity is unattractive to anyone who wishes to avoid dancing in the 'closet'.[15] It is most certainly a narrow position to some of the openly gay male dance artists such as Simo Heiskanen, Tuomo Railo, Ismo-Pekka Heikin-heimo and Lassi Sairela to name but a few, whose performances have successfully eroded fixed categories of gender and sexuality.

Hence, the production of male dancers through various mascu-linising body technologies in dance education is connected to a

14   See Chapter Seven on bullying and reconciling one's dancer identity with the identity outside the dance community.
15   Dancing in the closet is defined here as a condition when a non-heterosexual person in dance has not openly revealed her/his sexual orientation. That is, s/he has not 'come out' yet.

significantly more complex question about the legitimacy of dance art in Finland. Moreover, male dancing is intricately linked with the notion of social accountability in Finnish society where hetero-normative masculinism is a prevalent and dominant discourse.

Chapter Nine
Conclusions

From a queer theory perspective, this book has examined articulations in dance educational discourse and accounts of young males in dance. The aim has been to explicate tensions in boys' dancing to provide new understanding of the discourses that produce such tensions. The approach presented in this book is a multi-perspective one in the sense that combinations of methodologies and various theories, that can be located under the umbrella of social constructionism, have been applied for examining such complex phenomena. A literature review, focus groups and observation of dance classes and choreographies were used to collect multiple forms of data on articulations of boys' dance education and of male dance students' social position. An approach that combined a dance analytical perspective with elements from relevant discourse analytic perspectives was applied to examine extracts from the data in order to pull out discourses that underpinned the examined articulations.

In conclusion, it has been shown that the concept of 'boy' constitutes a nodal point for the discourse of boys' dance education. Other concepts in this discourse receive their meaning in relation to this privileged signifier. As 'boy' is a floating signifier – there are multiple and even contradictory views on young males – there is no unanimous view on boys' dance education. However, often these views are reductionist and essentialist in the sense that the male body as well as young males' personalities, identities, interests and motivations are believed to emerge from the fixed male 'nature'. In dance, boys receive additional meanings through their marginal position in dance education and also through the male dancers' marginal position in society. These discursively constructed meanings shape boys' dance education together with a myriad of other discourses.

In dance for boys, the dance student is subjugated to discursive practices that emerge, of course, through different genres and styles of dancing. In training, the male dancer's body is also subjected to discourses of play and games, sports training, nutrition and drama. More importantly, however, he is subjected to heteronormativity and the discourse of sex-difference through the biology-based as well as psychological essentialist discourses. He is also subjected to masculinism as a culturally dominant heteronormative discourse that is produced in boys' dancing through intertextual references from Western history writing, literature, popular culture, sports, the military discourse and nationalism. Such masculinism embraces masculinities of heroism, militarism, athleticism, patriotism, and the warrior masculinity. In opposition to these masculinities, effeminate masculinity and homosexuality are collapsed together and constructed as otherness through the homophobia and misogyny that are embedded deep in Western thinking. These biases are maintained through a nexus of discourses including, for example, Christianity, Enlightenment, medicine, psychology and eugenics. Furthermore, the male dance student's body becomes a vehicle that carries and disseminates discursive statements on gender and sexuality in a dance class and on stage.

In the West the male dancer, perceived stereotypically as an effeminate homosexual, has been marginalised and looked down upon since the 19th century. In dance educational institutions, attempts have been made to erase this common stereotype in order to get more boys involved. This has been done by 'straightening out' male dancing with masculinist performances. This book argues that heteronormative masculinism operates as a doxa in boys' dance education. The teaching content and methods in boys' dancing tend to accommodate the culturally prevalent masculinist norms that dominate in Finnish society. For example, multiple masculinities performed in dances that have been choreographed for male students are almost always constructed as heterosexual and masculinist. Non-heterosexual masculinities are rarely performed and even then such masculinities are marginalised or treated negatively. For this reason boys' dance education provides limited possibilities for students to identify themselves with in terms of gender and sexuality. Equally limited identity positions are provided for non-heterosexual audience members in dances that have been choreographed for male students to perform.

The acts of constructing the male dance student in a way that accommodates masculinist norms and of making him perform heterosexuality are political attempts to distance males in dance from connotations of effeminacy and homosexuality qualities that are perceived negatively in a heteronormative masculinist culture. This has been done in dance institutions by denying dance its own historical context and by constructing it, for example, as a sport or an adventure. It is clear that this has been done to get more males attracted to dance, which in itself is an attempt to masculinise the field of theatrical dance. Moreover, it has been politically advantageous to perform masculinism to gain theatrical dance a better or more legitimate status in a society where dance as an art has had a marginal position.

Individual male dance students apply masculinist rhetoric and performances of heterosexuality to position themselves in relation to others by calculating how others would respond to their performances of gender. Such rhetoric and performative acts function as self-protective coping strategies for boys to avoid a socially negative marking. Culturally dominant heteronormative masculinist discourse is not embodied habitually but for the reason that boys in dance want to have a recognised position and a 'voice' under the prevalent social code that excludes non-heterosexual masculinities. Thus, boys' freedom to perform gender and sexuality is limited to discourses that appear as socially valid capital in the social environments they interact in. Therefore, it can be seen that many boys distance themselves from females, effeminacy and homosexuality in order to maintain social accountability or credibility in a masculinist culture.

Through a juxtaposition of articulations on boys' dancing with texts on Western Enlightenment, Finnish political and cultural history and queer theory it was possible to argue that the politic that excludes femininity and homosexuality from boys' dance education is rooted deep in discourses that underpin Western thinking. In late 20th century Finland, such a politic was formed through culturally prevalent discourses that construct women as inferior and gays as perverts, criminals or mentally ill. While there is no valid justification

277

for such out-dated discourses, their persistence in articulations on boy and dance shows the power of heteronormative masculinism to turn boys' dancing into a site of oppression.

While gender research in dance has traditionally focused on women's oppressed position as well as representations of male and female dancers on stage, my research brings to light performances of masculinity and young males as oppressed subjects in dance education. This research has provided new insights on heteronormative masculinist discourse in dance education that can help teachers and other practitioners in the field of dance to become aware of such a discourse. The book can encourage teachers to seek more democratic dance educational practices although it is beyond the scope of this book to provide practical suggestions on how such practices should be constructed. Thus, here opens up a clear possibility to extend research on dance education and gender in the future.

There were some drawbacks in my research in terms of the use of secondary sources such as articles from newspapers and magazines. That is, such sources provided often interesting direct and indirect citations on boys' dancing. However, articles are always already interpretations made by their authors. As secondary sources, they did not provide a direct access to the constructed 'reality' of those teachers and students who were interviewed in the articles. Such texts provided, nevertheless, illuminating examples on discourses through which male dancing has been addressed and made sense of in society. Therefore secondary sources were included in this research as part of the corpus of data, which also included plenty of firsthand articulations from boys and their teachers. Moreover, multiple types of data were collected from various sources with a nexus of methodologies to ensure that the corpus of data was rich with different viewpoints.

The research took up parental views on male dancing and socially prevalent views on this subject more generally as boys, their teachers and some authors in the media discussed them in the data. The approach provided important understanding on how the male dance student's social position and the social significance of male dancing were constructed from those particular subject positions. However, the research did not include firsthand data on how parents or other people outside the realm of dance construct boys' dancing. Also, the corpus of data excluded female dance students' articulations on their male fellow-students. These omissions provide fertile possibilities for future research. It would be particularly important to gain discourse analytic understanding on how young males and men outside the realm of dance construct male dancing. It would be equally interesting to find out what female dance students articulate about the presence of male students in a co-educational dance class.

Considering the social environment that focus groups create, the focus group set up used in this research was not the best way to enable non-heterosexual participants to air their views. It was clear that not all participants, regardless of their sexual orientation, were willing to reveal their anti-heteronormative views in such an environment even if, in some groups, sympathetic views towards homosexuals were put forth. Only one of the students and one of the teachers that were interviewed for this research could be identified with certainty as gay in the sense that they had male partners. In both cases such certainty was obtained outside the interview situation. It is hardly likely that a closeted gay or bisexual boy or a man is willing to 'come out' in a focus group or to speak about his position as 'other' in relation to prevalent heteronormativity. Therefore it would be highly important for any future research to address non-heterosexual youths in dance with more feasible methodologies. Focus groups can be used, but the sampling has to have a non-heterosexual focus and the interviews should take place outside any dance institution in a safe environment.

The analyses that were undertaken in my research were limited in the sense that they produced scholarly interpretations from a selection of theoretical positions that have been described in Chapter One as well as elsewhere in this book. It was regarded as justified to use theoretical concepts provided by these positions to analyse boys' dancing because these positions seemed relevant to gender research. In addition, these positions were called forth and therefore also validated by the research questions and parts of the data that were considered as relevant to those questions.

The interpretations produced were contingent upon the body of data that was collected on boys' dancing from seven Finnish dance institutions and from a number of media accounts. It is clear that these interpretations cannot be taken to mirror how dance education for males is organised in all dance institutions in Finland or some other country. Institutional cultures can vary between different institutions and they can also vary from country to country. It is good to keep in mind - particularly because the analysed text extracts were selected from a period of almost 45 years - that institutional culture can also change within a single institution. Yet, the precise value of including an older text, Nyholm (1959)'s article that was examined in Chapter Eight, in the corpus of data was that it provided reasonably explicit examples of some discourses that have recognisable relevance to present-day articulations on boys' dancing. It is clear that older 'discourses do not just disappear or stop functioning' (Taylor 2001b, p. 317) when new discourses of masculinity and male sexuality have emerged in the late 20th century Finland.

The articulations of individual young males and dance teachers that were presented in this book cannot be taken unproblematically to mirror the 'real' views of these people, mainly because, from a social constructionist point of view, it is impossible to get inside other people's heads. Moreover, such articulations have been examined in this book to pull out underpinning discourses. Sometimes it would have required more than just a short text extract to provide a more complete account on how a particular subject elaborated on a particular topic in complex ways throughout an interview, for example. A different methodology that stems from conversation analysis would have been needed to study this kind of phenomena that was beyond the focus of my research. However, to avoid presenting articulations out of their context, contextual information was provided and sometimes more space was allowed for text and dance examples to provide more detailed descriptions.

Performances of masculinity and boys' position in folkdance and social dancing more generally were outside the scope of this book. A masculinity study that compares different types of dancing could provide highly interesting accounts not just on male positions and performed masculinities but also on different functions of dancing for male subjects. A more in-depth approach that compares different genres of dance within theatrical dance could provide detailed understanding on the range of embodiments and performances of masculinity in each genre and in theatrical dance more generally. It would be important to extend this field of research with a study that compares masculinities and male positions in dance education across different cultures to gain a better understanding on shifting discourses that underpin performances of masculinity in dance. It is equally important to analyse how gender and sexuality are performed in dances that are choreographed by non-heterosexual dance students. This should help us understand how, and to what extent, dancing provides space for bodies that resist heteronormativity in the context of dance education.

Throughout this book, I have come to understand that the Holy Grail of boys' dancing is not to be found. It is how such a Grail is articulated – the myths through which we produce dance education – that is important. By giving up our little egos and questioning critically politics that are taken for granted, oppressive dance practices can be replaced with more humane and democratic approaches that appreciate students as subjects who identify in multiple ways.

> Both the true hero and the mystic have to die to their egos, die to an idea of who they are in order to be reborn as something else and something greater ... It is the fate of heroes to lose their old way of living in order to allow a new higher, or mature life to enter the empty space left by their old selves. (Godwin 1994, p. 228)

Bibliography

Abraham, S. Characteristics of eating disorders among young ballet dancers. *Pyschopathology*, 29/4, 1996, pp. 223-229.

Adair, C. *Women and Dance: Sylphs and Sirens*. New York: New York University Press, 1992.

Adams, R. *Freaks and the American Cultural Imagination*. Chicago, IL: University of Chicago Press, 2001.

Adams, R. & Savran, D. (eds) *The Masculinity Studies Reader*. Malden & Oxford: Blackwell Publishers, 2002.

Adshead, J. *The Study of Dance*. London: Dance Books, 1981.

____. The Practice-Theory Dichotomy in Dance Education. *The Educational Forum*, 54/1 1989, pp. 35-45.

Adshead, J. et al (eds). *Dance Analysis: Theory and Practice*. London: Dance Books, 1988.

Adshead-Lansdale, J. Creative Ambiguity: Dancing Intertexts, in Adshead-Lansdale, J. (ed). *Dancing Texts: Intertextuality in Interpretation*. London: Dance Books, 1999, pp. 1-25.

Af Björkesten, M. Tufft program får även killar att dansa. *Hufvudstadsbladet*. 22.12.1997.

Ahjolinna, A. Uno Onkinen 14.11.1922 – 7.2.1994 in memoriam. *Tanssi*, 4/1994, p. 25.

Ahonen, P. Harsohamonen lehahtaa, Suomalaiset käsitykset kehollisuudesta ja sukupuolijärjestelmästä sekä niiden vaikutus legitoitumisprosessiin vuosina 1922-1935. Unpublished MA dissertation, University of Helsinki, 2000.

Alkins, R. Help – there's a boy in my class! *Dance Gazette*, 3, 217, 1994, pp. 48-49.

Althusser, L. *Lenin and Philosophy and Other Essays*. London: New Left Books, 1971.

Anttila, E. *Tanssin aika: Opas koulujen tanssikasvatukseen*. Helsinki: Liikuntatieteen Seuran julkaisu no 139, 1994.

____. Tanssikasvatuksen tutkimuksen uudet haasteet, in Sarje, A. (ed). *Näkökulmia tanssinopettamiseen; suomalaisten tanssitaiteilijoiden ja tanssin tutkijoiden kirjoituksia 1997*. Turku: P. Pakkanen, A. Sarje,

Opetusministeriö & Turun taiteen ja viestinnän oppilaitos, 1997, pp. 115-132.

Au, S. *Ballet and Modern Dance*. Revised and expanded edition. London: Thames & Hudson, 2002.

Austin, J.L. *How to do Things with Words*. Oxford: Oxford University Press. 1962.

Banes, S. *Dancing Women: Female Bodies on Stage*. New York: Routledge, 1998.

Barnes, C. Men in Modern Dance. *Dance Magazine*. October, 1991, p. 106.

Barr, S. & Lewin, P. Straddling Borders: The Proto-Narrative Unit, in Adshead-Lansdale, J. (ed) *Border Tensions: Dance and Discourse*, Proceedings of the Fifth Study of Dance Conference. Guildford: University of Surrey, 1995, pp. 19-29.

Barthes, R. The Death of the Author in *Image Music Text*. London: Fontana Press, 1977, pp. 142-154.

_____. Theory of the Text, in Young, R. (ed) *Untying the Text: A post-structuralist reader,* London: Routledge and Kegan Paul, 1981, pp. 31-47.

Bask, A. Baletin pojilla urheilijan kunto. *Myyntineuvottelija*. 1, 1992, pp. 27, 29-31.

Beauvoir de, S. *Toinen sukupuoli*. Jyväskylä: Tammi, 1999.

Bentley, C. *The Complete Book of Thunderbirds*. London: Carlton Books, 2000.

Bergman, M. Isto tanssittaa pojista miehiä. *Kodin Kuvalehti*. 19/ 2002, pp. 80-82, 84.

Best, D. The *Rationality of Feeling: Understanding the Arts in Education*. London & Washington D.C. The Falmer Press, 1992.

Billig, M. *Arguing and thinking: A rhetorical approach to social psychology*. 2nd Edition. Cambridge: Cambridge University Press, 1996.

Bird, S. Welcome to the Men's Club: Homosociality and the Maintenance of Hegemonic Masculinity. *Gender and Society* 10/2 1996, pp. 120-132.

Bly, R. *Iron John: A Book about Men*. Reading, MA: Addison-Wesley, 1990.

Bogdan, R. Freak Show: Presenting Human Oddities for Amusement and Profit. Chicago, IL: University of Chicago Press, 1988.

Bond, K. How 'Wild Things' Tamed Gender Distinctions. *Journal of Physical Education, Recreation and Dance*. 65/2, 1994, pp. 28-33.

_____. Some summarizing and musings from Karen, in Bond, K. & Stinson, S. *Issues in Observational Research*, an unpublished hand-out from a course on 'Researching Meaning in Dance Education', Helsinki: Theatre Academy, June 1997.

284

Boulton, M. J. Teachers' views on bullying: definitions, attitudes and ability to cope. *British Journal of Educational Psychology*. 67, 1997, pp. 223-233.

Bourdieu, P. *Sosiologian kysymyksiä*. Tampere: Osuuskunta Vastapaino, 1985.

Braisted, J.R. et al. The adolescent ballet dancer. Nutritional practices and characteristics associated with anorexia nervosa. *Journal of Adolescent Health Care*. 6/5, September 1985, pp. 365-371.

Breakwell, G. & Rose, D. Research: Theory and Method, in Breakwell, G., Hammond, S. & Fife-Schaw, C. (eds) *Research Methods in Psychology*. London, Thousand Oaks, New Delhi: Sage Publications, 2000, pp. 5-21.

Briggs, C. Learning how to ask: A sociolinguistic appraisal of the role of the interview in social science research. Cambridge: Cambridge University Press, 1986.

Briginshaw, V. Theorising the Performativity of Lesbian Dance, in *Proceedings of the 21st Conference of Society of Dance History Scholars*, University of Oregon, 1998, pp. 269-277.

____. Choreographing Lesbian Desire: Filling the Spaces, Bridging the Gaps, in *Proceedings of the 22nd Conference of Society of Dance History Scholars*, Albuquerque, New Mexico, 1999, pp. 95-101.

____. *Dance, Space and Subjectivity*. Houndmills: Palgrave Macmillan. 2001.

Brittan, A. *Masculinity and Power*. Oxford: Basil Blackwell, 1989.

____. A. Masculinities and Masculinism, in Whitehead, S. & Barrett, F. (eds) *The Masculinities Reader*. Cambridge: Polity Press, 2001, pp. 51-55.

Brod, H. & Kaufman, M. (eds) *Theorizing Masculinities*. Thousand Oaks: Sage Publishing, 1994.

Brohm, J-M. *Sport: A Prison of Measured Time*. London: Pluto Press, 1989.

Brooks, A. Postfeminisms: Feminism, cultural theory and cultural forms. London & New York: Routledge, 1997.

Brown, C. *Inscribing the Body: Feminist Choreographic Practices*. An unpublished PhD thesis. Guildford: University of Surrey, 1994a.

____. Re-tracing our steps: The possibilities for feminist dance histories, in Adshead-Lansdale, J. & Layson, J. (eds) *Dance History: An Introduction*. 2nd Edition. London & New York: Routledge, 1994b, pp. 198-216.

Buckland, T. (ed) Dance in the Field: Theory, Methods and Issues in Dance Ethnography. Basingstoke: Macmillan, 1999.

Burr, V. *An Introduction to Social Constructionism.* London & New York: Routledge, 1995.

____. V. *Gender and Social Psychology.* London & New York: Routledge, 1998.

Burt, R. The Male Dancer: Bodies, Spectacle, Sexualities. London & New York: Routledge, 1995.

____. R. Dissolving in Pleasure: The Threat of the Queer Male Dancing Body, in Desmond, J. (ed) *Dancing Desires: Choreographing Sexualities on & off the Stage.* Madison & London: University of Wisconsin Press, 2001a, pp. 209-241.

____. The Trouble with the Male Dancer…, in Dils, A. & Cooper Albright, A. (eds) *Moving History / Dancing Cultures: A Dance History Reader.* Middletown: Wesleyan University Press, 2001b, pp. 44-55.

Butler, J. Gender Trouble: Feminism and the Subversion of Identity. New York & London: Routledge, 1990.

____. Bodies That Matter: On Discursive Limits of 'Sex'. New York & London: Routledge, 1993.

____. Critically Queer, in Phelan, S. (ed.) *Playing with Fire: Queer Politics, Queer Theories.* New York & London: Routledge, 1997, pp. 11-29.

Cameron, D. 1996. Sukupuoli ja kieli: Feminismi ja kielentutkimus. [Feminism & Linguistic Theory]. Tampere: Vastapaino, 1996.

Carabine, J. Unmarried Motherhood 1830-1990: A Genealogical Analysis, in Wetherell, M., Taylor, S. & Yates, S.J. (eds) *Discourse as Data.* London, Thousand Oaks, New Delhi: Sage Publications. 2001, pp. 267-310.

Carey, M. & Smith, M. Capturing the Group Effect in Focus Groups: A Special Concern in Analysis. *Qualitative Health Research*, 4,1, 1994, pp. 123-127.

Carrigan, T., Connell, B. & Lee, J. Toward a New Sociology of Masculinity. *Theory and Society*, vol 14, 5, 1985, pp. 551-604.

Carroll, J. & Lofthouse, P. *Creative Dance for Boys.* London: Macdonald & Evans Ltd. 1969.

Carspecken, P.F. Critical Ethnography in Educational Research: A Theoretical and Practical Guide. New York & London: Routledge, 1996.

Carter, A. 'Winged and shivering': images of dancers in the Alhambra and Empire Ballets 1884-1915. An unpublished PhD Thesis, Guildford: University of Surrey, 1993.

_____. Bodies of knowledge: dance and feminist analysis, in Campbell, P. *Analysing performance: A critical reader*. Manchester & New York: Manchester University Press, 1996, pp. 43-55.

Carter, R. *Mapping the Mind*. London: Weidenfeld & Nicolson, 1998.

Case, S.E., Brett, P. & Foster, S.L. (eds) Cruising the Performative. Interventions into the Representation of Ethnicity, Nationality and Sexuality. Bloomington & Indianapolis: Indiana University Press, 1995.

Cashmore, E. *Making Sence of Sport*. London: Routledge, 1990.

Charpentier, S. *Sukupuoliusko. Valta, sukupuoli ja pyhä avioliitto lesbo- ja homokeskustelussa*. Jyväskylä: Jyväskylän yliopisto, Nykykulttuurin tutkimuskeskuksen julkaisuja 69, 2001.

Cixous, H. The laugh of the medusa, *Signs*, summer, 1976, pp. 875-893.

_____. Sorties. In: La jeune née. Union Générale d'Editions 10/18, 1975, reprinted in Marks, E. and de Courtivron, I. (eds) *New French Feminisms: An Anthology*. Brighton: Harvester Press, 1985.

Collins Concise Dictionary. Glasgow: HarperCollins Publisher, 2001.

Collinson, D. & Hearn, J. 'Men' at 'work': multiple masculinities/multiple workplaces, in Mac an Ghaill, M. (ed) *Understanding Masculinities*. Buckingham & Philadelphia: Open University Press, 1996, pp. 61-76.

_____. Naming Men as Men: Implications for Work, Organisation and Management, in Whitehead, S. & Barrett, F. (eds) *The Masculinity Reader*. Cambridge: Polity, 2001, pp. 144-169.

Comaroff, J. & Comaroff, J. *Ethnography and the Historical Imagination*. Oxford & Bolden: Westview Press, 1992.

Connell, R.W. Gender and Power: Society, the Person and Sexual Politics. Cambridge: Polity Press, 1987.

_____. The State, Gender and Sexual Politics: Theory and Appraisal, in Radtke, H.L. & Stam, H.J. (eds). *Power/Gender: Social Relations in Theory and Practice*. London, Thousand Oaks, New York: Sage, 1994, pp. 136-173.

_____. *Masculinities*. Cambridge: Polity Press, 1995.

_____. *The Men and the Boys*. Cambridge: Polity Press, 2000.

_____. The Social Organization of Masculinity, in Whitehead, S. & Barrett, J. (eds) *The Masculinities Reader*. Cambridge: Polity Press, 2001, pp.30-50.

Connor, S. *Postmodernist Culture: An Introduction to Theories of the Contemporary*. Oxford: Blackwell (2nd edition), 1997.

Cooper Albright, A.C. Mining the Dancefield: Spectacle, Moving Subjects and Feminist Theory. *Contact Quarterly*. 15/2, 1990, pp. 32-40.

____. *Choreographing Difference: The Body and Identity in Contemporary Dance.* Middletown, CT: Wesleyan University Press, 1997.

____. Techno Bodies or Muscling with Gender in Contemporary Dance. *Choreography and Dance*, 5/1, 1998, pp. 39-51.

Cox, L.M. & Lyddon, W.J. Constructivist conceptions of self: A discussion of emerging identity constructs. *Journal of Constructivist Psychology.* 10, 1997, pp. 201-219.

Coyle, A. Discourse Analysis, in Breakwell G.M. et al (eds) *Research Methods in Psychology.* London: Sage Publications, 1995, pp 243-258.

Cranny-Francis, A. et al (eds) *Gender Studies: Terms and Debates.* Houndsmills & New York: Palgrave Macmillan, 2003.

Cratty, B.J. *Perceptual and motor development in infants and children.* Englewood Cliffs, NJ: Prentice-Hall, Inc. 2nd edition, 1979.

Culler, J. *Ferdinand de Saussure.* Helsinki: Tutkijaliitto, 1994.

Daly, A. The Balanchine woman: Of Hummingbirds and Channel Swimmers. *The Drama Review*, 31/1, (T113), summer, 1984, pp. 8-21.

____. At Issue: Gender in Dance. *The Drama Review*, 31/2, summer, 1987, pp. 22-23.

____. To Dance Is "Female". *The Drama Review* 33/4, winter, 1989, pp. 23-27.

____. Unlimited Partnership: Dance and Feminist Analysis. *Dance Research Journal*, 23,1, 1991, pp. 2-5.

____. Dance History and Feminist Theory: Reconsidering Isadora Duncan and The Male Gaze, in Senelick, L. (ed) *Gender in Performance: The Presentation of Difference in the Performing Arts.* Hanover & London: Tufts University Press, 1992, pp. 239-259.

____. "Woman," Women, and Subversion: Some Nagging Questions from a Dance Historian. *Choreography and Dance*, Vol 5/1, 1998, pp. 79-86.

____. Feminist Theory across the Millennial Divide. *Dance Research Journal.* 32, 1, 2000, pp. 39-42.

Davies, B. Becoming Male or Female, in Jackson, S. & Scott, S. (eds) *Gender: A Sociological Reader.* London & New York: Routledge, 2002, pp. 280-290.

Davies, B. & Harré, R. Positioning: The Discursive Production of Selves, in Wetherell et al (eds) *Discourse Theory and Practice: A Reader.* London, Thousand Oaks, New Delhi: Sage Publications. 2001, pp. 261-283.

De Lauretis, T. *Technologies of Gender: Essays on Theory, Film and Fiction.* Bloomington & Indianapolis: Indiana University Press, 1987.

Dempster, E. Women writing the body: let's watch a little how she dances, in Sheridan, S. (ed) *Grafts: Feminist Cultural Criticism*. London: Verso, 1988, pp. 35-54.

Denzin, N.K. *Interpretative Ethnography: Ethnographic Practices for the 21st Century*. Thousand Oaks, London, New Delhi: Sage Publications, 1997.

Desmond, J. (ed) *Meaning in Motion: New Cultural Studies of Dance*. Durham & London: Duke University Press. 1997.

____. (ed) *Dancing Desires: Choreographing Sexualities On & Off Stage*. Madison, WI: University of Wisconsin Press, 2001.

Dollimore, J. *Sexual Dissidence: Augustine to Wilde, Freud to Foucault*. Oxford: Clandon Press. 1991.

Donald, R. Masculinity and Machismo in Hollywood's War Films, in Whitehead, S. & Barrett, F.J. (eds) *The Masculinities Reader*. Cambridge: Polity, 2001, pp 170-183.

Dreyfus, H.L. & Rabinow, P. (eds) *Michel Foucault: Beyond Structuralism and Hermaneutics*. Hemel Hempstead: Harvester Wheatsheaf, 1986.

Dunning, E. *Sport Matters. Sociological Studies of Sport, Violence and Civilization*. London & New York: Routledge, 1999.

Dyer, R. Gayness and Gender, in Holopainen, T. et al (eds) *What's that got to do with my gender?* Turku: Turun yliopiston ylioppilaskunnan julkaisusarja. 1989, pp. 51-58.

____. 'I seem to find the happiness I seek', Heterosexuality and Dance in the Musical, in Thomas, H. (ed) *Dance, Gender and Culture*. Houndmills & London: Macmillan Press Ltd, 1993, pp. 49-65.

____. *The matter of Images: Essays on Representation*. London & New York: Routlege, 1994.

____. The White Man's Muscles, in Adams, R. & Savran, D. (eds) *The Masculinity Studies Reader*. Malden & Oxford: Blackwell, 2002, pp. 262-273.

Eichberg, H. *Liikuntaa harjoittavat ruumiit*. Tampere: Vastapaino, 1987.

Eklund, M. *Lärarens syn på samundervisning i gymnasiet*. Åbo: Åbo Akademi University Press, 1999.

English, R. Alas alack: The representation of the ballerina. *New Dance*. 15, 1980, pp. 18-19.

Erickson, F. What Makes School Ethnography 'Ethnographic'? *Anthropology and Education Quarterly*, vol 15, 1984, pp. 51-66.

Eräsaari, L. Sikiö ruudussa, in Jokinen, E. (ed) *Ruumiin siteet: kirjoituksia eroista, järjestyksestä ja sukupuolesta*. Tampere, Vastapaino, 1997, pp. 189-215.

Feuchtner, B. A Dancer Switches Sides: Bart De Block slips into a tutu and pirouettes away. *Ballet International/Tanz Aktuell*, 8-9, August, 1998, pp. 28-31.

Finnish Military Defence 2002. Helsinki: Information Division of the Defence Staff, 2002.

Flick, U. *An Introduction to Qualitative Research*. London: Sage, 1998.

Foster, S.L. Choreographing history, in Foster, S.L. (ed) *Choreographing History*. Bloomington and Indianapolis: Indiana University Press, 1995, pp 3-21.

____. The ballerina's phallic pointe, in Foster, S.L. (ed) *Corporealities, Dancing Knowledge, Culture and Power*. London & New York: Routledge, 1996, pp. 1-24.

____. (ed) *Corporealities: Dancing, Knowledge, Culture and Power*. New York & London: Routledge, 1996.

____. Choreographies of Gender, in Goodman, L. & de Gay, J. (eds) *The Routledge Reader in Politics and Performance*. London & New York: Routledge, 2000, pp. 208-212.

____. Closets Full of Dances: Modern Dance's Performance of Masculinity and Sexuality, in Desmond, J. (ed) *Dancing Desires: Choreographing Sexualities on & off the Stage*. Madison & London: University of Wisconsin Press, 2001, pp. 147-207.

Foster, S.L. et al. Introduction, in Foster, S.L. (ed) *Corporealities: Dancing, Knowledge, Culture and Power*. New York & London: Routledge, 1996b, pp. xi-xvii.

Foucault, M. *The Archaeology of Knowledge*. London & New York: Tavistock Publications. 1972 [1969].

____. *The History of Sexuality, Volume 1: An Introduction*. Harmondsworth: Penguin, 1978.

____. *Power/Knowledge: Selected Interviews and Other Writings 1972 – 1977*. C. Cordon (ed.) New York: Pantheon Books, 1980a.

____. Prison Talk, in Foucault, M. *Power/Knowledge, Selected Interviews and Other Writings*. Gordon, G. (ed). New York: Pantheon Books. 1980b, pp. 37-54.

____. The Eye of Power, in Foucault, M. *Power/Knowledge, Selected Interviews and Other Writings*. Gordon, G. (ed). New York: Pantheon Books. 1980c, pp. 146-165.

____. Afterword: The subject and power, in Dreyfus, H. and Rabinow, P. (eds) *Michel Foucault: Beyond Structuralism and Hermaneutics,* Brighton: Harvester, 1982, pp. 208-226.

290

_____. The Order of Discourse. Inaugural Lecture at the College de France, in Shapiro, M.J. (ed) *Language and Politics*. Oxford: Blackwell, 1984a, pp. 108-138.

_____.The Repressive Hypothesis, in Rabionow, P. (ed) *The Foucault Reader*. New York: The Pantheon Books, 1984b, pp. 301-329.

_____. Nietzsche, Genealogy, History, in Rabionow, P. (ed) *The Foucault Reader*. New York: The Pantheon Books, 1984c, pp. 76-100.

_____. What Is an Author?, in Rabionow, P. (ed) *The Foucault Reader*. New York: The Pantheon Books, 1984d, pp. 101-120.

_____. *Madness and Civilization: A History of Insanity in the Age of Reason*. New York: Vintage Books, 1988. [1961].

_____. *The Order of Things: An Archaeology of the Human Sciences*. New York: Vintage Books, 1994. [1966].

_____. *Discipline and Punish: The Birth of Prison*. New York: Vintage Books, 1995. [1975].

_____. The Ethics of the Concern of the Self as a Practice of Freedom, in Rabinow, P. (ed). *Ethics: Subjectivity and Truth*. New York: The New Press, 1997a, pp. 281-301.

_____. Sex, Power, and the Politics of Identity in Rabinow, P. (ed). *Ethics: Subjectivity and Truth*. New York: The New Press, 1997b, pp. 163-173.

_____. Society Must Be Defended in Rabinow, P. (ed). *Ethics: Subjectivity and Truth*. New York: The New Press, 1997c, pp. 59-71.

_____. The Punitive Society, in Rabinow, P. (ed). *Ethics: Subjectivity and Truth*. New York: The New Press, 1997d, pp. 23-37.

_____. Technologies of the Self, in Rabinow, P. (ed). *Ethics: Subjectivity and Truth*. New York: The New Press, 1997e, pp. 223-251.

_____. *Society Must Be Defended*. London: Allen Lane, 2003.

Franko, M. *Dancing Modernism / Performing Politics*. Bloomington & Indianapolis: Indiana University Press, 1995.

Frosch, J. Dance Ethnography, Tracing the Weave of Dance in the Fabric of Culture, in Horton Fraleigh, S. & Hanstein, P. (eds) *Researching Dance: Evolving Modes of Inquiry*. London: Dance Books, 1999, pp. 249-280.

Frosh, S. *Sexual Difference: Masculinity & Psychoanalysis*. London & New York: Routledge, 1994.

Frosh, S., Phoenix, A. & Pattman, R. *Young Masculinities: Understanding Boys in Contemporary Society*. Houndsmills: Palgrave, 2002.

Frow, J. Intertextuality and ontology, in Worton, M. & Still, J. *Intertextuality: Theories and practices*. Manchester & New York: Manchester University Press, 1990, pp. 45-55.

Gardiner, J. Introduction, in Gardiner, J. (ed) *Masculinity Studies and Feminist Theory: New Directions.* New York: Columbia University Press, 2002, pp. 1-29.

Gergen, K. Constructionism and Realism: How Are We to Go On?, in Parker, I. (ed.) *Social Constructionism, Discourse and Realism.* Thousand Oaks: Sage, 1998, pp. 147-156.

____. *An Invitation to Social Construction.* London: Sage Publications. 1999.

Godwin, M. *The Holy Grail: Its Origins, Secrets & Meaning Revealed.* New York: Viking Studio Books, 1994.

Gordon. T. & Lahelma, E. Kansalaisuus, kansallisuus ja sukupuoli, in Alasuutari, P. & Ruuska, P. (eds) *Elävänä Euroopassa. Muuttuva suomalainen identiteetti.* Tampere: Vastapaino. 1998, pp. 251-280.

Grange le, D., Tibbs, J. & Noakes T.D. Implications of a diagnosis of anorexia nervosa in a ballet school. *International Journal of Eating Disorders.* 15/4, May 1994, pp. 369-376.

Grant, J. Dancing men. *New Dance.* Spring, 1985, pp. 18-20.

Gray, J. *Men are from Mars, Women are from Venus.* New York: HarperCollins Publisher, 1992.

Gray, J.A. *Dance Instruction: Science Applied to the Art of Movement.* Champaign, Il.: Human Kinetic Books. 1989.

Green, J. & Stinson, S.W. Postpositivist Research in Dance, in Horton Fraleigh, S. & Hanstein, P. (eds) *Researching Dance: Evolving Modes of Inquiry.* London: Dance Books, 1999, pp. 91-123.

Griffin, C. *Typical Girls: Young Women from School to the Job Market.* London: Routledge & Kegan Paul, 1985.

Gronow, J. "In food we trust" – kulutuksen vaarat ja riskit. *Tiede & Edistys.* 1, 1998, pp. 1-7.

Grossberg, L. On the Road with three Ethnographers. *Journal of communication Inquiry.* 13/2, 1989, pp. 23-26.

Grönfors, M. Miehen arin alue, Maskuliinisuus, seksuaalisuus ja väkivalta, in Jokinen, A. (ed) *Mies ja muutos: Kriittisen miestutkimuksen teemoja.* Tampere: Tampere University Press, 1999, pp. 223-236.

Hakanen, A. *Perustietoa persoonallisuuden psykologiasta.* Turku: Täydennyskoulutuskeskus, Turun yliopisto, 1992.

Halberstam, J. The Good, the Bad, the Ugly: Men, Women and Masculinity, in Gardiner, J. (ed) *Masculinity Studies & Feminist Theory: New Directions.* New York: Columbia University Press, 2002, pp. 344-367.

Hall, P. *Den svenskaste historia*, Oskarshamn: Carlsson, 2000.

Hall, S. Representation, meaning and language, in Hall, S. (ed) *Representation: Cultural Representations and Signifying Practices*. London, Thousand Oaks, New Delhi: Sage Publications/The Open University. 1997, pp. 15-64.

_____. *Identiteetti*. Tampere: Vastapaino, 1999.

_____. Foucault, Power, Knowledge and Discourse, in Wetherell et al (eds) *Discourse Theory and Practice, A Reader.* London, Thousand Oaks, New Delhi: Sage Publications, 2001, pp. 72-81.

Halonen, J. *Mieliruumis*. Unpublished MA dissertation. Helsinki: Theatre Academy, 2000.

Hamilton, L. *Advice for Dancers: Emotional Counsel and Practical Strategies*. New York: Jossey-Bass, 1998.

_____. Coming Out in Dance: Paths to Understanding. *Dance Magazine*. LXXIII, 11, November, 1999, pp. 72-75.

Hammersley, M. & Atkinson, P. *Ethnography: Principles in Practice*. 2nd edition. London & New York: Routledge. 1995.

Hankaniemi, A. Pitkä oppimäärä balettitanssijaksi. *Keskipohjanmaa*. 10.8.1999.

Hanna, J.L. Resopnse to Ann Daly's attack on 'Patterns of Dominance: Men, Women, and Homosexuality in Dance', *The Drama Review*, 31/2 (T114), summer, 1987, pp. 24-25.

_____. *Dance, Sex and Gender: Signs of Identity, Dominance, Defiance, and Desire*. Chicago & London: The University of Chicago Press, 1988.

Hapuli, R. *Nykyajan sininen kukka. Olavi Paavolainen ja nykyaika*. Helsinki: Suomalaisen kirjallisuuden seura, 1995.

Hargreaves, J. (ed) *Sport, Culture and Ideology*. London: Routledge & Paul Kegan, 1982.

Harré, R. The Language Game of Self-Ascription: A Note, in Gergen, K.J. & Davis, K.E. (eds) *The Social Construction of the Person*. New York, Berlin, Heidelberg, Tokyo: Springer-Verlag, 1985, pp. 259-263.

Harri, T. Tanssi tarvitsee urheilun ja akrobatian energiaa. *Länsiväylä*. 17.11.1993a.

_____. Kenraali Raiko taistelee ja tanssii. *Länsiväylä*. 17.11.1993b.

Haukinen, P. et al (eds). *Taidetanssi Suomessa, koreografit, pedagogit, tanssijat*. Helsinki: Suomen Tanssialan Keskusliitto, 1992.

Hayashi, M. Dance Education and Gender in Japan. *Choreography and Dance*. Vol 5, 1, 1998, pp. 87-102.

Haywood, C. & Mac an Ghaill, M. Schooling Masculinities, in Mac an Ghaill, M. (ed) *Understanding Masculinities*. Buckingham & Philadelphia: Open University.

293

Helkama, K., Myllyniemi, R. & Liebkind, K. *Johdatus sosiaalipsykologiaan*, 3rd edition, Helsinki: Edita, 1999.

Helsingin Sanomat. Joutsenkuningatar ja urheilijaprinssi. *Helsingin Sanomat*, 22 May 1959, p. 14.

____. Pienen kansan tulee keskittyä sisäisiin tehtäviin. *Helsingin Sanomat*, 31 May 1959, p. 18.

Herek, G. On Heterosexual Masculinity: Some Psychical Consequences of the Social Construction of Gender and Sexuality, in Kimmel, M. (ed). *Changing Men: New Dimensions in Research on Men and Masculinity*. Newburry park Sage, 1987, pp. 68-82.

Hietaniemi, H. Poikien omat tanssikuviot. *Kotilääkäri*. 10/1989, pp. 60-72.

____. Tästä pojasta tulee tanssija. *Kodin Kuvalehti*. 15/1992, pp. 64-67.

Hietalahti, U. Ville Sallinen jo kiinni tanssiammatin syrjässä. *Etelä-Saimaa*. 3.4.1996.

Hiltunen, R. Finland, in Berger, N.J., Krickler, K., Lewis, J. & Wuch, M. (eds) *Equality for lesbians and gay men: A relevant issue in the civil and social dialogue*. A report of ILGA-Europe, The European Region of the International Lesbian and Gay Association. Brussels: ILGA – Europe, 1998, pp. 42-45.

Hodgens, P. Interpreting the dance, in Adshead, J. et al (eds) *Dance Analysis: Theory and Practice*. London: Dance Books, 1988, pp. 60-89.

Hoikkala, T. (ed) *Miehen kuvia. Välähdyksiä nuorista miehistä Suomessa*. Helsinki: Gaudeamus, 1996.

Holland, J. et al. *The Male in the Head: young people, heterosexuality and power*. London: the Tufnell Press, 1998.

Horrocks, R. *Masculinity in Crisis: Myths, Fantasies and Realities*. Houndmills: The Macmillan Press Ltd, 1994.

Humm, M. *The Dictionary of Feminist Theory*. London: Harvester Wheatsheaf, 1989.

Hutcheon, L. *The Politics of Postmodernism*. London: Routledge, 1989.

Huttunen, J. Full time fathers and their parental leave experiences, in Björnberg, U. & Kollind, A-K. (eds) *Men's family relations. Report from an international seminar*. Monograph from the Department of Sociology no 60, Göteborg University. Stockholm: Almqvist & Wiksell, 1996.

____. Muuttunut isyys, in Jokinen, A. (ed) *Mies ja muutos: Kriittisen miestutkimuksen teemoja.*Tampere: Tampere University Press, 1999, pp. 169-193.

Hänninen, J. Modernin miehen seksuaalinen liikkumatila, in Jokinen, A. (ed) *Mies ja muutos: Kriittisen miestutkimuksen teemoja.*Tampere: Tampere University Press, 1999, pp. 194-220.

Härkönen, S. Sonja Tammelan tanssiopisto juhlii pyöreitä vuosia valoisissa merkeissä. *Etelä-Saimaa.* 21.08.1999.

Ikäheimo, K. Realistisia tanssinäytelmiä kaiken kansan katsottavaksi – Tanssiteatteri Raatikon ensimmäinen vuosikymmen 1972-1982, in Pauniaho, P. (ed) *Raatikko tanssii... Näkökulmia Tanssiteatteri Raatikon historiaan ja nykypäivään 1972-1997.*Oulu: Kustannus Pohjoinen, 1998, pp. 15-24.

Innanen, K. Nuorena on jalat venytettävä. *Kaleva.* 02.08.1997.

Irigaray, L. *This sex which is not one.* Ithaca, N.Y.: Cornell University Press, 1985.

Jackson, S. *Heterosexuality in Question.* London: Sage Publications, 1999.

Jakobson, M. *Pelon ja toivon aika: 20. vuosisadan tilinpäätös II.* Helsinki: Otava, 2001.

Janhonen, U. Häiriköt heitettiin ulos *Helsingin Sanomat* 28.06.1996a.

_____. "Miehillä on tiukemmat otteet", Kuopiossa on tanssittu poikajoukossa jo kymmenen vuotta. *Helsingin Sanomat,* 28.6.1996b.

Jaworski, A. & Coupland, N. (eds) *The Discourse Reader.* London & new York: Routledge, 1999.

Jenkins, K. *On "What is History?", From Carr and Elton to Rorty and White.* London: Routledge, 1995.

Jessor, R. Ethnographic Methods in Contemporary Perspective. In: Jessor, R., Colby, A. & Shweder, R.A. (eds) *Ethnography and Human Development: Context and Meaning in Social Inquiry.* Chicago: Chicago University Press. 1996, pp. 3-14.

Jokela-Nazimov, A-M. Pasi Leppänen toivoisi poikia balettikouluun. *Iltasanomat.* 10.12.1991.

Jokinen, A. (ed) *Mies ja muutos: Kriittisen miestutkimuksen teemoja.*Tampere: Tampere University Press, 1999.

Jokinen, A., Juhila, K. & Suoninen, E. *Diskurssianalyysin aakkoset.* Tampere: Vastapaino, 1993.

_____. *Diskurssianalyysi liikkeessä.* Tampere: Vastapaino, 1999.

Juvonen, T. *Varjoelämää ja julkisia salaisuuksia.* Tampere: Vastapaino, 2002.

Jääskeläinen, L. Pojat ovat poikia. *Tanssi,* 1/1993, pp. 4-6.

Kaikkonen, R. Poikien tanssissa ei "lillutella", *Helsingin Sanomat.* 15.11.1996.

Kaiku, J-P. Operans balettskola gör trendig nutidsdans, *Hufvudstadsbladet.* 25.5.1996.

Kaiku, J-P. & Sutinen, V. Murtumia ja moninaisuutta: Suomalaisen nykytanssin freelancerkenttä 1980- ja 1990-luvulla in Helavuori, H-L., Kukkonen, J., Raatikainen, R. & Vuorenmaa, T-J. (eds) *Valokuvan tanssi. Suomalaisen tanssin kuvat.* Oulu: Pohjoinen, 1997, pp. 205-214.

Kallas, A. *The Wolf's Bride: A Tale from Estonia.* Translated from Finnish by Alex Matson in collaboration with Bryan Rhys. London: Johathan Cape, (1928)/1930.

Kangas, S. Taistelulajeista löytyy avian selvää tanssia. *Kaleva.* 9.10.1994.

Karhunen, P. *Regional Arts Councils as Supporters of the Arts in Finland.* Facts about the Arts 2, Helsinki: Arts Council of Finland, 1990.

Karhunen, P. & Smolander, A. *Tanssitaiteilija lähikuvassa: Tutkimus asemasta ja toimeentulosta 1990-luvun vaihteessa - The Social and Economic Position of Finnish Dance Artists.* Helsinki: Taiteen keskutoimikunta, Arts council of Finland, 1995.

Karnakoski. K. *Tanssin ja rakastin.* Jyväskylä: Gummerus, 1983.

Karvonen, L. et al. *Naisen kuvia.* Vantaa: Kansan Sivistystyön Liitto, 1998.

Kauhanen, A-L. & Lyytinen, J. *Parasta ennen 01012015: Tulevaisuuden tekijät – Suomi 2015.* Helsinki: Sitra, 2003.

Kehily, M.J. & Nayak, A. Lads and Laughter: Humour and the Production of Heterosexual Hierarchies. *Gender and Education.* 9, 1997, pp. 1, 67-87.

Keyworth, S.A. Critical autobiography: 'straightening' out dance education. *Research in Dance Education.* 2/2, 2001, pp. 117-137.

Kimmel, M. Rethinking "Masculinity": New Directions in Research, in Kimmel, M. (ed). *Changing Men: New Directions in Research on Men and Masculinity.* Newbury Park: Sage Publications, 1987, pp. 9-24.

Kinnunen, T. *Pyhät bodarit: yhteisöllisyys ja onni täydellisessä ruumiissa.* Helsinki: Gaudeamus, 2001.

Kitzinger, J. The methodology of Focus Groups: the importance of interaction between research participants. *Sociology of Health & Illness.* 16/1, 1994, pp. 103-121.

_____. Qualitative Research: Introducing focus groups. *British Medical Journal.* 311, July, 1995, pp. 299-302.

Kivi, A. *Seitsemän veljestä.* Helsinki: Suomalaisen kirjallisuuden seura, 2000 (1870).

Kivinen, R., Latikka, A-M. & Oja-Koski, R. *Ihminen, tavoitteet ja toiminta.* Turku: Turun yliopiston täydennyskoulutuskeskus, 1994.

Klemola, T. *Ruumis liikkuu – liikkuuko henki? Fenomenologinen tutkimus liikunnan projektista.* Tampere: Fitty, 1998.

Knif, C-J. *Improvisations roll i nutidsdansen och dess betydelse i sökandet efter min egen dans.* Unpublished MA dissertation. Helsinki: Theatre Academy, 2000.

Knuutila, S. Häviämisen häpeä, in Sironen, E., Tiihonen, A. & Veijola, S. (eds) *Urheilukirja.* Tampere: Vastapaino, 1995, pp. 87-96.

Koegler, H. Dancing in the Closet: The Coming Out of Ballet. *Dance Chronicle.* Vol 18, 2, 1995, p. 231-238.

Komiteamietintö 1965, A 8, Valtion taidekomitean mietintö. Helsinki: Valtion painatuskeskus, 1965.

Kunnas, K. *Hanhiemon iloinen lipas.* Helsinki: WSOY, 1954.

Kuopio Dance and Music Festival/Kuopio Dance Festival, Festival Brochures, Kuopio: Kuopio Dance and Music Festival/Kuopio Dance Festival, 1987-2003.

Kuopio Dance and Music Festival/Kuopio Dance Festival, Dance Camp for Boys, Brochures, Kuopio: Kuopio Dance and Music Festival/Kuopio Dance Festival 1987-2003.

Laakso, L. Oudot linnun poikaset: Poikien tanssikurssi Kuopiossa. *Keskisuomalainen* 24.06.1988.

Laclau, E. & Mouffe, C. *Hegemony and Socialist Strategy: Towards a Radical Democratic Politics.* London: Verso, 1985.

Lahelma, E. *Sukupuolten eriytyminen peruskoulun opetussuunnitelmassa.* Helsinki: Yliopistopaino, 1992.

Lammassaari, T. Miehet pelkäävät turhaan tanssia. *Aamulehti.* 20.10.1992.

Lampi, I. Pojatkin tanssivat – kun opetat oikein, in Viitala, M. (ed) Olen liikkeellä... purkaudun liikkeellä... ilmaisen liikkeellä... luon liikkeellä... ...tanssin. Oulu: Kirjapaino Osakeyhtiö Kaleva, 1991, p. 12.

_____. Mistä on miehen opetus tehty?, in Lampi, I. et al. (eds) *Popeda: poikien tanssipedagogiikka-työryhmän muistio.* Vantaa, Helsinki: Vantaan tanssiopisto & Suomen kansallisoopperan balettioppilaitos, 2002, p. 4.

Lancaster, R. Subject Honor, Object Shame, in Adams, R. & Savran, D. (eds) *The Masculinity Reader.* Malden & Oxford: Blackwell Publishers, 2002, pp. 41-68.

Lankolainen, E. Tanssileiri vetää ennätysmäärän poikia. *Savon Sanomat,* 14.6.2003.

Lechte, J. *Fifty Key Contemporary Thinkers: From structuralism to postmodernity.* London & New York: Routledge, 1994.

Lee, R. *Doing research on sensitive topics.* London, Thousand Oaks, New Delhi: Sage Publications, 1993.

297

Lehikoinen, K. Tanssi poikien liikuntakulttuurissa. *Tanssi.* 1/1993, pp. 9-11.

_____. Fragile Roughness: Representations in Kenneth Kvarnström's *Fem Danser.* Unpublished MA-dissertation. Guildford: University of Surrey, 1996.

_____. Fragile Masculinities and the Sex Role Theory in Dance for Boys: A Critical Discourse, in Anttila, E. (ed) *Proceedings of the 1997 Conference of Dance and Child International.* Kuopio, Finland: daCi, 1997, pp. 195-201.

_____. Fragile Masculnitities: Reading Kvarnström, in *Proceedings of the 22nd Conference of Society of Dance History Scholars,* Albuquerque, New Mexico, 1999, pp. 129-137.

Lehman, P. (ed) *Masculinity: bodies, movies, culture.* New York & London: Routledge, 2001.

Lehtiranta, L. Baletin urheilullisuus vie poikia tanssikouluun. *Vantaan Sanomat,* 17.1.1993.

Lehtola, V. Lähtijät ja jääjät, in Heikkinen, V. Mantila, H. & Varis, M. (eds) *Tuppisuinen mies: Kirjoitelmia sukupuolesta, kielestä ja kulttuurista.* Helsinki: Suomalaisen kirjallisuuden seura, 1998, pp. 228-238.

Lehtonen, J. Young non-heterosexual men and models for homosexual identity formation. *Psykologia.* 33/6, 1998, pp. 421-429.

_____. Pojista miehiä koulun heterojärjestyksessä, in Jokinen, A. (ed) *Mies ja muutos: Kriittisen miestutkimuksen teemoja.*Tampere: Tampere University Press, 1999, pp. 121-148.

_____. *Seksuaalisuus ja sukupuoli koulussa - näkökulmana heteronormatiivisuus ja ei-heteroseksuaalisten nuorten kertomukset.* Helsinki: Yliopistopaino, 2003.

Lehtonen, M. *Pikku jättiläisiä.* Tampere: Vastapaino, 1995.

_____. Maskuliinisuus kansallisuus ja identiteetti in Jokinen, A. (ed) *Mies ja muutos, Kriittisen miestutkimuksen teemoja.* Tampere: Tampere University Press. 1999, pp. 74-88.

Leinonen, J. Tinasotilas Pähkinänsärkijässä: Baletin Jouluaatto. *Nuorten sarka.* Suomen 4H-liitto, Joulukuu, 1994.

Lipiäinen, P. Pojat hikoilivat baletissa. *Keskisuomalainen.* 20.11.1996.

Lloyd, G. *The Man of Reason. 'Male' and 'Female' in Western Philosophy.* London: Routledge (2nd edition), 1993.

_____. G. *Miehinen järki. "Mies" ja "nainen" länsimaisessa filosofiassa.* Tampere: Vastapaino, 2000.

Lofland, J. & Lofland, L. *Analyzing Social Settings: A Guide to Qualitative Observation and Analysis.* 3rd edition. Belmont: Wadsworth Publishing, 1995.

Luhtanen,T. *Tanssijana Paula Tuovisen duetossa.* Unpublished MA dissertation. Helsinki: Theatre Academy, 1998.

Mac an Ghaill, M. *The Making of Men: Masculinities, Sexualities and Schooling.* Buckingham & Philadelpia: Open University Press, 1994.

___. (ed) *Understanding Masculinities.* Buckingham & Philadelphia: Open University Press, 1996.

Macleod, C. Deconstructive discourse analysis: Extending the methodological conversation. *South African Journal of Psychology.* 32/1, 2002, pp. 17-25.

Majors, R. Cool Pose: Black Masculinity and Sports, in Whitehead, S. & Barrett, F. (eds) *The Masculinity Reader.* Cambridge: Polity Press, 2001, pp. 209-217.

Makkonen, A. A Struggle for a Survival. A historical and contextual study of Finnish free dance during the period 1945-1962. An unpublished MA dissertation. Guildford: University of Surrey, 1990.

___. Mitä tapahtui Suomen vapaassa tanssissa 1940- ja 1950-luvulla? *Tanssi,* 1/1991, pp. 14-15.

Matza, D. *Becoming Deviant.* Englewood Cliffs, NJ: Prentice-Hall, 1969

McKay, J. Exercising hegemonic masculinity: sport and the social construction of gender, in Lupton, G. et al (eds), *Society and Gender: An Introduction to Sociology,* Sydney: Macmillan, 1992.

Meidän Kajaani, Tanssi vei Minnan sydämen. *Meidän Kajaani.* 5/2001, p. 3.

Merton, R. K. The focussed interview and focus groups. *Public Opinion Quarterly.* 51, 1987, pp. 550-566.

Merz, R. 'Swan Lake' Goes All-Male, *Ballett International/Tanz Aktuell,* 8-9/1998, pp. 10-13.

Middleton, P. *The Inward Gaze: Masculinity and Subjectivity in Modern Culture.* London: Routledge, 1992.

Miettinen, J. *25 Tanssin Juhlaa: Kuopio Tanssii ja Soi 1970-1994, Kuopio Dance and Music Festival.* Iisalmi: Kuopio Tanssii ja Soi, 1994.

___. Sukkahousuprinsseistä ikuisuuteen. *Tanssi.* 4, 1994b, pp. 21-23.

Mills, S. *Discourse.* London & New York: Routledge, 1997.

___. *Michel Foucault.* London & New York: Routledge, 2003.

Mitchell, H. Men with Tights. *Dance International.* Spring, 1999, pp. 14-18.

Monahan, J. In a Woman's World? *Dance & Dancers,* no 417, September, 1984, pp. 24-25.

Moore, C. & Yamamoto, K. *Beyond Words.* London & New York: Routledge, 1988.

Morgan, D. Family, Gender and Masculinities, in Whitehead, S. & Barrett, F. (ed) *The Masculinities Reader*. Cambridge: Polity Press, 2001, pp. 223-232.

Moring, K. Samurait valtasivat Aleksanterinteatterin, *Helsingin Sanomat*. 8.4.1993.

Mosse, G.L. *The Image of Man: The Creation of Modern Masculinity*. New York & Oxford: Oxford University Press, 1996.

Mulvey, L. Visual Pleasure and Narrative Cinema, *Screen*, 16/3, Autumn, 1975, pp. 6-18.

Mumaw, B. & Sherman, J. How It All Began: Ted Shawn's First Modern All-Male Dance Concert. *Dance Magazine*. July, 1982, pp. 42-46.

Mäkinen, E. Siivet kantapäissä, Kotiliesi, 13-14/2003, pp. 88-92,94.

Mäkinen, H. Ei voi tehdä balettia jollei tunne nuotteja. *Helsingin Sanomat*, 20 May 1959a, p. 16.

_____. Oopperan balettikoulussa on poikia vain kuudesosa. *Helsingin Sanomat*, 4 November 1959b, p. 6.

Nardi, P. "A Vicarious Sense of Belonging", The Politics of Friendship and Gay Social Movements, Communities, and Neighbourhoods, in Whitehead, S. & Barrett, J. (eds) *The Masculinities Reader*. Cambridge: Polity Press, 2001, pp. 288-306.

Nayak, A. & Kehily, M. J. Masculinities and Schooling: Why are Young Men so Homophobic, in Steinberg, L., Epstein, D. & Johnson, R. (eds) *Border Patrols: Policing the Boundaries of Heterosexuality*. London: Cassell, 1997, pp. 138-161.

Nieminen, P. Neljä tietä tanssiharrastukseen – tutkimus tanssin sosiaalistumisesta ja tanssijoiden harrastusprofiileista, in Sarje, A. (ed). *Näkökulmia tanssinopettamiseen; suomalaisten tanssitaiteilijo-iden ja tanssin tutkijoiden kirjoituksia 1997*. Turku: P. Pakkanen, A. Sarje, Opetusministeriö & Turun taiteen ja viestinnän oppilaitos, 1997, pp. 31-51.

_____. *Four Dance Subcultures. A study of Non-professional Dancers' Socialization, Participation Motives, Attitudes and Stereotypes*. Studies in Sport, Physical education and Health. Jyväskylä: University of Jyväskylä, 1998.

_____. Motives for dancing among Finnish folk dancers, competitive ballroom dancers, ballet dancers and modern dancers. *European Journal of Physical Education*, Vol 3, 1, 1998b, pp. 22-34.

Niiranen, H. Pojat ja naisopettaja, in Lampi et al (eds) *POPEDA, Poikien tanssipedagogiikka –työryhmän muistio*, Vantaa & Helsinki: Vantaan

Tanssiopisto & Suomen Kansallisoopperan Balettioppilaitos, 2002, pp. 6-7.

Novack, C.J. *Sharing the Dance: Contact Improvisation and American Culture.* Madison: The University of Wisconsin Press, 1990.

____. Ballet, Gender and Cutural Power, in Thomas, H. (ed.) *Dance, Gender and Culture.* Houndsmills & London: Macmillan Press Ltd, 1993, pp. 34-48.

Nyholm, L. Tanssitaiteen ongelmia IV. *Tanssitaide Danskonst* 4, 1959, pp. 4-6.

Nykänen, A. Kovat kundit tanssivat. *Helsingin Sanomat.* 15.6.2003, p. D7.

Opetushallitus. Taiteen perusopetuksen opetussuunnitelman perusteet. 1992.

____. Ammatillisen peruskoulutuksen opetussuunitelman ja näyttötutkinnon perusteet. Tanssialan perustutkinto 2001. Määräys 13/011/2001. Helsinki: Opetushallitus, 2001.

____. Taiteen perusopetuksen tanssin laajan oppimäärän opetussuunnitelman perusteet 2002. Määräys 38/011/2002. Helsinki: Opetushallitus, 2002.

Pakkanen, P. Tanssitaide koulukulttuurin kuokkavieraana – Liikkeitä suomalaisen tanssitaidekasvatuksen historiasta 1900-1992, *Liikunta & Tiede*, 2/2001a, pp. 9-17.

____. Tanssipedagogi oman työnsä tutkijana, *Liikunta & Tiede*, 2/2001b, p. 10.

____. Näkymätön tanssitaide, Koulukelpoikseksi kesytetty tanssi, *Liikunta & Tiede*, 2/2001c, p. 13.

Palmén, J. Miehiä ilmassa. Baletti on poikien juttu siinä missä jalkapallokin, todistavat ylpeät pojat. *Helsingin Sanomat, NYT viikkoliite.* 8/2002, pp. 10-12.

Parker, I. *Discourse dynamics: Critical analysis for social and individual psychology.* London: Routledge. 1992.

Parker, I. & The Bolton Discourse Network (eds). *Critical textwork: an introduction to varities of discourse and analysis.* Buckingham: Open University Press, 1999.

Parkkinen, M-L. *Ulos kaapista: Tositarinoita homoseksuaalisuuden kohtaamisesta.* Helsinki: Like, 2003.

Pateman, C. The Fraternal Social Contract, in Adams, R. & Savran, D. (eds) *The Masculinity Studies Reader.* Malden & Oxford: Blackwell Publishers, 2002, pp. 119-134.

Pauniaho, P. (ed). *Raatikko tanssii... Näkökulmia Tanssiteatteri Raatikon historiaan ja nykypäivään.* Oulu: Kustannus Pohjoinen, 1998.

Phelan, S. Introduction, in Phelan, S. (ed.) *Playing with Fire: Queer Politics, Queer Theories.* New York & London: Routledge, 1997, pp. 1-8.

Philips, L. & Jørgensen, M. *Discourse Analysis as Theory and Method.* London, Thousand Oaks, New Delhi: Sage Publications, 2002a.

_____. Laclau & Mouffe's Discourse Theory. In: Philips, L. & Jørgensen, M. *Discourse Analysis as Theory and Method.* London, Thousand Oaks, New Delhi: Sage Publications, 2002b, pp. 24-59.

Pietinen, V. Valtteri ei häpeä balettiharrastustaan. *Helsingin Sanomat.* 23.09. 1997.

Pleck, J. *The Myth of Masculinity.* Cambridge, MA: MIT Press, 1981.

Plummer, K. *The Gender Coding of Modern Dance: Its Significance in the Hidden Curriculum of Dance in Education.* Unpublished MA thesis. University of South Wales, 1995.

Polhemus, T. Dance, Gender and Culture, Thomas, H. (ed.) *Dance, Gender and Culture.* Houndsmills & London: Macmillan Press Ltd, 1993, pp. 3-15.

Pollack, W. *Real Boys: Rescuing Our Sons from the Myths of Boyhood.* New York: Random House, 1998.

Porna, I. *Taiteen perusopetuksen vuosikirja 2000.* Helsinki, Suomen kuntaliitto, 2000.

Porna, I. & Korpipää, S. *Taiteen perusopetuksen toimeenpano kunnissa.* Taiteen perusopetuksen toimeenpanokoulutus 11 läänissä 11-31.3.1992. A hand-out. Helsinki: Kaupunkiliitto & Kunnallisliitto, 1992.

Potter, J. & Wetherell, M. *Discourse and Social Psychology: Beyond Attitudes and Behaviour.* London, Thousand Oaks, New Delhi: Sage Publications, 1987.

Powney, J. & Watts, M. *Interviewing in educational research.* London: Routledge & Kegan Paul, 1987.

Puhakainen, J. *Kesytetyt kehot.* Tampere: Tampere University Press, 1997.

_____. *Lapsen Aika: Puheenvuoro lasten liikunnasta ja urheilusta.* Helsinki: Like, 2001.

Raatikko Dance School. *Raatikon tanssikoulun opetussuunnitelma.* An unpublished curriculum of the Dance School of Raatikko, Raatikon tanssikoulu, Vantaa (n.d.).

Raatikko Dance School & Tikkurila Theatre. *Star Track.* Programme notes. Tikkurila, Vernissa. 15.11. 1996.

Radley, A. Relationships in detail: the study of social interaction, in Miell, D. & Dallos, R. (eds) *Social Interaction and Personal Relationships.* London: Sage Publications, 1996, pp. 23-100.

Rainer, Y. *A Woman Who... Essays, Interviews, Scripts.* Baltimore & London: The John Hopkins University Press, 1999.

Raiskio, P. Selkä pettää, polvi särkyy... *Tanssi* 3/1990, pp. 6-7.

Rajankovsky, F. *The Tall Book of Mother Goose*. New York: Harper & Row, 1942.

Rehunen, S. et al. *Kuntotestauksen perusteet*. Finland: Liite Ry, 1998.

Repo. R. *Tanssien tulevaisuuteen*. *Tutkimus suomalaisen tanssitaiteen legitimaatiosta ja tanssin koulutusjärjestelmän vakiintumisesta*. Taiteen keskustoimikunnan julkaisuja nro 6. Helsinki: Valtion painatuskeskus, 1989.

Reunamäki, H. Tanssi on poikaa! *Savon Sanomat*. 2.7. 2000, p. 16.

Risner, D. Rehearsing Heterosexuality: *Unspoken* Truths in Dance Education. *Dance Research Journal*. 34/2, Winter, 2002a, pp. 63-78.

_____. Re-educating Dance Education to its Homosexuality: an invitation for critical analysis and professional unification. *Research in Dance Education*, 3, 2, 2002b, pp. 181-187.

_____. Sexual Orientation and Male Participation in Dance Education: Revisiting the Open Secret. *Journal of Dance Education*. 2/3, 2002c, pp. 84-92.

Roberts, S. Men in Ballet. *Ballet Today*. October, 1955, p. 22.

Rodgers, R.A. Men and the Dance: Why do we question the image? *Dance Magazine*. June, 1966, pp. 33-36.

Rosenberg, T. Byxbegär. Göteborg: Anamma. 2000.

Runonen, C. Poikaenergiaa Vantaalta lavan täydeltä Mikkelissä. *Länsi-Savo*. 27.1.2001, p. A10.

Ruoppila, I. Alkusanat, in Lyytinen, P., Korkiakangas, M. & Lyytinen, H. (eds) *Näkökulmia kehityspsykologiaan: Kehitys kontekstissaan*. Helsinki: WSOY, 1995, pp. 18-27.

Russell, B. *Länsimaisen filosofian historia 2*. Porvoo: WSOY, 1996.

Räsänen, A. Terveempiä tanssijoita, parempia tuloksia: Urheiluvalmennuksesta apua tanssiin. *Uusi Suomi*. 8.8.1986.

_____. Balettikoulu / The ballet school, in Räsänen, A. & Hakli, K. *Suomen kansallisbaletti tänään, The Finnish National Ballet Today*. Helsinki: WSOY, 1995, pp. 52-59.

_____. *Suomen Kansallisoopperan balettikoulu 75 vuotta, Finnish National Opera Ballet School 75 years*. Helsinki: Kirjapaino Libris Oy, 1997.

_____. Pojista oman elämänsä tanssijoiksi. *Helsingin Sanomat*. 2. February, 2000a.

_____. Yksilölle tilaa! Kansallisoopperan balettioppilaitos elää muutosvaihetta. *Helsingin Sanomat*. 1. April, 2000b.

Räty, J. Tanssiminen ei vie keltään miehisyyttä. *Helsingin Sanomat*. 24.5.2003. p. A5.

Saarela, M. Tositarinoita nukkumalähiöstä. *Etelä-Saimaa*. 27.01.2001a, p. 9.

____. Vantaan tanssikoulussa pojista tehdään miehiä. *Etelä-Saimaa.* 27.01.2001b, p. 9.

Saarinen, E. *Länsimaisen filosofian historia huipulta huipulle _Sokrateesta Marxiin.* Porvoo: WSOY, 1985.

Salih, S. *Judith Butler.* London & New York: Routledge, 2002.

Salmenhaara, E. *Suomen musiikin historia 2.* Porvoo: WSOY, 1996.

Salosaari, P. *Multiple Embodiment in Classical Ballet: Educating the Dancer as an Agent of Change in the Cultural Evolution of Ballet.* Helsinki: Teatterikorkeakoulu, 2001.

Sampson, E. The Deconstruction of the Self, in Shotter, J. & Gergen, K. (eds.) *Texts of Identity.* London, Newbury Park, New Delhi: Sage Publications, 1989, pp. 1-19.

Sarbin, T.R. The narrative as root metaphor for psychology, in Sabrin, T.R. (ed) *Narrative Psychology: The Storied Nature of Human Conduct,* New York: Praeger, 1986, pp. 3-21.

Sarje, A. Koululaisten luovan tanssin suhdeverkostot "Lapset ja taiteilijat – luovia yhdessä" projektissa. In Sarje, A. (ed). *Näkökulmia tanssinopettamiseen; suomalaisten tanssitaiteilijoiden ja tanssin tutkijoiden kirjoituksia 1997.* Turku: P. Pakkanen, A. Sarje, Opetusministeriö & Turun taiteen ja viestinnän oppilaitos, 1997, pp. 17-30.

____. *Suomalaisen tanssin taidemaailman sosiaalinen muutosdynamiikka vuosien 1988 ja 1996 välillä; teorioiden vertailua taiteen kehityksen selittäjinä.* Helsinki: Helsingin yliopiston sosiaalipsykologian laitos, 1999.

Saukkonen, P. Suomalaisten kulttuurinen yhtenäisyys on myytti. *Helsingin Sanomat.* 16 September, 2002, p. A4.

Schechner, R. *Performance Studies: An Introduction.* London & New York: Routledge, 2002.

Scott, J. *Gender and the Politics of History.* Revised Edition. New York & Chichester: Columbia University Press, 1999.

Scraton, S. Equality, Coeducation and Physical Education in Secondary Schooling, in Evans, J. (ed) *Equality, Education and Physical Education.* London & Washington: The Falmer Press, 1995, pp. 139-153.

Segal, L. Sexualities, in Woodward, K. (ed) *Identity and Difference.* London, Thousand Oaks, New Delhi: Sage Publications/The Open University, 1997, pp. 183-234.

____. Back to the boys? Temptations of the good gender theorist. *Textual Practice.* 15/2, 2001, pp. 231-250.

304

Seidler, V. *Rediscovering Masculinity: Reason, Language and Sexuality.* London: Routledge, 1989.

____. *Unreasonable Men: Masculinity and Social Theory.* London: Routledge, 1994.

Sevänen, E. *Vapauden rajat. Kirjallisuuden tuotannon ja välityksen yhteiskunnallinen säätely Suomessa vuosina 1918-1939.* Helsinki: Suomalaisen kirjallisuuden seura, 1994.

Shapiro, S.B. (ed.) *Dance, Power, and Difference*: Critical and Feminist Perspectives on Dance Education. Champaign: Human Kinetics Books, 1998.

Shotter, J. Social Accountability and Self Specification, in Gergen, K.J. & Davis, K.E. (eds) *The Social Construction of the Person.* New York, Berlin, Heidelberg, Tokyo: Springer-Verlag, 1985, pp. 167-189.

____. Social Accountability and the Social Construction of 'You', in Shotter, J. & Gergen, K. (eds.) *Texts of Identity.* London, Newbury Park, New Delhi: Sage Publications, 1989, pp. 133-151.

____. 1997. The Social Construction of Our Inner Selves. *Journal of Constructivist Psychology.* 10/1997, pp. 7-24.

Shotter, J. & Gergen, K. (eds.) *Texts of Identity.* London, Newbury Park, New Delhi: Sage Publications, 1989.

Silenius, L. Ei mitään sipsuttelua. *Etelä-Suomen Sanomat.* 14.9.1991.

Sinfield, A. Should there be Lesbian and Gay Intellectuals? in Bristow, J. & Wilson, A.R. (eds) *Activating Theory: Lesbian, Gay, Bisexual Politics.* London: Lawrence & Wishart, 1993, pp. 16-29.

Singer, Robert, N. *Motor learning and human performance: An application to motor skills and movement behaviors.* New York: Macmillan Publishing Co, 3rd edition, 1980.

Sinkkonen, J. *Pienistä pojista kunnon miehiä.* Juva: WSOY, 1990.

Sklar, D. Reprise: On Dance Ethnography. *Dance Research Journal.* 32,1, 2000, pp. 70-77.

Slugoski. B.R. & Ginsburg, G.P. Ego Identity and Explanatory Speech. In Shotter, J. & Gergen, K.J. (eds). *Texts of identity.* London: Sage, 1989, pp. 36-55.

Smart, B. *Postmodernity.* London: Routledge, 1993.

Smith, C. On Authoritarianism in the Dance Classroom, in Shapiro, S.B. (ed.) *Dance, Power, and Difference*: Critical and Feminist Perspectives on Dance Education. Champaign: Human Kinetics Books, 1998, pp. 123-146.

Smith, J. Semi-Structured Interviewing and Qualitative Analysis, in Smith, J., Harré, R. & Van Langehove, L. (eds) *Rethinking Methods in*

Psychology. London, Thousand Oaks, New Delhi: Sage Publications, 1995, Ch 2.

Soikkeli, M. Miesrakastajan emansipatorisuus kirjallisuudessa ja kulttuurissa, in Jokinen, A. (ed) *Mies ja muutos: Kriittisen miestutkimuksen teemoja.*Tampere: Tampere University Press, 1999, pp. 149-168.

Sokura, T. Kummallista…, in programme notes of the *Tanssiva poika 2000* gala, Martinus Hall, Vantaa, 4.6.2000, Vantaa Dance Institute.

Spurgeon, D. The Men's Movement, in E. Anttila (ed.) 1997. *The Call of Forests and Lakes: Proceedings of the 1997 Conference of Dance and The Child International*. Kuopio, Finland: daCi, 1997, pp. 8-17.

Stinson, S. Journey toward a Feminist Pedagogy for Dance. *Women & Performance: A Journal of Feminist Theory*, 6,1, 1993, pp. 131-146.

____. Places Where I've Been: Reflections on Issues of Gender in Dance Education, Research and Administration. *Choreography and Dance*. 5, 1, 1998, pp. 117-127.

Stinson, S., Blumenfeld-Jones, D. & Jan Dyke, J. Voices of Young Women Dance Students: An Interpretive Study of Meaning in Dance. *Dance Research Journal*, 22, 2, 1990, pp. 13-22.

Stoller, R. J. *Sex and Gender: On the Development of Masculinity and Femininity*. New York: Science House, 1968.

____. *Sex and Gender, vol. 2: The Transexual Experiment*. New York: Jason Aranson, 1976.

Strinati, D. *An Introduction to Theories of Popular Culture*. London: Routledge, 1995.

Stålström, O. *Homoseksuaalisuuden sairausleiman loppu*. Gaudeamus: Helsinki, 1997.

Suhonen, T. Kaunoliiketaiteesta tanssirealismiin. Suomalaisen tanssin historiaa, in Helavuori, H-L. et al (eds). *Valokuvan tanssi. Suomalaisen tanssin kuvat 1890-1997. Dance in Finnish Photography*. Oulu: Pohjoinen, 1997, pp. 11-34.

Säävälä, H. Mieheyden psykologiaa, in Jokinen, A. (ed) *Mies ja muutos: Kriittisen miestutkimuksen teemoja.*Tampere: Tampere University Press, 1999, pp. 52-73.

Tajfel, H. (ed) *Differentiation between social groups: studies in the social psychology of intergroup relations*. London: Academic Press, 1978.

Talvitie L. Mikä ihmeen vapaa-aika? Lätkäpojalle ja balettitytölle harrastus on koko elämä. *Ilta Sanomat*. 10.02.1990.

Tavris, C. *Anger: The Misunderstood Emotion*. Simon & Schuster, New York, NY, 1982.

Taylor, S. Locating and Conducting Discourse Analytic Research, in Wetherell, M., Taylor, S. & Yates, S.J. (eds) *Discourse as Data.* London, Thousand Oaks, New Delhi: Sage Publications. 2001a, pp. 5-48.

_____. Evaluating and Applying Discourse Analytic Research, in Wetherell, M., Taylor. & Yates, S.J. (eds) *Discourse as Data.* London, Thousand Oaks, New Delhi: Sage Publications. 2001b, pp 311-330.

Teiz, C. Knee Problems in Dancers, in Solomon, R., Minton, S. & Solomon, J. (eds) *Preventing Dance Injuries: An Interdisciplinary Perspective.* Reston, VA: American Alliance for Health, Physical Education, Recreation and Dance, 1990, pp. 39-73.

Tenhunen, I. Taistelutanssin mestari. *Budoexpress.* 2/1994, pp. 8-9.

Tervo, M. *Geographies in the making: Reflection on sports, the media, and national identity in Finland.* A PhD thesis, Oulu: University of Oulu, 2003.

Thomas, H. An-Other Voice: Young Women Dancing and Talking, in Thomas, H. (ed) *Dance, Gender and Culture.* Houndmills and London: Macmillan Press Ltd, 1993, pp. 69-93.

_____. *Dance, Modernity and Culture: Explorations in the Sociology of Dance.* London & New York: Routledge, 1995.

_____. Do You Want to Join the Dance? Postmodernism/Poststructuralism, the Body, and Dance, in Morris, G. (ed) *Moving Words: Re-writing Dance.* London & New York: Routledge, 1996, pp. 63-87.

_____. *The Body, Dance and Cultural Theory.* Houndmills & New York: Palgrave Macmillan, 2003.

Tiihonen, A. Oikeita miehiä - ja urheilijoita? Urheilun miestutkimusta, in Jokinen, A. (ed) *Mies ja muutos: Kriittisen miestutkimuksen teemoja.* Tampere: Tampere University Press, 1999, pp. 89-120.

Tiihonen, M. Poika, tee tanssisoolo Tikkurilasta avaruuteen. *Ilta-Sanomat.* 16.11.1996.

Tomkins, A. Man Dancing. *Animated.* Spring, 1997, p. 21.

Tossavainen, J. Pikku-Frankit tanssivat aikuisuuteen Vernissassa: Vantaalla pojatkin ovat innostuneet tanssista. *Helsingin Sanomat.* 25.4.1998.

_____. Tositarinoita mieheksi kasvamisesta: True Stories on Vantaan poikien ja Isto Turpeisen työvoitto. *Helsingin Sanomat.* 4.2.2000, p. B10.

Tourunen, J. Machoballerina joutuu koville. *VK-lehti.* 5, 1988, pp. 24-25.

Treusch-Dieter, G. Sex, Swan and Gender, *Ballett International/Tanz Aktuell,* 8-9/1998, pp. 14-17.

Tudeer, A. Läsa balett med Foucault, som fan läser bibeln in Pakkanen et al (eds) *Askelmerkkejä tanssin historiasta, ruumiista ja sukupuolesta.* Helsinki: Taiteen keskustoimikunta, 1999, pp. 65-77.

Tuohinen, T. Isät, pojat ja pärjäämisen henki, in Hoikkala, T: (ed) *Miehenkuvia, Välähdyksiä nuorista miehistä Suomessa.* Helsinki: Gaudeamus, 1996, pp. 66-100.

Turpeinen, I. *Tanssiva mies 1990: sattumista tanssiammattiin.* Tanssinopettajien täydennyskoulutus TO2:n opinnäyte. Helsinki: Teatterikorkeakoulun täydennyskoulutuskeskus, 1990.

_____. Tanssin taikaa, in Grönholm, I. (ed) *Ilmaisun monet kielet.* Helsinki: Opetushallitus, 1994, pp. 110-117.

_____. Poikia, taikarumpuja ja bokkeneita Raatikon tanssikoulussa, in Sarje, A. (ed). *Näkökulmia tanssinopettamiseen; suomalaisten tanssitaiteilijoiden ja tanssin tutkijoiden kirjoituksia 1997.* Turku: P. Pakkanen, A. Sarje, Opetusministeriö & Turun taiteen ja viestinnän oppilaitos, 1997, pp. 8-16.

_____. Suuri kohtaaminen, in Ranta-Meyer, T. & Kaikkonen, M. (eds) *Lahjakkuus lentoon.* Helsinki: Sibelius akatemian koulutuskeskus, 1998, pp. 55-60.

_____. *Tuotantokirja: True Stories – poikien seikkailu.* An unpublished choreographer's notebook. 2000.

Van Dijk, T.A. Principles of critical discourse analysis. *Discourse and Society* 4, 1993, pp 249-83.

Van Ulzen, K. Real Men Do Dance. *Dance Australia.* December 1995/January 1996, pp. 16-20.

Vienola-Lindfors, I. & af Hällström, R. *Suomen Kansallisbaletti 1922-1972.* Helsinki: Musiikki Fazer, 1981.

Viitala, M. *Tanssia elämyksen Ehdoilla: Dance as an Art Experience.* Helsinki: Svoli-Palvelu Oy. 1998.

Virtanen, J.P. Hirviporukan mies, in Hoikkala, T. (ed) *Miehen kuvia. Välähdyksiä nuorista miehistä Suomessa.* Helsinki: Gaudeamus, 1996. pp. 180-185.

Vuori, J. Tanssin vaatimukset muuttuvat. *Turun Sanomat.* 27.11.1996.

Walker, K.S. Male Dancers Then and Now. *Dance Expression.* June, 2000, p. 4.

Weedon, C. *Feminist Practice and Poststructuralist Theory.* Oxford: Blackwell, 1987.

Weeks, J. The Paradoxes of Identity, in Goodman, L. & de Gay, J. (eds) *The Routledge Reader in Politics and Performance.* London & New York: Routledge, 2000, pp. 162-166.

____. *Sexuality*. 2nd Edition. London & New York: Routledge, 2003.

Weir, L. Post-modernizing Gender: from Adrienne Rich to Judith Butler, in Radtke, H.L. & Stam, H.J. (eds). *Power/Gender: Social Relations in Theory and Practice*. London, Thousand Oaks, New York: Sage, 1994, pp. 210-218.

Wellings, K., Branigan, P. & Mitchell, K. Discomfort, discord and discontinuity as data: using focus groups to research sensitive topics. *Culture, Health & Sexuality*, 2,3, 2000, pp. 255-267.

Wetherell, M. Themes in Discourse Research: The Case of Diana in Wetherell et al (eds). *Discourse Theory and Practice: A Reader*. London, Thousand Oaks, New Delhi: Sage Publications. 2001a, pp. 14-28.

____. Editor's introduction to Part Three: Minds, Selves and Sense Making in Wetherell et al (eds). *Discourse Theory and Practice: A Reader*. London, Thousand Oaks, New Delhi: Sage Publications. 2001b, pp. 186-197.

____. Debates in Discourse Research. *Discourse Theory and Practice: A Reader*. London, Thousand Oaks, New Delhi: Sage Publications. 2001c, pp.380-399.

Wetherell, M., Taylor, S. & Yates, S.J. (eds) *Discourse Theory and Practice: A Reader*. London, Thousand Oaks, New Delhi: Sage Publications. 2001a.

____. (eds) *Discourse as Data*. London, Thousand Oaks, New Delhi: Sage Publications. 2001b.

Whitehead, S. *Men and Masculinities*. Cambridge: Polity Press, 2002.

Whitehead, S. & Barrett, J. The Sociology of Masculinity, in Whitehead, S. & Barrett, J. (eds) *The Masculinities Reader*. Cambridge: Polity Press, 2001, pp. 1-26.

Wigert, A. Några tankar om pojkars och flickors sätt att attackera dans. In Gronlund, E. et al (eds). *Forskning i förelse: Tio texter om dans*. Stockholm: Carlssons, 1999, pp. 13-21.

Williams, R. *Marxismi, kulttuuri ja kirjallisuus*. Transl. Mikko Lehtonen. Vastapaino, Tampere, 1988.

Wilton, T. Which one's the man? The heterosexualisation of lesbian sex, in Richardson, D. (ed) *Theorising heterosexuality: Telling it straight*. Buckingham & Philadelphia: Open University Press, pp. 125-142.

Windschuttle, K. *The Killing of History: How Literary Critics and Social Theorists are Murdering Our Past*. New York: The Free Press. 1996.

Wittgenstein, L. *Philosophical Investigations*. New York: The Macmillan Company, 1965.

Wolf-Light, P. The Shadow of Iron John. *Achilles Heel.* 17, autumn, 1994, pp.14-17.

Wooffitt, R. Researching Psychic Practitioners: Conversation Analysis. In: Wetherell et al (eds) *Discourse as Data, A Guide for Analysis.* London, Thousand Oaks, New Delhi: Sage Publishing, 2001, pp. 49-92.

Worton, M. & Still, J. (eds) *Intertextuality: Theories and Practices.* Manchester & New York: Manchester University Press, 1990.

Wulff, H. *Ballet Across Borders: Career and Culture in the World of Dancers.* Oxford: Berg, 1998.

Ylikangas, H. *Käännekohdat Suomen historiassa. Pohdiskeluja kehityslinjoista ja niiden muutoksista uudella ajalla.* Juva: WSOY, 1986.

Yli-Sirniö, M. Oopperan balettikoulussa koko elämä on tanssia. *Ilta-Sanomat*, 14.5.1996.

Electronic sources:

Charpentier, S. Gender, Body and the Sacred: Heterosexual Hegemony as a Sacred Order in *Queen: a Journal of Rhetoric and Power.* Vol. 1/1, 2000. <http://www.ars-rhetorica.net> (13.Jan. 2003).

FINLEX, The Constitution of Finland 11 June 1999 (731/1999), an unofficial translation in http://finlex.fi/pdf/saadkaan/ E9990731.PDF (7. Nov. 2003).

Gergen, K.J. Constructionist Dialogues and the Vicissitudes of the Political. <http://www.swarthmore.edu/SocSci/kgergen1/text7. html> (14. Nov. 2002) and in I. Velodity (forthcoming) London: Sage.

Heikkala, J. et al. Liikunnan ja urheilun tarina. *Liikunnan ja urheilun maailma* 17/2003, Suomen liikunta ja urheilu. http://www.slu. fu/mp/db/file_library/x/IMG/17059/file/liik%5fja%5furh%5ftarina%5f 72%5fdpi.pdf (30.11.2003)

Hiltunen 1998; SETA ry, Tietopankki – Tasa-arvo ja asenteet, http: //www.seta.fi/fi/setafi47.htm 10.7.2002.

Internetix. <http://www.internetix.fi/opinnot/opintojaksot/9historia/sosiaa liturva/index.htm> (15.2.2003).

Keinänen, M. Tanssia harrastavat pojat kaipaavat paljon tukea. News, YLE TV2, 15.6.2003, at 6 pm.

Kuopio Dance Festival. Dancing Boy 2003 Residential Course. <(http://www.kuopiodancefestival.fi/english/index2en.html> (24.4.2003).

Lampi, I. et al. (eds) *Popeda: poikien tanssipedagogiikka-työryhmän muistio.* Vantaa, Helsinki: Vantaan tanssiopisto & Suomen kansallisoopperan balettioppilaitos, 2002. (A Word-file saved on a CD-ROM).

Mattila, M. *Kuopio tanssii ja soi,* Loma-Suomi täsmä, YLE RADIO1, 13 June 2001, 08:42 am, length 6'42''.

Mirage Studios, USA. <http://www.ninjaturtles.com> (08.08.2003).

Netfit <http//:www.netfit.co.uk/plyometrics_web.htm> (15.6.2003).

Opetusministeriö. Education: The Finnish Educational Policy. <http://www.minedu.fi/minedu/education/ > (15.2.2003).

Rauhamaa, R. *Kantapään kautta: tanssivan miehen tie.* YLE TV1 Opetusohjelmat & Ikoni ja Indeksi Ay, 1994.

SETA ry. Tietopankki – Tasa-arvo ja asenteet. <http: //www.seta.fi/fi/setafi47.htm> (10 July 2002).

Smolander, J. Integratiivinen nationalismi – porvarillisen Suomen hyvinvointi-ideologia toisen maailmansodan jälkeen. *Ennen ja Nyt:Historian tietosanomat,* 1,4, 2001. <http://www.ennenjanyt .net/4-01/smolander.htm#N_9_ > (27.10.2003).

Teatterimuseo. Maggie Gripenbergin arkisto http://www.teatterimuseo .fi/3/gripenberg.html#Maggie (15.4.2003).

The Research Institute for Olympic Sports http://www.kihu. jyu.fi /english/ (16.2.2003).

Turpeinen, I. http://www.kolumbus.fi/isto.turpeinen/index2htm. (15.3. 2003).

YLE, *Kuopio tanssii ja soi Loma-Suomi täsmä,* in YLE RADIO1, 13.06.2001, 08:42 am.

YLE, *Levottomat jalat,* in YLE TV1, 21.5.2003.

Index

314

322

326

328

329